Shared Prosperity

in America's Communities

THE CITY IN THE TWENTY-FIRST CENTURY

Eugenie L. Birch and Susan M. Wachter, *Series Editors*

A complete list of books in the series
is available from the publisher.

SHARED PROSPERITY IN AMERICA'S COMMUNITIES

Edited by

Susan M. Wachter

and

Lei Ding

UNIVERSITY OF PENNSYLVANIA PRESS

PHILADELPHIA

Published by
University of Pennsylvania Press
Philadelphia, Pennsylvania 19104-4112
www.upenn.edu/pennpress

Printed in the United States of America
on acid-free paper
1 3 5 7 9 10 8 6 4 2

Library of Congress Cataloging-in-Publication Data
ISBN 978-0-8122-4785-5

CONTENTS

Introduction

The rise in income inequality in the United States in recent decades has heightened the degree to which place matters in the geography of economic opportunity. By almost every measure imaginable, we are a nation divided, and the geography of opportunity matters more than ever for the propagation and persistence of poverty.

Despite the nation's GDP doubling in the past thirty years, median family income and wages trail far behind. And income inequality is increasingly aligned with *place*. Neighborhoods and metropolitan areas have become more polarized, creating stark differences in levels of poverty, income, health outcomes, job opportunities, lifetime earning potential, as well as educational attainment.

This is a book about the place-based disparity of opportunity and what communities can do to build shared prosperity. Part I of the book lays out the issues of social and economic mobility, showing the challenges of the changing geography of inequality. Part II offers a portfolio of strategies to address the challenges of place-based inequality. Part III shows how communities across the nation are implementing change and building a future of shared prosperity.

Chetty, in the first chapter of this volume, demonstrates that social mobility varies substantially across the nation. While there are areas in the United States where mobility is higher than in most other countries, in other areas the chance of a child moving from the bottom to the top quintile of income is lower than 5 percent, less than in any other developed nation on record. Why does social mobility vary? Chetty identifies location-based factors associated with regional differences in mobility: segregation by race and ethnicity, income inequality, school quality, social capital, and family structure.

As the chapters by Jargowsky and Kneebone show, geographic stratification in income inequality and segregation by race and ethnicity have grown over time. Gains of the 1990s have been reversed, as segregation by income and race—particularly for children—has increased. Jargowsky points to social isolation, social disorganization, and poor quality education at the neighborhood level as mechanisms that propagate poverty over generations. And Kneebone documents that poverty has become more concentrated in neighborhoods in metropolitan areas (particularly in smaller metros and some suburbs).

As Diamond shows, the geography of opportunity is increasingly stratified across metros, as well. Nationally, discordance between economic growth and stagnating wages in the lower- and middle-income brackets reflects both an increase in returns to skills and an increasing inequality in educational outcomes. While the increasing returns to educational attainment are well known, Diamond shows why the new knowledge-based economy has also led to an increase in skill segregation across metro areas and the consequences of this new regionally based wage and income stratification. High-tech and high-skill regions offer both higher wages and a higher quality of life, including higher-quality education. However, in high-skilled regions, access to affordable housing is decreasing, discouraging lower-skilled and non-college graduate workers from in-migrating. The result is an increase in the sorting of high- and low-income residents across metro areas. This limits low-skill workers' access to higher-paying jobs and to positive knowledge spillovers existing in high-skill cities. This new segmentation in the metro level geography of opportunity adds to neighborhood-based effects that reproduce inequality.

Addressing these place-based factors that limit social mobility can benefit all. As Chetty states:

> Improving opportunities for children from disadvantaged families to succeed should be a priority for policy makers not just because it is one of the core principles of American society but also because improving mobility can have substantial economic payoffs. Unlike other policy issues that involve sharp tradeoffs, increases in absolute upward income mobility can benefit everyone in society. Children from disadvantaged backgrounds naturally benefit directly from having higher levels of income. But affluent individuals can benefit as well, because income growth among the least affluent members of society contributes to economic growth and reduces the number of individuals receiving transfers from the government, saving taxpayers money.

Part II offers context- and location-specific policies to help accomplish this. Introducing this section, Turner lays out "place-conscious" strategies to overcome poverty—aimed at "reintegrating" economically stratified neighborhoods through opportunity-improving initiatives. The subsequent chapters address components of reforms in housing policies, education, labor market preparation, and economic development. Massey discusses the gains, and particularly the educational gains, from inclusionary housing policies. Jargowsky et al. present case studies in educational reform from pre-K through K-12 to show effective strategies to close achievement gaps and to improve educational outcomes. Carnevale and Smith examine how to overcome shortages of skilled workers while connecting students to higher education opportunity to improve their skill base, while Bartik offers economic development strategies that better link workers to jobs.

Part III shows how cities and regions are adopting holistic strategies to realize potential benefits of shared economic prosperity. Nowak lays out joint approaches from the "inside out" and the "outside in" to this end: the first restores place-based amenities and services from public institutions to increase opportunity in disinvested communities; the second promotes higher levels of social mobility by linking people to regional opportunities. Rubin, Blackwell, and Schildt identify regional strategies for inclusive growth that address the nexus of access to jobs and affordable housing and that support economic development through public and private entrepreneurship. Pastor and Benner describe "epistemic communities" which, through a region-wide lens, have identified strategies to link people to jobs and housing and economic opportunity through region-wide inclusive growth strategies.

This inclusive growth is the answer to disparity. In the face of division, both socioeconomic and geographic, by restoring the experience of community, the American community can share in resulting prosperity. Inclusivity begins at the neighborhood level and extends to regional levels through collective action and partnerships at all levels. In this book, you will see how communities, cities, and regional alliances of cities are taking up the challenge of addressing economic inequality to build a nation of opportunity for all.

PART I

Social and Economic Mobility in America's Communities

CHAPTER 1

Socioeconomic Mobility in the United States: New Evidence and Policy Lessons

Raj Chetty

Since the eighteenth century, the United States has been hailed as a "land of opportunity," a society where all children can succeed, regardless of their family background. However, modern empirical research reveals that the rate of upward income mobility in the United States is actually lower than in many other countries (Corak 2013; Boserup et al. 2013). A child born in the bottom quintile of the income distribution, for example, has a 7.5 percent chance of reaching the top quintile in the United States.[1] In Denmark, a child born in the bottom fifth has an 11.7 percent chance of reaching the top fifth (Boserup et al. 2013); in Canada, the figure is 13.5 percent (Corak and Heisz 1999). Hence, children in Canada have almost twice as high a chance of realizing the "American Dream" of moving up the income ladder as children in America.[2]

Improving opportunities for children from disadvantaged families to succeed should be a priority for policy makers not just because it is one of the core principles of American society but also because improving mobility can have substantial economic payoffs. Unlike other policy issues that involve sharp tradeoffs, increases in absolute upward income mobility can benefit everyone in society. Children from disadvantaged backgrounds naturally benefit directly from having higher levels of income. But affluent individuals can benefit as well, because income growth among the least affluent members of society contributes to economic growth and reduces the number of individuals receiving transfers from the government, saving taxpayers money.

This chapter presents a summary of recent research that offers lessons about how to improve economic mobility in the United States. It draws primarily on evidence from the Equality of Opportunity Project, which presents comprehensive statistics on mobility in the United States based on anonymous earnings records for forty million children and their parents. These statistics reveal that mobility is lower in the United States than in other developed countries and has been consistently low for children born during the past three decades.

Though mobility has been stagnant over time, there is significant geographic variation in mobility within the United States: some areas of the country exhibit rates of upward mobility on par with the most mobile countries in the world, such as Denmark and other Northern European countries, while other areas of the country have lower rates of upward mobility than those measured in any country in which data have been analyzed. Therefore, while some areas in the United States certainly deserve to be called lands of opportunity, others are better described as lands of persistent inequality.

The first section of this chapter summarizes trends in intergenerational mobility in the United States in recent decades. Next, I discuss how upward mobility varies across areas of the country. The third section summarizes the key characteristics (segregation, income inequality, school quality, social capital, and family structure) that are correlated with the variation in socioeconomic mobility across the country. The chapter concludes by discussing potential directions for future research and policy—including place-based initiatives and investments in improving the quality of primary education—that can increase upward mobility.

Trends in Intergenerational Mobility in the United States

Chetty et al. (2014a) show that percentile-based measures of intergenerational mobility did not change significantly for children born between 1971 and 1993 (see Figure 1.1). Consider, for example, the likelihood of a child with parents in the bottom quintile of the income distribution growing up to earn an income in the top quintile of the distribution. This probability is 8.4 percent for children born in 1971, compared with 9.0 percent for those born in 1986.

A comparison of the likelihood of attending college by children from the highest-income families to children from the lowest-income families tells a

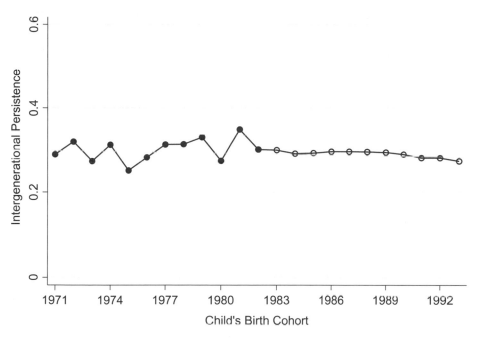

Figure 1.1. Trends in intergenerational mobility in the United States. Chetty et al. 2014a.

similar story about the stability of intergenerational mobility over time, with children from higher-income families much more likely to attend college regardless of their birth year. Children born to families in the top 1 percent of the income distribution in 1984 were 74.5 percentage points more likely to attend college than those born to families in the bottom 1 percent. The corresponding gap in college attendance rates for the 1992 birth cohort was 69.2 percent.

Figure 1.1 illustrates the stability of intergenerational mobility for children born between 1971 and 1993 (for children born after 1986, estimates are predictions based on college attendance rates). The Y-axis, "intergenerational persistence," is a measure of the gap in average income percentiles for children born in the poorest versus the richest families. On average, children with parents in the bottom 1 percent of the income distribution grow up to earn an income approximately 30 percentiles lower than their peers with parents in the top 1 percent of the income distribution. This difference has remained relatively steady across the birth cohorts studied.

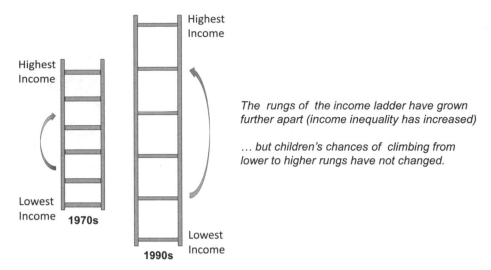

Figure 1.2. The rungs of the income ladder have grown farther apart (income inequality has increased), but children's chances of climbing from lower to higher rungs have not changed.

Hertz (2007) and Lee and Solon (2009) find that intergenerational mobility was relatively stable between the 1950 and 1970 birth cohorts. Together with the results in Figure 1.1, these findings suggest that rank-based measures of social mobility—that is, children's chances of climbing from the bottom to the top of the income distribution—have not changed significantly over the second half of the twentieth century in the United States.

However, it is important to note that income inequality—as measured, for instance, by the difference in income levels between the lowest- and highest-earning households—increased substantially over the second half of the twentieth century (Piketty and Saez 2003). Because of the increase in income inequality, the consequences of the "birth lottery"—the parents to whom a child is born—are larger today than in the past. Imagine the income distribution as the ladder in Figure 1.2, with each percentile resting on a different rung. The distance between each rung has grown (inequality has increased), but each child's chances of climbing up the rungs have remained the same (rank-based mobility has not changed).

Because of the increase in inequality, the stability in rates of mobility means that children's economic prospects depend more heavily on their parents' incomes today than they did in the past. The fact that mobility is significantly lower in the United States than in most other developed countries (Corak 2013) is thus a more imperative problem today than it was half a century ago, as the consequences in terms of income differences are now much larger.

The stability in mobility over time has led some to question whether social mobility can be meaningfully influenced by policy (G. Clark 2014). Is mobility in the United States destined to be low relative to other countries because of certain characteristics unique to this country? Next, I turn to evidence on differences in mobility across communities, which paints a more positive picture and suggests it may actually be feasible to achieve high levels of upward mobility in the United States.

Geographical Differences in Mobility

In Chetty et al. (2014b), we characterize geographical variation in intergenerational mobility across the United States by dividing the country into 741 "commuting zones" (CZs). Commuting zones are geographical aggregations of counties that are similar to metro areas but also cover rural areas. We construct measures of intergenerational mobility for each of these areas by classifying children based on their location at age sixteen, so that their assigned locations reflect where they grew up. Within each local area, we rank both children and parents according to their positions in the *national* income distribution relative to others in the same birth cohort. As a result, we measure how much children eventually earn relative to their peers across the nation rather than in their local area.

We find that economic mobility varies substantially across the country, as illustrated by the map in Figure 1.3. This heat map was constructed by computing the probability that a child reaches the top fifth of the income distribution conditional on having parents in the bottom fifth of the income distribution. The areas are split into deciles, with lighter colors indicating areas with higher levels of upward mobility, and darker colors representing areas where children from low-income families are less likely to move up in the income distribution. In areas with the highest rates of mobility (areas denoted by the lightest color on the map), children growing up in a family in the bottom fifth have more than a 16.8 percent chance of reaching the top fifth. That number is higher than in most other countries with the highest rates of mobility. At the other end of the spectrum, the darkest-colored

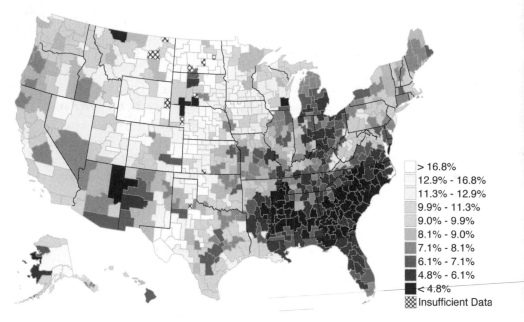

> 16.8%
12.9% - 16.8%
11.3% - 12.9%
9.9% - 11.3%
9.0% - 9.9%
8.1% - 9.0%
7.1% - 8.1%
6.1% - 7.1%
4.8% - 6.1%
< 4.8%
Insufficient Data

Figure 1.3. The geography of intergenerational mobility. Chetty et al. 2014b.

areas, children have less than a 4.8 percent chance of moving from the bottom fifth to the top fifth of the income distribution. The rates of upward mobility in these areas are lower than in any developed country for which data have been analyzed to date. More broadly, these differences in the chance of reaching the top quintile represent the very different lifetime outcomes for children born into disadvantaged families depending on where their parents live.

What broad geographic patterns do we see in Figure 1.3? The most immediately apparent pattern is regional variation. Children in the bottom quintile have less than a 5 percent chance of reaching the top quintile in much of the Southeast and the Rust Belt. In other areas, such as the Great Plains and the West Coast, children in the bottom quintile have more than a 15 percent chance of reaching the top quintile.

While the variation across regions is substantial, there is also a great deal of local area variation across places that are in close geographic proximity and have similar sociodemographic characteristics. For example, Ohio and Pennsylvania are fairly similar in terms of demographics and economic

Table 1.1. Upward Mobility in 50 Largest Metro Areas: Top 10 and Bottom 10

Rank	Commuting zone	Odds of reaching top fifth from bottom fifth (%)	Rank	Commuting zone	Odds of reaching top fifth from bottom fifth (%)
1	San Jose, CA	12.9	41	Cleveland, OH	5.1
2	San Francisco, CA	12.2	42	St. Louis, MO	5.1
3	Washington DC	11.0	43	Raleigh, NC	5.0
4	Seattle, WA	10.9	44	Jacksonville, FL	4.9
5	Salt Lake City, UT	10.8	45	Columbus, OH	4.9
6	New York, NY	10.5	46	Indianapolis, IN	4.9
7	Boston, MA	10.5	47	Dayton, OH	4.9
8	San Diego, CA	10.4	48	Atlanta, GA	4.5
9	Newark, NJ	10.2	49	Milwaukee, WI	4.5
10	Manchester, NH	10.0	50	Charlotte, NC	4.4

Source: Chetty et al. (2014b).

structure, yet Pennsylvania is dramatically better than Ohio in terms of rates of social mobility.

Finally, urban areas tend to have lower rates of social mobility than rural areas. The higher social mobility of children born in rural areas is generally accompanied by geographic mobility with these children moving to large metropolitan areas, often out of their state of birth. The most successful children growing up in rural areas are able to move up but generally also move out.

There is also substantial variation in upward mobility across cities, even among large cities that have comparable economies and demographics. Table 1.1 lists upward mobility statistics for the 50 largest metro areas, focusing on the 10 cities with the highest and lowest levels of upward mobility. Salt Lake City, Boston, and San Jose have rates of mobility similar to the most upwardly mobile countries in the world, while other cities—such as Charlotte, Atlanta, and Milwaukee—offer children very limited prospects of escaping poverty. The odds of moving from the bottom to the top are two to three times as large growing up in a city like Salt Lake City or San Jose rather than Milwaukee or Atlanta.

In ongoing work, Chetty, Hendren, Kline, and Saez (2014) find that if a child moves from a city with low upward mobility (such as Milwaukee) to a city with high upward mobility (such as Salt Lake City), her own income in adulthood rises in proportion to the time she is exposed to the better environment. Chetty, Hendren, and Katz (2015) find similar evidence of substantial neighborhood exposure effects when analyzing children's long-term outcomes in the Moving to Opportunity Experiment. These findings indicate that much of the difference in upward mobility across areas is driven by a causal effect of differences in the local environment rather than differences in the characteristics of the people who live in different cities. Hence, it is critical to tackle social mobility at the community level rather than simply at the national level.

The variation in economic mobility across cities in the United States is reason for optimism. If we can make every city in America have mobility rates like San Jose or Salt Lake City, the United States would become one of the most upwardly mobile countries in the world. This naturally leads to the next question: what makes some places in America have much higher rates of upward mobility than others?

Correlates of the Spatial Variation in Mobility

To understand the determinants of mobility, in Chetty et al. (2014b), we explore correlations between upward mobility and various factors that have been discussed in prior work by sociologists and economists. We identify several characteristics that are strongly correlated with higher or lower levels of intergenerational mobility across communities; however, we caution that these factors cannot necessarily be interpreted as causal mechanisms as our analysis does not control for many other potentially confounding factors.

The first pattern we document is that upward income mobility is significantly lower in areas with larger African American populations. However, race matters at the community level, not just the individual level: in areas with large African American populations, both African American and white individuals are less likely to move up in income distribution (Chetty et al. 2014b: fig. IX). One possible explanation (among many others) for such a community-level effect of race is the legacy of racial segregation. Areas with high levels of racial segregation also experience higher levels of income segregation, which means that in these areas, lower-income residents are also less likely to live in proximity to higher-income residents. Such income segregation may adversely affect both white and black low-income individuals. Standard measures of racial and income segregation and upward mobility are negatively correlated (Chetty et al. 2014b), consistent with research by Massey and Denton (1993), Cutler and Glaeser (1997), and Graham and Sharkey (2013). This finding suggests that interventions to promote mixed-income and integrated neighborhoods deserve careful consideration, although further work is required to determine the causal effects of such policy changes. We also find that upward mobility is lower in cities with more sprawl, as measured by average commute times to work, perhaps because of spatial mismatch between residential locations and jobs (Kain 1968). Together, these findings lead us to identify segregation as the first strong correlate of differences in upward mobility across areas.

Another strong correlate with upward mobility is the level of income *inequality* in an area. Cities with a smaller middle class tend to also have much lower levels of social mobility. Higher Gini coefficients are associated with lower rates of upward mobility, consistent with the "Great Gatsby curve" documented across countries (Krueger 2012; Corak 2013). In contrast, we find no correlation between upper tail inequality and social mobility across areas: top 1 percent income shares are not highly correlated with rates of upward mobility, either across countries or across CZs in the United States. These findings suggest that the factors that contribute to the erosion of the middle class may impede economic mobility more than the factors that lead to income growth at the highest end of the income distribution.

The fact that middle-class inequality is more strongly correlated with mobility across generations than is upper tail inequality may explain why social mobility has remained stable despite the increase in inequality in recent decades. The increase in inequality in the United States has come largely from the extreme upper tail (e.g., the top 1 percent). Given the cross-sectional correlations, we would not have predicted a large decline in social mobility in the United States over the past three decades, consistent with what we actually find in the data.

A third strong correlate with upward mobility is the difference in *school quality* between areas: as one might expect, places with better public schools tend to have higher levels of social mobility. We measure the quality of the elementary and secondary school system by average test scores (controlling for parent income levels), dropout rates (again controlling for parent income levels), and average class sizes. By all these measures, areas with better quality

K-12 education exhibit higher rates of upward mobility. Correspondingly, areas with higher local tax rates, which are predominantly used to finance public schools, also have higher rates of mobility.

Social capital is a fourth strong correlate of economic mobility. The strength of social networks and community involvement in an area can be measured by proxies popularized by Putnam (1995) and collaborators. These proxies include the share of religious individuals and level of participation in local civic organizations. We find that areas with higher levels of social capital—such as Salt Lake City—have much higher rates of social mobility.

Interestingly, one of the original proxies for social capital used by Putnam (1995) in "Bowling Alone"—the number of bowling alleys in an area—is very strongly correlated with rates of mobility. This notable correlation serves to illustrate a point that needs to be kept in mind with all the findings discussed in this section: the relationships being measured are correlations, which are not necessarily causal effects. It is unlikely that the best way to increase upward mobility is to build more bowling alleys.

A fifth strong correlate is *family structure*. The single strongest correlate of social mobility is the fraction of single mothers in an area, with areas with more single mothers exhibiting much lower rates of upward mobility. Importantly, however, the correlation is similar when we estimate absolute upward mobility on the subsample of children whose parents are married. That is, children from married families who live in areas with a large number of single parents have lower chances of moving up in the income distribution. This again suggests that the key mechanisms at play operate at the community level and not just at the household level.

We find little or no correlation between upward mobility and the average income levels in an area, rates of migration, access to higher education, or local labor market conditions.[3] We find a small correlation between upward mobility and local tax and government expenditure policies, but this correlation is much weaker than the five main factors discussed above.

While these correlations suggest that differences in local policies and community structures could have important effects on upward mobility, one cannot draw policy lessons directly from these correlations without further research into causal pathways. For example, there are many possible reasons that areas with higher rates of segregation have lower rates of upward mobility, such as a lack of access to jobs (in which case investments in better public transportation may be helpful) or higher levels of discrimination in hiring practices in these areas (in which case transportation may have no effect at all). Nevertheless, the evidence discussed above does shed some light on the types of policies that can improve mobility. I turn to these implications in the next and final section.

Policy Implications

Combined with other evidence from research, the results summarized above yield several potential lessons for policies to improve upward mobility in America.

Place-Based Initiatives

Place matters in enabling intergenerational mobility. Since rates of upward mobility vary widely across cities, place-based policies that are implemented by cities and regions are necessary to effect change. As discussed in the chapters that follow, such policies may include targeted tax credits, efforts to revitalize local communities, funding for improvements in local schools, and investments in infrastructure. While the research reviewed in this chapter points to the importance of local place-based initiatives, there is potentially an important role for the federal government in encouraging the type of policies that can improve mobility as well. For example, the federal government could provide matching grants to local communities that undertake specific initiatives to improve mobility with demonstrable impacts in these areas.

Focus on Childhood Environments

The data show that much of the spatial variation in children's outcomes emerges before they enter the labor market. In particular, children in areas with low income mobility also have higher teenage birth rates and lower college attendance rates. These findings indicate that the differences in mobility are driven by factors that affect children while they are growing up. Hence, it is important to prioritize investments that change childhood environments rather than focusing exclusively on providing jobs and economic opportunities for adults who are already working. Jobs matter, but ladders to opportunity begin well before children start to work.

Invest in Improving the Quality of Education

Among the factors correlated with mobility discussed above, improvements in the quality of education have the clearest causal effects on upward mobility. For example, in a study that tracked more than one million children from childhood to early adulthood, Chetty, Friedman, and Rockoff (2014) find that better teachers—as measured by test-score based value-added metrics—substantially increase students' earnings and college attendance rates and lower rates of teenage birth. They estimate that an excellent teacher generates more than $1.4 million of earnings gains for a single classroom of students over their lifetime. These findings imply that programs that increase teacher salaries and provide incentives for local school districts to recruit and retain higher quality teachers are likely to be valuable. As discussed by Jargowsky et al. (this volume), other studies have presented evidence from randomized experiments which show that investments in improving preschools (e.g., Heckman et al. 2010a) and reducing the size of classrooms (e.g., Chetty et al. 2011; Fredriksson et al. 2013; Dynarski et al. 2013) can have significant long-term payoffs. Importantly, such investments in education have substantial returns throughout childhood, not just in the earliest years. In particular, the benefits of having a high value-added teacher appear to be just as large in middle and high school as they are in the earliest year of elementary school.

Collect and Disseminate Information on Local Performance

One of the most cost-effective ways to improve mobility may be to collect and publicize local statistics on economic mobility and other related outcomes. Simply drawing attention to the areas that need improvement can motivate local policy makers to take action. Moreover, without such information, it is difficult to determine which programs work and which do not. The federal government is well positioned to construct such statistics at minimal cost with existing data and harnessing the power of big data to measure the impact of new interventions. The government could go further by offering awards or grants to areas that have substantially improved their rates of upward mobility. Shining a spotlight on the communities where children have opportunities to succeed can enable others to learn from their example and increase opportunities for economic mobility throughout America.

Conclusion

In the United States as a whole, chances of moving up in the income distribution relative to their parents for children entering the labor market today are similar those for children born in the 1970s. While mobility has been stable over time, there are stark differences in opportunities for upward economic mobility across communities in the United States. Cities such as Salt Lake City and San Jose exhibit levels of mobility similar to those observed in developed countries with the highest level of intergenerational mobility, while other cities such as Charlotte and Atlanta have lower levels of mobility than any country for which data have been analyzed to date. The large differences in intergenerational mobility across space point to the potential value of policies that target the five key community-level characteristics correlated with differences in mobility across areas: segregation, income inequality, school quality, social capital, and family structure.

The large differences in intergenerational mobility across areas of the United States create an opportunity and a challenge. The fact that some areas within America have greater social mobility than most other countries in the world demonstrates that we have an opportunity to greatly improve social mobility in the United States. If we can make each city in America like San Jose or maybe even Dubuque, Iowa—where a remarkable 17 percent of children born to the lowest-income families reach the very top of the U.S. income distribution—we would transform American society.

The challenge for researchers is to identify exactly what causes differences in social mobility across space, in order to be able to develop interventions to improve mobility. The challenge for practitioners is to implement those policy changes and make them politically and practically feasible. Overcoming these challenges could dramatically change social mobility in the United States and create opportunities for success for every child from Charlotte to San Jose.

CHAPTER 2

Neighborhoods and Segregation

Paul A. Jargowsky

This chapter presents the landscape of racial and ethnic segregation and of economic segregation in America, phenomena that work against the creation of a more equitable society. It begins with a description of data and methods, and then continues with a description of neighborhood segregation in America in terms of race and ethnicity and of income. It then goes on to explore two related trends that play a major role in the success, or failure, of policies to promote shared prosperity: the concentration of poverty and the especially high segregation of school-age children. The chapter concludes with implications for policy, arguing that the underlying systems and processes that produce high-poverty urban contexts must be addressed in order to create a more equitable society, with equal access to neighborhood institutions and resources.

Overview

Figure 2.1 outlines the societal forces that shape neighborhoods' effects for life chances and socioeconomic mobility. In any given location—such as a metropolitan area or school district—there is a certain amount of racial and ethnic diversity and a level of economic inequality. For a variety of reasons, including preferences, housing discrimination, and the location of affordable housing, people are not distributed evenly across neighborhoods within the larger area. As Robert Park (1926) argued long ago, persons attempt to convert perceived social distances into physical distances. Segregation by race

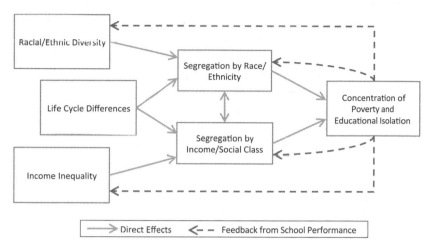

Figure 2.1. Effects of segregation by race and class.

and ethnicity tends to create racially homogeneous neighborhoods. Segregation by income level, driven in part by the geographic distribution of housing units of different market values, produces a variety of neighborhoods at different economic levels. Both economic and racial segregation may vary by the life cycle status of families (W. Clark and Onaka 1983). For example, overall segregation may be reduced if whites move into central city neighborhoods with a high percentage of minority residents. However, these "urban pioneers" tend to be childless young professionals or "empty nesters" who are less concerned about issues related to school quality (Ellen, Horn, and O'Regan 2013). Hence, as shown in Figure 2.1, children tend to be more segregated than their parents by both race and income.

Figure 2.1 also indicates that racial and economic segregation contribute to each other (Jargowsky 2014a; Quillian 2012). When minority groups are poor relative to the majority population, segregation by race and ethnicity has the effect of segregating the poor as well. Similarly, if the poor tend to be disproportionately composed of minority group members, segregation by social class will also automatically generate a degree of racial segregation. As argued below, racial segregation contributes about one-third of economic segregation in the typical U.S. metropolitan area. In contrast, economic segregation generates only about 10 percent of racial segregation.

Taken together, segregation by race and segregation by class results in concentrated poverty—high-poverty ghettos and barrios. More than 12.4

million persons lived in census tracts with poverty rates of 40 percent or more in 2010, a staggering 72 percent increase since 2000.[1] In these neighborhoods, more than half of children live in female-headed families and fewer than half of adult men are in the labor force (Jargowsky 2013). These neighborhoods are often characterized by vacant housing, drug and alcohol abuse, crime and violence, and failing schools (Wilson 1987; Sampson 2012a). Jargowsky et al. (this volume) discuss the long history of educational failure in poor urban neighborhoods and a variety of approaches and policies that have been advanced to compensate and ameliorate those conditions. Children in high-poverty neighborhoods are also significantly less healthy, further impeding their ability to learn (Currie 2011). Schools are for the most part locally funded, so school districts in declining central cities and older suburbs have limited resources to address educational decline. In our system of fiscal federalism, the federal government plays a limited role in educational funding, particularly at the elementary and secondary levels.

Thus, neighborhood decline contributes to school decline, but the process does not stop there, as indicated by the feedback arrows shown in Figure 2.1. The social conditions of high-poverty neighborhoods generally, and the poor performance of inner-city schools in particular, serve as a further inducement toward segregation. Those with means, and those with realistic alternatives, seek safer neighborhoods with better amenities and better schools. Students who fail academically will be unprepared to function in the modern labor market, limiting social mobility and increasing economic inequality. Finally, the failure of schools in a given school district as well as the broader social conditions may lead to "white flight" to suburban school districts, affecting the overall racial and ethnic composition of the school district overall. The neighborhood context of school failure as well as social conditions more broadly are, therefore, both caused by racial and economic segregation and represent forces that sustain and worsen segregation, racial isolation, and economic inequality.

Data and Methods

This chapter examines trends in racial and economic segregation and economic inequality over the period 1990–2010. The data used in this analysis come from the "long form" of the 1990 Census of Population and Housing, Summary File 3 (SF3); the corresponding file for the 2000 Census, which is based on a one-in-seven sample of the U.S. population; and the American Community Survey (ACS) five-year file for the period 2008–2012. We chose to use the ACS for 2008–2012 because the long form was discontinued after 2000 and replaced by the ACS and, while the ACS releases data annually, for small geographic areas (like the census tracts we are using as proxies for neighborhoods), the annual data release consists of the aggregation of sixty monthly samples over five calendar years to protect the confidentiality of survey respondents. The five-year ACS file for the period 2008–2012 centers around the year 2010.

To measure segregation, we use the Index of Dissimilarity (D)—the most commonly used measure of the evenness of the distribution of groups across neighborhoods (O. D. Duncan and B. Duncan 1955). While there are many other measures of segregation, those that measure evenness are highly correlated with D in practice (Massey and Denton 1988a). D is given by

$$D_{xy} = 0.5 * \sum_{i=1}^{n} \left| \frac{x_i}{X} - \frac{y_i}{Y} \right|,$$

where x_i and y_i are the populations of two different groups, X and Y, in neighborhood i. X and Y represent the total population of the two groups, respectively, across all n neighborhoods in the primary geographic unit (normally metropolitan areas). D, which ranges in value from 0 to 1, is easily interpreted: a D value of 1 indicates complete segregation, of 0 indicates perfect integration, and of 0.5 indicates that 50 percent of one group or the other would have to move to achieve perfect integration.

Census tracts, as noted above, serve as our proxy for neighborhoods. Census tracts are small geographic units that contain 4,000 persons on average (White 1987). Our analysis includes 384 metropolitan areas and metropolitan divisions, based on the 2010 definitions (OMB 2010). We apply these 2010 boundaries retroactively to the data from 1990 and 2000.

One complicating factor in measuring racial segregation is changes in the definition of racial groups over time. In the 1990 Census, respondents could identify only one race. Since 2000, respondents can identify as many racial groups as they desire.[2] In practice, about 2 percent of non-Hispanic respondents select more than one racial group. Given the inherent ambiguity in classifying those who choose more than one race, the category "black" in this analysis refers to people who indicated "Black" as their race in 1990, or who chose the category "Black or African American" alone in the 2000 Census or ACS surveys. Asians are treated in the same way. To avoid double counting, the analyses in this chapter are based, to the extent possible, on mutually exclusive categories of Hispanic, on the one hand, and non-Hispanic whites, blacks, and Asians, on the other hand.

To measure economic segregation and the concentration of poverty, we rely on the federal definition of poverty-level income, currently almost $24,000 per year for a family of four (Department of Health and Human Services 2014). Persons residing in families with income below the poverty threshold are considered poor, and those at or above the poverty line are considered nonpoor. In the 2000 Census and ACS surveys, it is possible to identify non-Hispanic whites by poverty status. In the 1990 data, we approximate non-Hispanic whites by poverty status by subtracting Hispanic and other race groups from the poor and nonpoor population figures.

The Dimensions of Neighborhood Differentiation

Segregation by Race and Ethnicity

The average segregation of blacks from whites in U.S. metropolitan areas fell from 0.64 in 1990 to 0.62 in 2000 and 0.60 in 2010 (the center point of the ACS sample spanning 2008–2012), as shown in Table 2.1. While the decline is encouraging, a segregation level of over 0.60 is still very high—60 percent of all blacks (or 60 percent of all whites) would have to be relocated to achieve an even distribution of whites and blacks across neighborhoods within metropolitan areas. Few groups in American history have ever experienced such high levels of segregation, let alone sustained such high levels over many decades (Massey 1990). Indeed, at the pace of the decline in black/white segregation since 1990, it would take 150 years to achieve a low level of segregation (0.30 or less) of blacks from whites. Logan and Stults (2010), in their analysis of racial segregation, concluded that progress had come to a "standstill."

Other researchers (e.g., Cutler, Glaeser, and Vigdor 1999; Glaeser and Vigdor 2012; Vigdor 2013) view the changes more positively. In part, their more favorable readings are based on examining the segregation of blacks from "non-blacks," rather than from whites. "Non-blacks" includes other minority groups, such as Hispanics and the increasing number of Hispanic immigrants who compete with blacks for the same limited stock of affordable housing in the central city and older inner-ring suburbs. Yet segregation of blacks from non-Hispanic whites, the majority group that has the lion's share

Table 2.1. Index of Dissimilarity, U.S. Metropolitan Areas

	Index of dissimilarity		
Segregation of Whites from:	**Blacks**	**Hispanics**	**Asians**
1990 Census	0.64	0.45	0.42
2000 Census	0.62	0.47	0.44
2008–2012 ACS	0.60	0.48	0.48
Segregation of Blacks from:		**Hispanics**	**Asians**
1990 Census		0.56	0.64
2000 Census		0.50	0.59
2008–2012 ACS		0.49	0.60
Segregation of Hispanics from:			**Asians**
1990 Census			0.50
2000 Census			0.50
2008–2012 ACS			0.54

1990 and 2000 U.S. Census; 2008–2012 ACS.
Figures are weighted averages of 384 metropolitan areas.
Calculations by the author.

of resources and community amenities, is more relevant to the question of black people's access to community resources and, in particular, black children's access to quality education.

Table 2.1 also shows that the segregation of other minority groups—not only African Americans—from whites is increasing. Hispanic/white segregation increased modestly from 0.45 to 0.48 between 1990 and 2010; this may be driven by immigration by Hispanics directly into barrio neighborhoods in gateway cities. White/Asian segregation has increased from 0.42 to 0.48 over the same period.[3]

Over the same period, segregation of minority groups from each other declined for the most part, resulting in more multiracial and multiethnic neighborhoods. The segregation of blacks from Hispanics declined from 0.56 to 0.49, and the segregation of blacks from Asians declined from 0.64 to 0.60. The exception is segregation of Hispanics from Asians, which increased from 0.50 to 0.54 between 1990 and 2010. While the integration of minority groups with each other is an interesting development, it does not address the question of access to the neighborhood institutions and resources of non-Hispanic whites.

In larger metropolitan areas with substantial black populations, the story is more discouraging. In a number of major cities, particularly in the Midwest

Table 2.2. Highly Segregated Metropolitan Areas

Metropolitan area	White/Black index of dissimilarity			Black population, 2008–2012*
	1990	2000	2008–2012	
Milwaukee-Waukesha-West Allis, WI	0.84	0.84	0.82	251,557
Detroit-Livonia-Dearborn, MI	0.86	0.87	0.81	727,260
New York-White Plains-Wayne, NY-NJ	0.83	0.82	0.80	2,381,601
Newark-Union, NJ-PA	0.84	0.82	0.80	442,053
Gary, IN	0.91	0.86	0.78	128,769
Chicago-Joliet-Naperville, IL	0.85	0.82	0.78	1,413,447
Philadelphia, PA	0.82	0.79	0.76	867,718
Cleveland-Elyria-Mentor, OH	0.83	0.79	0.75	403,714
Buffalo-Niagara Falls, NY	0.81	0.79	0.74	131,685
St. Louis, MO-IL	0.78	0.76	0.73	498,777
Nassau-Suffolk, NY	0.78	0.76	0.73	251,622
Boston-Quincy, MA	0.75	0.74	0.73	235,073
Miami-Miami Beach-Kendall, FL	0.72	0.72	0.71	460,472

1990 and 2000 U.S. Census; ACS 2008–2012.
*Metropolitan areas with at least 100,000 Blacks.

and Northeast, segregation remains at historically high levels. Table 2.2 lists U.S. metropolitan areas where black/white segregation exceeds 0.70. Four metropolitan areas, including New York and Detroit, have black/white dissimilarity of 0.80 or higher. Another nine metropolitan areas, including Chicago and Philadelphia, exceed 0.70.

Economic Segregation

Table 2.3 shows the average Index of Dissimilarity of the poor from the nonpoor within racial and ethnic groups across all U.S. metropolitan areas. The interpretation of the measure is analogous to the racial case; the Index of Dissimilarity of the poor from the nonpoor expresses the proportion of the poor that would have to move to achieve an even distribution of the poor across neighborhoods (Abramson and Tobin 1994; Abramson, Tobin, and VanderGoot 1995). The absolute level of poor/nonpoor segregation is lower than the black/white segregation figure, but these figures cannot be compared directly. Income is continuous, so that someone just above the poverty line

Table 2.3. Index of Dissimilarity of the Poor from the Nonpoor

Year	White	Black	Hispanic	Asian
1990 Census	0.310	0.370	0.460	0.610
2000 Census	0.300	0.360	0.370	0.560
2008–2012 ACS	0.330	0.430	0.420	0.630

1990 and 2000 U.S. Census; ACS 2008–2012.
Weighted averages of 384 metropolitan areas.

is hardly distinguishable from someone just below it. Moreover, individual incomes fluctuate over time and so a person might be poor in one period and not poor the next. Thus, the numerical values for the Index of Dissimilarity between the poor and nonpoor are not directly comparable to values for segregation of one racial group from another. Instead, we focus on the trend over time.

There is a trend toward increasing poor/nonpoor segregation *within* racial and ethnic groups. Economic segregation among whites increased from 0.31 in 1990 to 0.33 in the most recent data; among blacks it increased more substantially from 0.37 to 0.43; and among Asians, who have the highest level of segregation of the poor from the nonpoor, it increased from 0.61 to 0.63. Hispanics were the only group to show a decrease in segregation based on poverty status. The increase in economic segregation within racial groups continues the trend from earlier decades. Using a different measure of economic segregation, Jargowsky (1996) reported that economic segregation increased 24 percent for non-Hispanic whites, 41 percent for blacks, and 27 percent for Hispanics between 1970 and 1990. Reardon and Bischoff (2011b), also using a different measure, reported a 72 percent increase in economic segregation for blacks between 1970 and 2000, compared to a 26 percent increase for whites.[4]

We get a more disaggregated view of economic segregation by breaking the household income distribution into several social classes. Households are divided into four groups based on total household income: 1) less than $25,000; 2) $25,000 to $49,999; 3) $50,000 to $99,999; and 4) more than $100,000. For ease of presentation, we refer to the first group as "poor households," the second group as "working class," the third group as "middle class," and the last group as "affluent."[5]

As shown in the first three columns of Table 2.4, poor white households are least segregated from white working-class households (0.22) and most segregated from white affluent households (0.40). Nevertheless, the figures for white households reveal modest to low levels of segregation by income even when comparing poor to affluent households. The racial and ethnic differences in the levels of economic segregation across income classes are quite striking. The *lowest* levels of segregation between black income classes (poor versus working class, 0.39) is almost as high as the *most* segregated white income group pairing (poor versus affluent, 0.40). Black poor households are highly segregated from affluent black households, with an index of dissimilarity of 0.65. Hispanics and Asians have even higher levels of economic segregation between poor and affluent households, 0.67 and 0.73 respectively. William Julius Wilson (1987) argues that middle- and higher-income households in a community constitute a "social buffer" that helps lower-income households weather economic downturns. These figures show that minority poor households are much less likely than white poor households to benefit from the presence of wealthier households of their own group. The economic isolation of minority poor households is particularly relevant in the educational context. Higher-income families, with higher than average social capital and more flexible employment hours, are more likely to take an active role in neighborhood schools—volunteering, raising funds, and participating in the parent-teacher association (Heymann and Earle 2000).

The next four columns of Table 2.4 examine the segregation of other race and ethnic groups of various income levels from whites of various income levels. Remarkably, *all* black, Hispanic, and Asian households, even affluent ones, are highly segregated from white affluent households. Segregation of black poor from affluent white households is nearly total, with an index of dissimilarity of 0.79. As high as this figure is, it is not driven primarily by the greater than four-to-one income difference between affluent and poor households. The segregation of black and white *affluent* households is 0.68, meaning that two-thirds of all affluent black households would have to move to achieve an even distribution with white affluent households. To the extent that better-off black families are integrating neighborhoods, they tend to move to inner-ring suburbs, not the neighborhoods of wealthier whites (Lacy 2007; Pattillo-McCoy 2000). The persistence and enduring strength of the color line cannot be denied when white households earning less than $25,000 can share neighborhoods with affluent white families far more easily than black families making over $100,000. Hispanics and Asians, two groups that are less segregated from whites than blacks in the aggregate figures, are nearly as segregated as blacks from *affluent* whites. Segregation of these groups

Table 2.4. Segregation of Households by Income Level,
U.S. Metropolitan Areas, 2008–2012

	Within-group segregation			Segregation from whites			
	Working	Middle	Affluent	Poor	Working	Middle	Affluent
Non-Hispanic White							
Poor	0.22	0.29	0.40				
Working class		0.19	0.32				
Middle class			0.22				
Affluent							
Black							
Poor	0.39	0.50	0.65	0.66	0.70	0.74	0.79
Working class		0.40	0.57	0.63	0.64	0.67	0.73
Middle class			0.50	0.63	0.62	0.63	0.68
Affluent				0.71	0.68	0.67	0.68
Hispanic							
Poor	0.43	0.52	0.67	0.60	0.63	0.67	0.73
Working class		0.43	0.61	0.54	0.54	0.58	0.66
Middle class			0.55	0.54	0.51	0.52	0.59
Affluent				0.63	0.59	0.57	0.57
Asian							
Poor	0.62	0.67	0.73	0.72	0.74	0.75	0.78
Working class		0.57	0.65	0.65	0.64	0.65	0.67
Middle class			0.55	0.63	0.61	0.59	0.60
Affluent				0.71	0.67	0.64	0.60

ACS 2008–2012.
Weighted by total households. See text for description of income brackets.

from affluent whites diminishes somewhat as their income level rises, but even affluent Hispanic and Asian households are still much less likely to live with affluent whites than poor whites.

The Interaction of Racial and Economic Segregation

It has long been recognized that racial segregation by itself generates a certain amount of economic segregation because the segregated minority groups are poorer on average than whites (Massey and Eggers 1990; Massey and Fischer 2000). Likewise, given that the poor and nonpoor populations have different racial compositions, economic segregation also generates racial segregation (Massey 1990). For example, if some neighborhoods have affordable housing and others do not, even if the poor and nonpoor sort randomly into the units they can afford, some degree of racial segregation will be produced. The question is how much does each form of segregation contribute to the other? Are we dealing with one underlying problem with two different manifestations, or two independent processes?

Jargowsky (2014a), using ACS 2007–2011 data, decomposed economic segregation into a part that is attributable to sorting *by* race and a part that is due to sorting by income *within* race. On average across 384 metropolitan areas, about 37 percent of economic segregation is mechanically produced by racial segregation. The rest is due to residential sorting of the poor and nonpoor *within* racial and ethnic groups. Among the twenty largest metropolitan areas, the percentage of economic segregation that is tied to racial segregation ranges from 23 to 59 percent. It is not surprising that the contribution of racial segregation to economic segregation is highest in metropolitan areas with large black populations and high levels of black/white residential segregation. While racial segregation clearly plays a role in generating economic segregation, it is also clear that the bulk of economic segregation—close to two-thirds, on average—is independent of racial sorting.

Figure 2.2 graphically depicts the decomposition of economic segregation into the part that is due to sorting by race and the remainder that is due to sorting within race for the twenty largest metropolitan areas sorted by overall level of economic segregation. Interestingly, the part of economic segregation that is due to sorting *within* race—depicted on the left—is relatively constant across these large metropolitan areas, reflecting that there is some degree of economic segregation within all racial groups. Some metropolitan areas, however, have a substantially higher contribution to economic segregation that stems from sorting *by* race—depicted on the right. Figure 2.3 shows a very strong positive correlation ($r = 0.65$, $p < 0.000$) between the overall economic segregation (poor versus nonpoor, all races) and black/white segregation for the hundred metropolitan areas with the highest percentage black.

In theory, economic segregation can also generate racial segregation. The poor are disproportionately composed of members of minority groups and the nonpoor are disproportionately white. Thus if the poor and nonpoor are segregated, some racial segregation will be produced as well. Table 2.5 displays the results of a decomposition of metropolitan racial segregation into the part due to the segregation of the poor from the nonpoor and the part due to racial sorting *among* the poor and the nonpoor. Panel A shows the

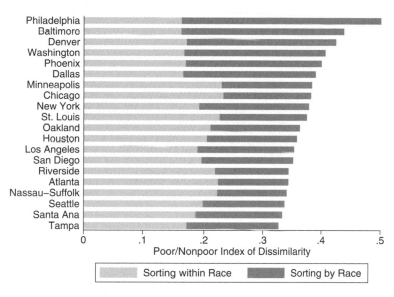

Figure 2.2. Decomposition of economic segregation, 20 largest metropolitan areas. Jargowsky 2014, based on American Community Survey 2007–2011 file.

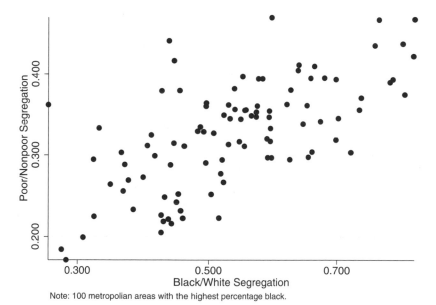

Note: 100 metropolian areas with the highest percentage black.

Figure 2.3. Economic and racial segregation, 100 metropolitan areas with highest percentage black. Jargowsky 2014, based on American Community Survey 2007–2011 file.

Table 2.5. Racial Segregation, Actual and Due to Economic Segregation

		Black	Hispanic	Asian
Panel A: Actual racial/ ethnic segregation				
	White	0.601	0.481	0.480
	Black		0.496	0.610
	Hispanic			0.543
Panel B: Due to economic segregation				
	White	0.059	0.054	0.016
	Black		0.018	0.046
	Hispanic			0.041
Panel C: Proportion due to economic segregation				
	White	9.8%	11.2%	3.3%
	Black		3.6%	7.5%
	Hispanic			7.6%
N		384	384	384

Jargowsky (2014a).
Average of 384 metropolitan areas, weighted by population.

average metropolitan Index of Dissimilarity among pairs of racial and ethnic groups. Panel B shows the racial segregation induced by poor/nonpoor segregation. Panel C shows the proportion of racial segregation associated with economic segregation of the poor from the nonpoor, that is, Panel B divided by Panel A. The results are striking: very little of the observed racial segregation is caused by economic segregation. The level of black-white segregation due to the residential sorting of poor and nonpoor persons is only 0.059, compared to the actual figure of 0.601. At the metropolitan level, therefore, less than 10 percent of the measured level of black/white racial segregation comes from economic segregation. Only 11.2 percent of Hispanic/white segregation is contributed by economic segregation. Furthermore, less than 4 percent of the Index of Dissimilarity between blacks and Hispanics is due to economic segregation. In part, this reflects that both groups have elevated poverty rates. The contribution of economic segregation to the racial segregation of Asians is less than 8 percent in all comparisons. In contrast to economic segregation, only a small fraction of sorting by race is a byproduct of sorting by income.

In conclusion, economic segregation per se contributes very little to racial segregation, except in a few smaller metropolitan areas with small black populations. In contrast, racial segregation seems to be a significant force in creating economic segregation, accounting for about one-third of such segregation in the typical metropolitan area. At the same time, two-thirds of economic segregation on average is *not* driven by racial segregation. These are related but independent spatial processes, both of which contribute to the tendency of poor and minority children in particular to live in racially and economically isolated communities, as will be discussed further in the following section.

Segregation of School-Age Children

As a natural consequence of life-cycle selection, school-age children will be more segregated than persons overall, both racially and economically. Residential decisions of adults are affected by the presence and age of children in their families (W. Clark and Onaka 1983; Rossi 1955). Families with children, regardless of race, seek higher-quality schools and safe environments, and are less likely than childless families to locate in neighborhoods with higher poverty rates. Whites who have children are less likely to be urban pioneers in integrated urban neighborhoods (Ellen, Horn, and O'Regan 2013).

The effect of these life-cycle interactions with segregation can be seen in Figure 2.4, which shows the segregation of children enrolled in different levels of education: kindergarten and pre-K, elementary school (grades 1–8), and high school (grades 9–12), compared to persons not enrolled in those levels of schooling, based on an analysis of the 2007–2011 ACS data (Jargowsky 2014a). All bars in the chart represent the weighted average Index of Dissimilarity for 384 metropolitan areas for the specified groups. Segregation of children enrolled in school is substantially higher than in the corresponding non-enrolled populations. For example, the Index of Dissimilarity for whites and blacks not attending pre-K through 12th grades is 0.582, whereas black and white children enrolled in elementary school have a 23 percent higher Index, 0.717. White and black high school students are even more segregated, with a segregation score of 0.738. The difference may be related to the finding, reported by Kimelberg (2014), that highly educated middle-class parents worry more about issues of academic quality and school safety at the high school than the elementary level.

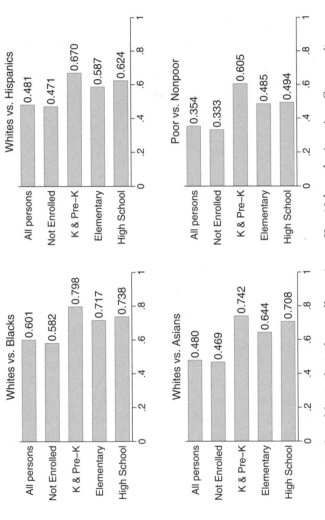

Figure 2.4. Index of dissimilarity by enrollment in pre-K to 12th grade. American Community Survey, 2007–2011; Jargowsky 2014.

The residential segregation of children enrolled in kindergarten and pre-kindergarten is influenced both by the segregation of families with children in that age range and by the choices families make about enrolling those children. Apparently, families exercise their choices in ways that further increase segregation: children enrolled in kindergarten and pre-kindergarten have the highest black-white segregation, measured at 0.798 (37 percent higher than those not enrolled). This extreme figure is the nationwide average of 384 metropolitan areas.

Segregation of Hispanics and Asians from whites by school enrollment follows exactly the same pattern as black/white segregation, albeit starting from lower overall levels in the general population. Similarly, poor and non-poor children enrolled in school are more segregated than the poor and nonpoor persons not in school, as is also shown in Figure 2.3. Among children enrolled in prekindergarten, segregation of the poor from the nonpoor is 0.605, compared to 0.333 for poor and nonpoor persons not enrolled in school. Elementary and high school students also exhibit elevated segregation, with poor versus nonpoor dissimilarity of 0.485 and 0.494 respectively. The ACS data do not have sufficient detail to examine the racial/ethnic segregation of students separately for poor and non-poor students, but it seems clear that poor school-age minority students would be segregated on both dimensions from non-poor white students.

Thus, the generally reported segregation levels substantially underestimate the effective level of residential segregation for the school age population. Given the linkage between school composition and academic performance (Hanushek et al. 2003), the elevated levels of residential segregation among school-age children have important implications for equality of opportunity in education. Scholars and policy makers concerned with reducing disparities in educational attainment need to address both racial and economic segregation, given that both contribute independently to the educational isolation of low-income children.

Concentration of Poverty

Both economic and racial segregation contribute to a phenomenon known as "the concentration of poverty." The problems of poverty are exacerbated when poor people live in dysfunctional high-poverty neighborhoods where they are exposed to high levels of crime and violence and have limited access to educational and economic opportunities (Wilson 1996). Growing up in such neighborhoods can affect children's educational achievement (Ludwig et al. 2011; Jargowsky and El Komi 2011; Burdick-Will et al. 2011). The burdens of poverty are, therefore, more intense for the minority poor, who are both racially and economically isolated, than for many of the white poor, who experience low income but are less likely to have the added burdens of living in very poor neighborhoods (Grady and Darden 2012).

The concentration of poverty quantifies the extent to which poor persons are likely to live in high-poverty neighborhoods and attend the schools that serve these severely disadvantaged neighborhoods. High-poverty census tracts are those in which more than 40 percent of the population have incomes below the federal poverty line. These neighborhoods are characterized by high rates of single parenthood, low levels of educational attainment, and detachment from the labor force (Jargowsky 1997, chap. 4). Further, the lack of opportunities and role models in such neighborhoods contributes to a social milieu in which alcohol and drug abuse, gang membership, criminality, and other self-defeating behaviors become more prevalent (Wilson 1987, 1996). Thus, a good measure of the concentration of poverty is percentage of the poor in a given area that lives in neighborhoods, represented by census tracts, with poverty rates of 40 percent or more. By this measure, concentration of poverty rose dramatically during the 1970s and 1980s (Jargowsky and Bane 1991; Kasarda 1993; Jargowsky 1997). The increases were fastest in the Midwest and Northeast, areas that suffered from rapid deindustrialization and rising poverty. In fact, concentration of poverty is closely correlated with overall economic conditions at the metropolitan level. Concentration of poverty declined substantially during the 1990s, a decade of rapid economic growth and low unemployment (Jargowsky 2003; Kingsley and Pettit 2003).

Since 2000, the spatial concentration of poverty has surged again. The number of high-poverty census tracts—defined as those with poverty rates of 40 percent or more—fell 26.5 percent, from 3,417 in 1990 to 2,510 in 2000 (Jargowsky 2003). The sharp reduction in high-poverty neighborhoods observed in the 2000 Census, after the economy had run at nearly full employment during the last half of the 1990s, has since been completely reversed. The count of such tracts increased by 800 (32 percent) between 2000 and the 2005–2009 ACS data to nearly the level of 1990, even though these data span more than three years before the financial crisis hit in late 2008 (Jargowsky 2013). *The latest data, spanning 2008–2012, show that the number of high-poverty tracts has increased to 4,054, a 62 percent increase since 2000* (Jargowsky

2014b). There are more zones of concentrated poverty now than have ever been recorded before.

The racial/ethnic composition of the population of high-poverty neighborhoods has changed due to different rates of growth among demographic subgroups. For example, while the population in high-poverty neighborhoods has risen for all racial and ethnic groups, it has grown fastest among non-Hispanic whites: the count of whites in high-poverty areas more than doubled, increasing 122 percent between 2000 and the most recent data. In comparison, the black and Hispanic population of those areas increased 51 and 74 percent, respectively. As a result, whites now make up 26 percent of the population of high-poverty tracts, compared to 20 percent in 2000. The black population share has declined from 42 percent in 2000 to 37 percent in 2008–2012. The Hispanic share has remained constant at approximately 31 percent.

While the number of high-poverty neighborhoods has risen, the number of poor persons has risen overall, due to both population growth and the general rise in the poverty rate since 2000. To ask whether poverty is more concentrated, we must examine the percentage of the poor living in high-poverty areas. In the average metropolitan area, the percent of the poor living in high-poverty neighborhoods rose from 11.6 percent to 15.0 percent between 2000 and 2008–2012, although the concentration of poverty is still lower than in 1990, when it was 16.8 percent. As shown in Figure 2.5, it rose for all groups, though the increase was fastest for whites (rising from 5.1 to 8.4 percent). Despite the recent increase in whites living in high-poverty areas, concentration of poverty still differentially affects members of minority groups. The black poor are nearly three times more likely than the white poor to live in high-poverty neighborhoods: 24.6 percent compared to 8.4 percent. The Hispanic poor are twice as likely as the white poor to be in neighborhoods of concentrated poverty.

Understanding the Links to Metropolitan Development

The underlying systems and processes that produce high-poverty urban contexts must be addressed in order to further equal access to neighborhood institutions and resources. Unless the root causes of segregation are addressed, many programs and policies will be fighting an uphill battle, necessitating the commitment of substantial resources and heroic efforts. Take

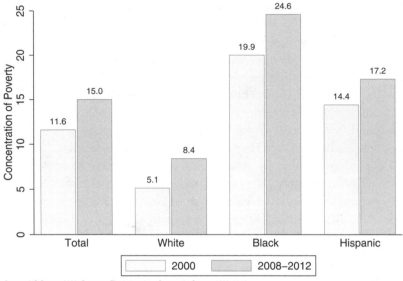

Source: US Census 2000, Summary File 3; American Community Survey, 2008–2012
Note: Weighted average of 384 Metropolitan Areas.

Figure 2.5. Concentration of poverty, U.S. metropolitan areas. Weighted average of 384 metropolitan areas. U.S. Census 2000, Summary File 3; American Community Survey, 2008–2012.

education policy for example: programs to reform and improve inner-city schools will be continuously undermined unless the root causes of segregation and the concentration of poverty are addressed.

The causes of the prevalence of high-poverty neighborhoods in urban centers are abundantly clear. Deindustrialization, of course, eroded the historic job base of many older industrial cities (Bluestone and Harrison 1982; Gillette 2011). Just as important, however, was the vast out-migration to the suburbs that began after World War II and accelerated in the 1960s when urban riots, violent crime, and racial tensions came to the fore (Mieskowski and Mills 1993; Massey and Denton 1988b).

Two factors are key to understanding the effect of the suburban explosion on central cities. First, suburban growth produced housing units much faster than needed to accommodate metropolitan population growth. Between 1970 and 1990, for example, most large central cities and some older inner-ring suburbs lost population rapidly, while successive new suburban rings gained population (Jargowsky 2002). Second, zoning was used to prevent low-income persons and racial minorities from leaving the confines of the central city (Galster 2012; Fischel 2004). In effect, while discrimination on the basis of race is strictly illegal, discrimination on the basis of income, through exclusionary zoning, is the law of the land. The results are selective out-migration, segregation by race and class, and concentration of poverty, as described above.

Conclusion

People of different races, ethnicities, and income levels are not distributed evenly across neighborhoods. Taken together, segregation by race and segregation by class result in concentrated poverty—high-poverty ghettos and barrios with poverty rates of 40 percent or more. These neighborhoods are often characterized by vacant housing, drug and alcohol abuse, crime and violence, and failing schools. These phenomena are part of a self-perpetuating process. The social conditions of high-poverty neighborhoods generally, and the poor performance of inner-city schools in particular, serve as a further inducement toward segregation. Those with means, and those with realistic alternatives, seek safer neighborhoods with better resources.

Segregation by race and class has serious implications for equal access to educational opportunity since school-age children are especially segregated and since they often attend schools near their homes, either because they are required to by geographic attendance zones or because of commuting time constraints. High-poverty neighborhoods are the ones that contain the most dysfunctional schools and school systems, leaving their students tragically unprepared for college or employment in the modern economy. Students who fail academically will be unprepared to function in the modern labor market, limiting their social mobility and increasing economic inequality. Racial and economic segregation causes, sustains, and worsens segregation, racial isolation, and economic inequality.

We cannot easily separate the contribution of schools and other aspects of segregated high-poverty neighborhoods to educational failure. Evidence suggests that both matter (Turner, this volume). Logic suggests that if there were a way to create and sustain high-quality schools in poor neighborhoods, gaps in educational outcomes for low-income and minority students would be substantially reduced. But given the tight connections and feedback loops between neighborhoods and schools, an effective solution to educational failure in the long term may require greater efforts to reverse economic and racial segregation. As Doug Massey (this volume) shows in the study of the outcomes of providing affordable housing in the affluent suburb of Mt. Laurel, New Jersey, low-income children who have the opportunity to live and attend schools in middle-class environments perform substantially better than their counterparts residing in segregated, high-poverty environments.

CHAPTER 3

The Changing Geography of Disadvantage

Elizabeth Kneebone

The 2000s brought significant changes to the demographic and economic fabric of the United States. The country has grown increasingly diverse in recent years, driven by a combination of immigration, declining births and increasing deaths among whites, and a boom in minority births. Already by 2012, almost half of children under five (49.9 percent) were people of color, and by 2043, the country as a whole is expected to tip to majority-minority (U.S. Census 2013).

The economic makeup of the country has changed as well. After a decade marked by two recessions that limped into slow and uneven economic recoveries, the number of people living below the federal poverty line ($23,492 for a family of four in 2012) rose to record levels. By 2012, 46.5 million people—15 percent of the population—lived in poverty, and more than one-third of the country (107.5 million) lived below twice the poverty line (DeNavas-Walt, Proctor, and Smith 2013).[1] At the same time, as wages for lower- and middle-income earners declined or stagnated, income and wealth became more concentrated at the top of the distribution, driving increases in income inequality that surpassed 1928's pre-Depression peak (Saez 2013).

However, these changes did not spread evenly across the country. They have played out differently across a diverse array of places, clustering and unfolding in ways that have influenced the growth (or decline) of communities over time. Moreover, many of the shifting dynamics that emerged since 2000 have changed the map of America's demographic and economic landscape in ways that challenge long-held notions of place and opportunity.

Background: The Spatial Impact of Demographic and Income Trends

In the 2000s, the population of the United States became increasingly metropolitan, continuing a long-running trend. Population growth in rural communities—those outside official metropolitan statistical areas—slowed in the 2000s. Since 2010 those communities have collectively shed residents. At the same time, the nation's hundred largest metro areas continued their dominance, particularly in the postrecession period. Since the late 2000s, major metro areas have grown at a faster clip than their smaller metropolitan counterparts, which experienced a steady slowdown in population growth over that period (W. Frey 2014).

Within the nation's largest metro areas, big cities have begun to reverse a decades-old pattern, as central city population gains outstripped growth outside central cities in recent years in places like Atlanta, Boston, New York, and Washington, D.C. (W. Frey 2013). While big cities work to sustain this resurgence, hoping to attract a growing number of millennials and aging boomers, shifts are also taking place outside of central cities. Traditionally perceived as bastions of white middle-class families, suburbia has become increasingly diverse, both demographically and economically.

At the start of the 2000s, in the nation's hundred largest metro areas 44 percent of African Americans lived in suburbs, reflecting in part the legacy of discriminatory housing policies that slowed suburbanization of black residents relative to the overall population and whites in particular. However, rapid growth in the African American population in suburbs over the decade, coupled with a net decline in big cities, significantly shifted the balance in metropolitan America. By 2010, 51 percent of black residents in the nation's major metro areas lived in suburbs, meaning that for the first time more than half of every minority group in large metro areas was suburban (W. Frey 2011).

Immigration has followed a similar pattern. Whereas cities and suburbs were home to a similar share of the nation's immigrants as recently as 1980 (41 and 43 percent, respectively), each decade since has seen a marked shift toward suburbs. This shift occurred as immigrants increasingly bypassed traditional gateway cities of the last century and settled directly in suburban enclaves. By 2010, the suburbs of 10 major metro areas—including Los Angeles, New York, and Chicago as well as Riverside, Houston, and Atlanta—accounted for more than half the nation's immigrant population. Within the nation's largest metro areas, more than 60 percent of immigrants lived in suburbia by the end of the 2000s (Singer 2013).

The age profile of these places is changing as well. Cities and suburbs alike saw their share of residents under eighteen decline slightly over the decade as the median age of the population ticked upward. Big cities in the nation's largest metro areas also saw their share of residents who were sixty-five and older decline as working-age residents made up a greater portion of city dwellers. In contrast, suburbs not only added to their share of working-age residents, but also "grayed" faster than cities, with their sixty-five and over population growing by 19 percent, or 2.7 million.[2]

Amid these demographic shifts, the landscape of poverty has changed markedly. For decades the images tied to discussions of poverty and place primarily have been those of distressed inner cities and declining and isolated rural communities. Indeed, historically, that is where the challenges of poverty have been most pronounced. In 1962, Michael Harrington's *The Other America* helped call attention to the plight of the "invisible" poor in urban and rural America. The disinvestment, declining population, and increasing crime that gripped many cities in the 1970s and 1980s exacerbated the challenges of urban poverty and led to growing concentrations of disadvantage in inner cities, as chronicled by the work of Paul Jargowsky and others in the 1990s (also see Jargowsky, this volume). William Julius Wilson's (1987) *The Truly Disadvantaged* and Douglas Massey and Nancy Denton's (1993) *American Apartheid* explored the pressures and policies that led to the concentrated and generational poverty in these distressed inner-city neighborhoods and the challenges faced by their residents. Likewise, the work of Cynthia Duncan (1999) and Janet Fitchen (1981) detailed the economic and social structures that contributed to deep and entrenched poverty in the nation's rural communities.

Cities continue to grapple with persistent and stubbornly high poverty rates. But as poverty grew to record levels in the 2000s, it has touched more people and places than before, although perceptions of where poverty is and whom it affects often have not kept pace with its growing reach. The poor population in suburbs grew by 65 percent between 2000 and 2012, more than twice the pace of growth in big cities and rural communities. By 2012, the suburbs were home to three million more poor residents than big cities and seven million more poor than rural areas. What is more, as suburban poverty

grew rapidly in the 2000s, it also moved beyond older, inner-ring suburbs that have long struggled with poverty alongside central cities—as
documented in the work of Myron Orfield and others—to newer, exurban
communities that may have previously seemed immune to these trends
(Kneebone and Berube 2013).

As Orfield's work suggests, the shift of poverty toward the suburbs has
been underway for decades. In the 1980s, the pace of growth in suburban
poor population began to outstrip urban increases, and each decade saw that
gap grow. The Great Recession helped push fast forward on the growth of suburban poverty—as suburbs bore the brunt of the recession alongside cities
more so than in past downturns—but the suburbs had already become home
to the majority of metropolitan poor by 2005 (Berube and Kneebone 2006). A
number of factors besides the recent downturn have helped drive these trends
over the years.

Part of this shift reflects the changing patterns in immigration mentioned
above. But even as immigrants contributed 30 percent to the overall population growth in suburbs in the 2000s, they made up just 17 percent of the
growth in suburban poor population, meaning this has been a phenomenon
largely driven by the native-born population (Suro, Wilson, and Singer 2011).

It also reflects shifting housing and labor market dynamics. In regions
where inner-city redevelopment and population are on the rise, housing price
pressures have prompted some residents to look further out in the region for
more affordable housing options. Housing subsidies have become more suburban as well. In the nation's largest metro areas, residents have increasingly
used portable housing choice vouchers to locate in suburban communities.
By 2008, roughly half of residents in voucher households lived in the suburbs,
although often in less opportunity-rich communities than their higher-income
counterparts (Covington, Freeman, and Stoll 2011). The housing-led downturn also took a deep toll on suburban communities. The subprime lending boom in the mid-2000s saw nearly three-quarters of subprime loans in
the nation's largest metro areas occur in the suburbs. In turn, suburbs have
been home to roughly three-quarters of foreclosures since the collapse of the
housing market (Schildt et al. 2013).

In addition, the geography of low-wage work became more suburban over
the last decade. Almost every major metro area saw jobs shift away from the
downtown during the 2000s, with industries like manufacturing, construction, and retail locating at least half their jobs more than ten miles from
downtown. Not only did the jobs base become more suburban, but so too did

the low-wage workforce. By 2012, two-thirds of employees in low-wage occupations lived in suburbs (Williams and Berube 2014).

Together these factors helped drive the rapid increases in suburban poverty that have taken place, particularly since 2000, as more low-income residents have moved to suburbia, and, perhaps more important, as more long-term residents slipped into poverty over time. However, even as it affects more communities, poverty has not "regionalized" evenly over time. Rather, it has clustered in long-struggling communities and in newly forming pockets of disadvantage, marking a resurgence of concentrated poverty across the country.

This shifting map of poverty and its reconcentration in recent years has serious implications for policy makers and practitioners working to build shared prosperity and access to opportunity across places. The remainder of this chapter focuses on analyzing the most recent data from the American Community Survey to better understand the distribution and trends within and across distressed neighborhoods in the nation's metropolitan and rural communities.

Findings: The Reconcentration of Poverty

After Progress in the 1990s, Concentrated Poverty Is on the Rise

As the 1990s drew to a close, a strong economy and a slate of targeted policies succeeded in not only reducing the number of poor in the United States, but also in decreasing the number of poor living in distressed, high-poverty neighborhoods (Kneebone, Nadeau, and Berube 2011). However, as the 2000s began they ushered in an economically tumultuous decade that largely erased that progress.

Nationally, the number of high-poverty neighborhoods—defined as census tracts with poverty rates of 40 percent or more—rose steeply over the course of the 2000s, growing from 2,080 in 2000 to 3,570 in 2008–2012.[3] As the number of distressed neighborhoods grew, so too did the number of residents living in such places. By the end of the first decade of this century, the number of people living in high-poverty neighborhoods had increased by more than 70 percent since the start of the decade (also see Jargowsky, this volume).

Similarly, the number of poor residents living in high-poverty neighborhoods rose by 78 percent, or 2.3 million people, more than twice the pace of growth in the overall poor population (32 percent) over the same time period.

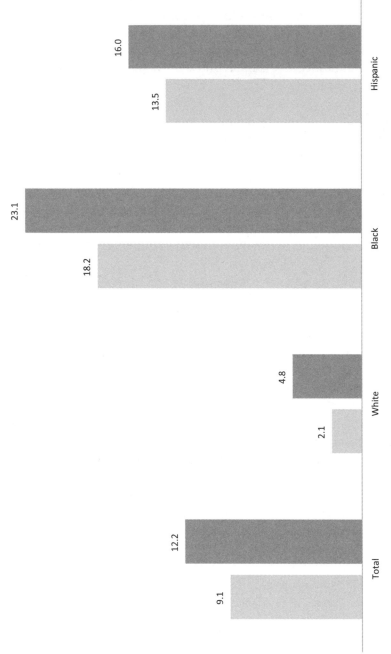

Figure 3.1. Share of poor residents in high-poverty neighborhoods by race and ethnicity. Brookings Institution analysis of decennial census and American Community Survey data.

By 2008–2012, 5.4 million residents faced the "double burden" of being poor in a very poor place. That figure represents only a fraction of the total poor population overall, but it is a share that has grown since 2000 (Figure 3.1).

Between 2000 and 2008–2012, the national concentrated poverty rate— or percentage of poor residents living in high-poverty neighborhoods—rose from 9.1 to 12.2 percent. While the growth of concentrated poverty in the 2000s was felt across racial and ethnic groups, deep disparities remain. The share of poor white residents living in high-poverty neighborhoods more than doubled over the decade but remained well below average at less than 5 percent. In contrast, the share of poor Hispanics in distressed neighborhoods was more than three times that rate, reaching 16 percent by 2008–2012. Poor black residents experienced the greatest uptick in their concentrated poverty rate, with an increase of 5 percentage points. By 2008–2012, almost one in four poor black residents (23.1 percent) lived in a high-poverty neighborhood.

The Nation's Largest Metro Areas Continue to Be Home to the Majority of Distressed Neighborhoods

Together, the nation's hundred largest metropolitan areas account for roughly two-thirds of the nation's population.[4] They are also home to more than two-thirds of the nation's high-poverty neighborhoods and a growing share of the country's poor population.

Between 2000 and 2008–2012, the poor population rose in each of the hundred areas except New Orleans.[5] At the same time, the number of poor living in high-poverty neighborhoods increased in 87 of the 100 largest metro areas, and 78 regions experienced an increase in their concentrated poverty rate.

While the growth of concentrated poverty touched every major census region, some were hit harder than others (Table 3.1). Together, Midwestern metro areas registered the steepest increase (8 percentage points), reaching a concentrated poverty rate of more than 18 percent and overtaking the Northeast for highest share of poor residents living in distressed neighborhoods by 2008–2012. Midwestern metro areas account for six of the ten largest increases in metropolitan concentrated poverty rates since 2000, with four of those metro areas clustered in Ohio (Table 3.2). Within the Midwest, all but one major metro area experienced an increase in their concentrated poverty rate, ranging from 1.1 percentage points in St. Louis, Missouri, to 22.6 percentage points in Toledo, Ohio.[6] Together, the number of poor

Table 3.1. Change in Population in High-Poverty Tracts by Census Region and Poverty Status, 100 Metro Areas

Region	Number of high-poverty tracts			Poor population in high-poverty tracts			Concentrated poverty rate		
	2000	2008–12	% change	2000	2008–12	% change	2000	2008–12	Change
Top 100 Metro Areas	1,538	2,447	59.1	2,279,337	3,753,609	64.7	11.2	13.8	2.6
Midwest (19)	345	756	119.1	345,663	901,003	160.7	10.3	18.3	8.0
Northeast (19)	453	519	14.6	740,018	845,010	14.2	15.4	15.6	0.2
South (38)	465	752	61.7	697,649	1,223,877	75.4	10.6	12.9	2.3
West (24)	275	420	52.7	496,007	783,719	58.0	8.8	10.6	1.8

Brookings analysis of decennial Census and ACS data.
*Changes are significant at the 90 percent confidence level.

Table 3.2. Top and Bottom Metro Areas for Change in Concentrated
Poverty Rate, 2000 to 2008–12

Metro areas	2000 to 2008–12		
	Concentrated poverty rate change	Change in poor population in extreme-poverty tracts	Change in number of extreme-poverty tracts
With Greatest Increases in Concentrated Poverty			
Toledo, OH	22.6	28,084	21
Youngstown-Warren-Boardman, OH-PA	21.2	20,259	15
Detroit-Warren-Livonia, MI	18.7	152,652	112
Dayton, OH	15.0	20,733	15
Tucson, AZ	12.8	25,767	11
Cleveland-Elyria-Mentor, OH	12.4	49,545	39
Greenville-Mauldin-Easley, SC	12.0	12,739	7
Syracuse, NY	12.0	12,290	10
Indianapolis-Carmel, IN	11.9	29,331	23
Hartford-West Hartford-East Hartford, CT	11.9	16,798	14
With Greatest Decreases in Concentrated Poverty			
McAllen-Edinburg-Mission, TX	−10.5	12,298	4
New Orleans-Metairie-Kenner, LA	−7.0	−21,567	−8
Virginia Beach-Norfolk-Newport News, VA-NC	−6.5	−8,713	−7
Ogden-Clearfield, UT	−4.9	−808	−1
New York-Northern New Jersey-Long Island, NY-NJ-PA	−3.8	−81,265	−51
Baltimore-Towson, MD	−3.4	−4,220	−8
Augusta-Richmond County, GA-SC	−2.8	1,019	1
Orlando-Kissimmee-Sanford, FL	−2.5	−2,712	−1
Washington-Arlington-Alexandria, DC-VA-MD-WV	−1.7	−1,191	−1
Atlanta-Sandy Springs-Marietta, GA	−1.4	26,097	17
Los Angeles-Long Beach-Santa Ana, CA	−1.3	−21,424	−4

Brookings analysis of decennial census and ACS data.
All changes significant at the 90 percent confidence level.

residents living in distressed neighborhoods in the Midwest climbed by
161 percent between 2000 and 2008–2012.

Large metro areas in the South and West also experienced steep upticks
in the number of poor residents living in high-poverty neighborhoods (75 and
58 percent, respectively), although their concentrated poverty rates rose by
more modest margins than in the Midwest. At the same time, ten of the eleven
metro areas that saw their concentrated poverty rates fall between 2000 and
2008–2012 were located in the South and West. Among this list, metro Atlanta
in particular stands out. Although the metro area's concentrated poverty rate
fell over this time period, the number of distressed neighborhoods in the region rose by seventeen, and 26,000 *more* poor lived in high-poverty tracts in
2008–2012 than at the start of the 2000s. The decline in the metro area's concentrated poverty rate largely reflects the rapid growth of poverty outside of
distressed neighborhoods, rather than progress in reducing distressed conditions. Among the top hundred metro areas, the Atlanta region experienced the second biggest increase in the poor population outside the urban
core between 2000 and 2012, which ballooned by 159 percent in twelve years.

New York was the only metro area outside the South and West that experienced a decline in its concentrated poverty rate between 2000 and 2008–
2012. However, almost every other Northeastern metro area posted an
increase.[7] The collective concentrated poverty rate for large metro areas in
the Northeast remained above average in 2008–2012 at 15.6 percent, but the
census region registered the smallest increase among the four over 2000
(0.2 percentage points). This is largely due to the outsized effect the New York
metro area has on the census region. Removing New York from the calculation actually nets an increase of 4.5 percentage points in the remainder of
the Northeast (from 11.1 percent in 2000 to 15.6 percent in 2008–2012). In
2000, metropolitan New York made up 64 percent of the poor population living in distressed neighborhoods in major Northeastern metro areas, but by
2008–2012 that share had fallen to 47 percent.

As Poverty Has Concentrated, Challenges of Concentrated
Disadvantage Have Spread to More Places

Large metro areas continue to house the bulk of distressed neighborhoods
and concentrated poverty, and central cities in particular remain home to the
highest concentrations of poverty. In 2008–2012, the concentrated poverty

rate in central cities was 23.3 percent, followed by small metro areas (12.7 percent) and suburban and rural communities (6.2 and 6.4 percent, respectively). However, patterns have been shifting in recent years—both within the nation's largest metro areas and beyond them.

In 2000, almost 62 percent of poor residents in high-poverty neighborhoods lived in big cities in the nation's largest metro areas. Another 10 percent lived in rural communities; the remainder were divided between suburbs and small metropolitan areas (Figure 3.2).[8]

Poor residents in distressed suburban neighborhoods and small metro areas more than doubled between 2000 and 2008–2012, growing by 128 percent and 145 percent, respectively, and eclipsing the urban growth rate of 51 percent. As a result, by 2008–2012, big cities accounted for just over half (52.5 percent, a decrease of 9.5 percentage points since 2000) of the poor population living in concentrated poverty while the small metro area and suburban shares had grown to 20.1 and 17.4 percent, respectively (up from 14.6 and 13.6 percent, respectively).

Among these geography types, small metro areas posted the biggest increase in the concentrated poverty rate (5.5 percentage points) over this time period. This uptick was fueled by increases in small metro areas like Lima and Springfield, Ohio; Erie and Reading, Pennsylvania; Topeka, Kansas; and Reno, Nevada—each of which experienced increases of 20 percentage points or more in concentrated poverty.

At the same time, suburbs in the nation's largest metro areas experienced an increase of 2.1 percentage points in concentrated poverty. While some of the regions with the largest suburban increases in concentrated poverty were in the Midwest, like Cleveland, Detroit, Toledo, and Youngstown, many Western and Southern metro areas make the list, like Fresno, Greenville, South Carolina, and El Paso, each of which experienced double-digit increases in their suburban concentrated poverty rate between 2000 and 2008–2012.

As poverty has grown and high-poverty neighborhoods have emerged in new places, including suburban communities and smaller metropolitan areas, the nature of distressed neighborhoods has changed as well. For one, the racial and ethnic makeup of high-poverty neighborhoods has shifted over time. By 2008–2012, residents of these neighborhoods were more likely to be white than in 2000, growing from 14 percent to 21.8 percent. At the same time, the share of African Americans in such neighborhoods fell from 44.9 to 38.5 percent, although they continued to make up the largest group living in distressed tracts. Residents of these neighborhoods were also more likely

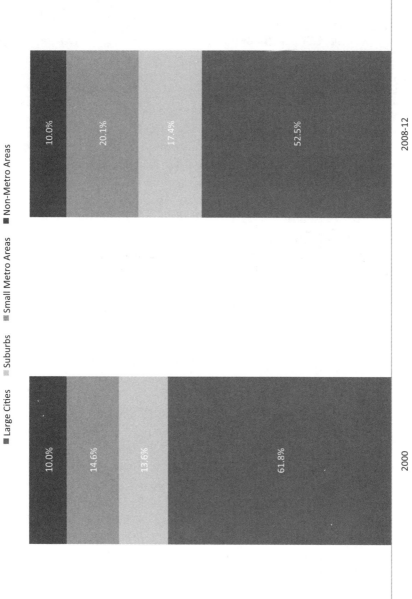

Legend: ■ Large Cities ■ Suburbs ■ Small Metro Areas ■ Non-Metro Areas

2000

10.0%
14.6%
13.6%
61.8%

2008-12

10.0%
20.1%
17.4%
52.5%

Figure 3.2. Change in geographic distributions of poor residents in high-poverty tracts.

to have reported receiving higher education than in the past. In 2000, 24.1 percent of residents in high-poverty neighborhoods had completed at least some college. By 2008–2012 that share had risen to 33.0 percent—compared to the national total, which increased from 51.8 to 57.5 percent during the same period. At the same time, the share of households in high-poverty neighborhoods that receive public assistance declined sharply, falling by half—from 18 percent of households to 9.5 percent—compared to the national total, which decreased from 3.4 to 2.7 percent during the same period.

Implications

An extensive literature has documented the myriad challenges and consequences that accompany the reality of being poor in a very poor neighborhood (Federal Reserve System 2008). It can be difficult to disentangle neighborhood effects from other complex factors that contribute to poverty. But research has shown that concentrated poverty brings with it additional challenges that can complicate the path out of poverty—from a lack of private investment, fewer job opportunities, and weaker employment networks in these neighborhoods to poorer health and education outcomes and higher violent crime rates for their residents. Recent work underscores the negative effects and intergenerational consequences of growing up in inner-city, racially segregated poverty, linking high incarceration rates among African Americans and racial disparities in educational outcomes to long-standing inequitable neighborhood conditions.[9]

Moreover, the concentration of poor residents into poor communities creates a physical divide between those residents and their wealthier counterparts that can in turn exacerbate misunderstanding and mistrust between those groups and undermine efforts to address poverty and the needs of poor neighborhoods. That spatial divide is one that has grown in recent years, as rising income inequality and a shrinking number of mixed-income and middle-class neighborhoods have left the wealthy and those with low incomes living increasingly segregated lives (R. Frey and Taylor 2012).

While the resurgence of concentrated poverty clearly has region-wide implications, within regions the ability of communities to address these challenges varies widely. Big cities have long faced these challenges, which can strain municipal budgets and services and put upward pressure on the tax burdens of local businesses and residents (Pack 1998). In response, they have spent decades building up the infrastructure, support systems, and civic and nonprofit capacity to address poverty and concentrated disadvantage. To aid in this effort, federal programs have been created since the War on Poverty to alleviate poverty in distressed inner-city neighborhoods. With varying levels of success, these policies have sought to improve conditions in high-poverty neighborhoods (e.g., by upgrading physical infrastructure or encouraging economic development), deliver critical services and work supports (e.g., affordable health care and child care options), or open up opportunities in other parts of the region for low-income families (e.g., through commute programs or housing vouchers) (Kneebone and Berube 2013). These efforts have made some degree of progress in deconcentrating poverty in urban areas and opening up opportunities for low-income and minority residents in suburbs that may have been previously inaccessible to them. For instance, Covington and her colleagues estimate that the shift of housing choice voucher recipients toward suburbs in the 2000s accounted for 23 percent of the increase in the suburban poor population over that time (Covington, Freeman, and Stoll 2011).

The rapid growth in poverty and its increasing concentration in suburban communities and smaller metropolitan areas have often occurred in places ill equipped to deal with these issues. Scott Allard and Benjamin Roth's research has documented the strained and patchy nature of the nonprofit safety net in suburbs, where providers stretch their services over greater distances (and often over multiple jurisdictions) and the range of supports available tends to be much more uneven than the continuum of services big cities provide (Allard and Roth 2010). The local governance capacity of these communities also tends to vary across the fragmented jurisdictional map that encompasses these places. Just as nonprofit capacity is limited or missing in many struggling suburban communities, many places often also lack the municipal staff, structures, and institutional experience to address the growing need in their communities.

In addition to services, resources like public transit tend to be less developed or lacking altogether outside major urban hubs. For those low-income suburbs that have access to transit, residents can reach just 4 percent of metro area jobs within a forty-five-minute commute (Tomer et al. 2011). The decentralization of employment may suggest better opportunities for low-income suburban residents to access nearby jobs, but job growth has often occurred in other parts of the region than where the low-income population is growing, and often in other suburbs as opposed to the downtown. As a result, Stephen Raphael and Michael Stoll found that low-income suburban residents tend to live in neighborhoods with fewer jobs than their higher-income counterparts, particularly poor black and Latino residents in the suburbs. Thus spatial mismatch challenges persist, especially in communities where affordable and reliable transportation options may be in short supply (Raphael and Stoll 2010).

These uneven and shifting patterns are affecting public schools across regions as well. Following trends in the larger low-income population, the population of students eligible for free and reduced price lunch has grown at a faster pace in suburbs than in cities in recent years, straining limited resources for school districts trying to address the multifaceted needs of a growing low-income population in the context of a weak suburban safety net. While low-income students in the suburbs often—although not always—have access to better schools than poor students in cities, income disparities plague suburban districts as well. The typical low-income student attends a school that performs at the 45th percentile on statewide exams compared to the typical middle- or higher-income student that attends a school testing at the 65th percentile (Kneebone and Berube 2013).

These issues—lack of capacity, services, and transportation, and struggling schools—point to areas of growing concern as concentrated poverty emerges in new and different places beyond its historic homes. As suburbs and smaller metro areas face poverty at levels they may not have seen in the past and increasingly struggle with issues of concentrated poverty, regions run the risk, absent target policy action, of creating new pockets of concentrated disadvantage in places disconnected from the types of supports and economic opportunities that can help ameliorate the worst effects of concentrated poverty and potentially provide a path out of poverty.

Yet, cities continue to grapple with entrenched and spreading concentrations of poverty within their own borders, so the answer is not to simply shift already insufficient resources from one distressed place to another. And while growing the pool of resources available is a much-needed step given the scale of today's need, the current political gridlock and budgetary debates in Washington make such increases at the federal level unlikely for the foreseeable future. To make limited resources stretch further to help more people in more places, policy makers and practitioners will need models that combine public and private investments in ways that do more than one thing in more than one place at the same time—working at a more effective scale and across policy silos and jurisdictional boundaries to connect residents and communities to regional economic opportunity.

Conclusion

The large-scale transformations underway in the United States are unfolding in *places*. The rapid pace at which the geography of poverty and opportunity has shifted within the United States since 2000 should serve both as a reminder of that fact and a call to action for policy makers and practitioners.

The community in which one lives affects the types of education options, job opportunities, services, and supports available to them. Put simply, place matters, and places change. And rarely do they do so in isolation. Rather, regional forces from population dynamics to housing and labor market trends intersect to create an evolving map of both barriers and access to opportunity.

As discussed in more detail in the following sections of the book, to promote truly sustainable and inclusive growth across these regions, policy and practice need to develop in place-conscious ways that can respond to the changing geography of poverty and opportunity and forge connections between the two. Failing to act runs the risk of leaving the most disadvantaged populations and places behind.

CHAPTER 4

U.S. Workers' Diverging Locations:
Causes and Inequality Consequences

Rebecca Diamond

Over the past three decades, the earnings of workers with a college education have substantially increased relative to those with less education. Over
the same period, workers have become increasingly spatially segregated by
education, with more highly educated workers living in metropolitan areas
with higher wage growth for both low- and high-skill workers, substantially
larger increases in housing costs, and more amenities, and less highly educated workers living in metropolitan areas with lower wage growth, lower
housing costs, and fewer amenities.[1] In addition, the economic trajectories
of increasingly high-skill cities are diverging from those with fewer college
graduates, with productivity in high-skill cities increasing faster than in low-
skill cities (Moretti 2013). This chapter explores the causes of the increased
geographic sorting by level of education and explores its effect on economic
well-being inequality.

Trends in well-being inequality, as measured by the difference in the utility derived from total consumption of goods and services, between low- and
high-skill workers have not traditionally been part of the policy debate on
inequality, although they should be: recognizing the importance of living
costs and amenities in determining the different levels of utility and therefore levels of well-being attained with a given income provides a more comprehensive picture of the evolution of inequalities. Living costs and amenities
are eminently place-specific; as a result, the increasing sorting of low- and
high-skilled workers across space has important well-being implications for
these two groups. Indeed, Diamond (2013) finds that the increased geographic

skill segregation from 1980 to 2000 has led to at least 30 percent more inequality than suggested by the increase in wage inequality alone. Increased
geographic sorting enabled college educated workers to access and consume
higher-quality local amenities than lower-skilled workers in low skill cities.
The benefits of these amenities more than compensated for the higher housing
prices paid by the college educated.

This chapter explores the causes of increased geographic sorting of workers of different skill levels across metropolitan areas and the consequences
of this sorting on the economic well-being of low- and high-skill workers.
Section 2 presents the historical trends in the location choices of college and
non-college graduates. Section 3 discusses the causes of increased geographic
skill-sorting over the past three decades. Section 4 analyzes the implication
of increased skill-sorting for economic well-being inequality between college
and non-college graduates. Section 5 discusses policy implications. Section 6
concludes.

Increasing Return to Skill and Diverging
Location Choices: Historical Facts

Wage inequality increased from 1980 to 2000; the increase in the wage gap
between high school and college graduates was an important component of
this overall increase. In 1980, college graduates earned on average 38 percent
more than high school graduates. By 2000, college graduates were earning
57 percent more than high school graduates (Diamond 2013), and by 2011 it
rose to 73 percent.[2]

This trend has attracted much study, with a large body of research dedi-
cated to teasing out the many causes of this increase in inequality. Explanations
include the advent of computers (Autor, Katz, and Krueger 1998), changing
labor market institutions (DiNardo, Fortin, and Lemieux 1996), and outsourcing of jobs to lower-wage countries (Autor, Dorn, and Hanson 2013).
See Goldin and Katz (2008) for a further review of these findings.

Over the same period during which the educational wage gap grew, there
was a concurrent geographic segregation by skill level—although somewhat
less attention has been paid to this phenomenon (Moretti 2004; Berry and
Glaeser 2005; Moretti 2013; Diamond 2013). Cities with initially high population shares of college graduates in 1980, such as Boston and Atlanta, disproportionately attracted college graduates over the following twenty years. Cities

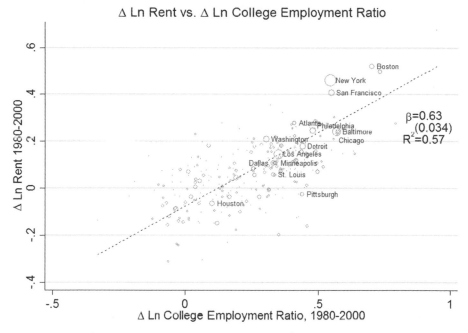

Figure 4.1. Change in rent versus change ln college employment ratio, 1980–2000.
Diamond 2013.

with smaller college populations in 1980, such as Albany, New York,, and
Harrisburg, Pennsylvania, lagged behind in attracting college graduates.
Among the top ten metropolitan areas with the largest share of college graduates in 1980, the share of college graduates between 1980 and 2000 grew by
12.2 percent on average. Conversely, the growth rate was only 1.9 percent in
the ten metropolitan areas with the lowest share of college graduates (Moretti
2013).

The divergence of workers' location choices is strongly related to the evolution of wages and rents across cities. Local housing rent increases from
1980 to 2000 are strongly associated with cities' increases in their share of
college graduates: for every 1 percent increase in the ratio of college graduates to non-college graduates (referred to as the "college employment ratio")
living in the city, a city experienced a 0.6 percent increase in rents (Figure 4.1).
This increase in housing costs, whether for homeownership or renting, has
an important role to play in the causality of increasing sorting of households
by income as discussed in the following section.

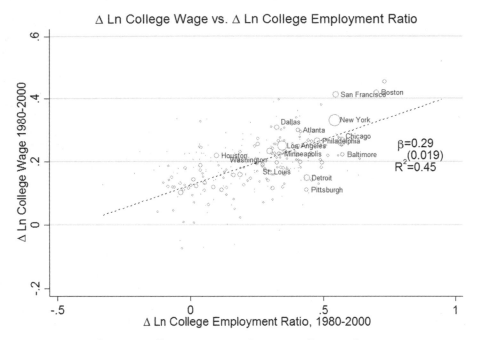

Figure 4.2. Change in college wage versus change in college employment ratio, 1980–2000. Diamond 2013.

Cities that experienced higher rates of growth in shares of college graduates have also experienced higher wage growth for both college *and* non-college workers. Diamond (2013) finds for each 1 percent increase in a city's college employment ratio, the city experienced a 0.3 percent increase in wages for college educated workers (Figure 4.2) and a 0.2 percent increase in wages for non-college educated workers (Figure 4.3).

Since wages for non-college educated workers are higher in cities with a higher college employment ratio, one might expect non-college educated workers to move to these cities in search of these higher wages. In fact, they used to; it is a relatively recent phenomenon that lower-skilled workers do not elect to move to areas offering them the highest wages. Ganong and Shoag (2013) show that in 1960, both college and non-college workers tended to migrate to areas offering the highest wages. But by the 1980s, workers without a college degree no longer elected to move to the highest-paying areas (while their more highly educated counterparts did).

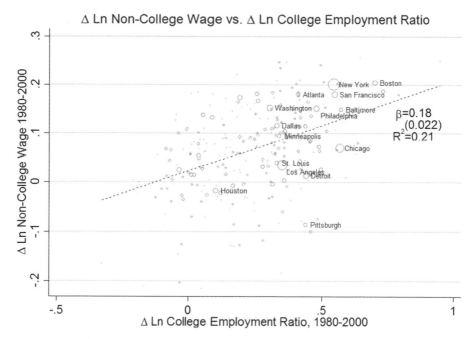

Figure 4.3. Change in non-college wage versus change in college employment ratio, 1980–2000. Diamond 2013.

There are many explanations for the decline in interstate migration. Molloy et al. (2014) find a decrease in the net benefits for workers to switch employers. They note that, as a result of changes in the labor market, the wage gains from geographic migration (for workers of all demographic and socio-economic characteristics) have become smaller. Ganong and Shoag (2013) find another explanation for the lower level of migration to high-wage regions in the 2000s versus the 1960s: the change in the cost of housing and local goods to which low-skill workers are particularly sensitive. In 1960, a 1 percent increase in a city's income per capita was associated with 0.95 percent increase in local housing prices. By 2010, this 1 percent increase in a city's per capita income was associated with 2.04 percent increase in local housing prices. Housing costs in high-wage, high-skill cities increased dramatically, which muted the incentive for low-skill workers to move to these higher-wage cities.[3]

At the same time, these increasingly expensive, high-skill cities experienced greater improvements in local amenities (and, as I will argue below, these amenities more than compensated residents for higher housing prices and contributed to an increase in their well-being). The amenities of a high-skill city include not just "classic" amenities (such as low crime rates and restaurant quality), but also the broad bundle of city characteristics which impact both work and home life. Diamond (2013) finds that increases in cities' shares of college graduates from 1980–2000 coincided with increases in the variety of local goods and services including bars, restaurants, dry cleaners, museums, and art galleries. These high-skill cities also experienced greater decreases in pollution and property crime rates than did low-skill cities. Indeed, high-skill cities likely offer many amenities which are difficult to empirically measure. For example, having highly educated neighbors may improve the quality of the local marriage market and the quality of local schools. There may be better job-related amenities in high-skill cities, such as higher expected future wage growth and a larger variety of job options.[4] Higher-skill cities offer not only the highest wages, but also a better quality of work life and home life.

Causes of Increased Skill Segregation Across Cities

The geographic divergence of skill across cities began in the 1980s and was strongly driven by the changing labor demands of different industries located across different cities (Moretti 2013; Diamond 2013). Due to a number of broad changes in the labor market from 1980 to 2000, many industries substantially changed their demands for college graduates' labor relative to their demand to hire non-college graduates. Important labor market changes from 1980 to 2000 included the advent of computers leading to skill-biased technological change, changes in labor market institutions such as the decline of unionization and the minimum wage, and the outsourcing of jobs overseas (Goldin and Katz 2008). For example, industries that more aggressively adopted computers and information technology (IT) tended to hire more college graduates, as these new technologies improved the productivity of tasks involving high cognitive ability and abstract thinking (Autor, Katz, and Krueger 1998). At the same time, computers and IT often automated tasks historically performed by lower-skilled workers. Thus, industries that aggressively pursued the adoption of computers and IT dramatically shifted their hiring away from non-college workers and toward more skilled college graduates.

This shift in labor demand is concentrated in historic high-tech hubs. Moretti (2013) shows that the cities that were historical geographic hubs of industries in which high-tech and R&D played an important role experienced larger shifts in their labor demand away from non-college workers toward college graduates, and experienced the largest increases in their shares of college graduates from 1980 to 2000. For example, the metropolitan area of San Francisco-Oakland-Vallejo was an economic hub for finance, engineering, research, and development services in 1980. Over the following decades, these industries dramatically increased their demand for college educated labor, helping drive the San Francisco MSA college share from 34 percent in 1980 up to 47 percent in 2000. Contrast this to Fresno, only a three-and-a-half-hour drive away. Fresno has historically been a hub for agriculture services and food processing and production. The surrounding farmland is home to many large-scale farms, which create many jobs in Fresno. However, food production jobs predominately do not require a college degree. Despite the overall population of Fresno doubling from 1980 to 2000, the share of college graduates *declined* from 24 percent in 1980 to 22 percent by 2000. The differential hiring demands of cities' local industries played a large role in attracting high- and low-skill workers to different cities, causing the divergence of skill across space.

The affordability of housing has been another important factor in the divergence of skill across space, with cities' elasticity of housing supply further fueling the geographic skill-sorting. As previously discussed, high-skill cities became comparatively more expensive to live in during the 1980s and 1990s. These increases in housing prices reflect a city's inability to accommodate an increase in housing demand with an increase in the housing stock due to supply constraints. In supply inelastic cities, housing prices will rise sharply in response to an influx of migrants. Many cities sharply increased their land-use regulations during this time period. Placing regulatory restrictions on the amount of allowed real estate development forces an increase in demand for housing to translate into skyrocketing housing prices.[5] Ganong and Shoag (2013) find that the cities that imposed larger restrictions on land-use regulation experienced larger increases in house prices as well as larger increases in their shares of college graduates. Indeed, college graduates' location decisions are less sensitive to increasing housing prices than are those of lower-skilled workers because lower-income households' marginal value of a dollar is higher.[6]

Combining data on local labor demands by industries and variations in cities' housing supply elasticities, Diamond (2013) estimates a model of how college educated and non-college educated workers trade off the relative benefits of cities' local wages, housing costs, and amenities (including public goods such as education) when electing where to live. In addition, this study estimates how local wages, housing costs, and amenities themselves respond to changes in the size of local college educated and non-college educated populations.

Consistent with Moretti (2013), Diamond (2013) finds that the primary driver of the increased skill segregation is changes in the labor demands of industries located in different cities. The study also finds that, even though local wage changes initially caused workers' migration, cities that attract a higher share of college graduates endogenously experience improvements in local amenities. When a city's share of college graduates increases, the quality and variety of the local goods and services increase, including increases in per capita amounts of clothing stores, bars, restaurants, movie theaters, grocery stores, and public goods including, importantly, education. An increase in the share of college graduates also leads to declines in property crime rates and pollution levels, all of which raise the cost of housing and therefore discourage the in-migration of non-college graduates.

Consider, for example, the metropolitan areas of Detroit and Boston. The economic downturn in Detroit has been largely attributed to the decline of auto manufacturing (Martelle 2012). But the decline is more than a loss of high-paying jobs—it also includes the decline of a broad range of public goods. In 2009, Detroit public schools had the lowest scores ever recorded in the twenty-one-year history of the national math proficiency test (Winerip 2011). Compare that dismal record to Detroit's public school system in the early twentieth century when manufacturing was booming and the system was lauded as a national model of urban education (Mirel 1999).

By comparison, Boston has increasingly attracted high-skill workers with its cluster of biotech, medical device, and technology firms. In the mid-1970s, Boston public schools were declining in quality, driven by racial tensions from integrating the schools (Cronin 2011). In 2006, however, the Boston public school district won the Broad Prize, which honors the urban school district that demonstrates the greatest performance and improvement in student achievement. The prosperity of Boston and decline of Detroit go beyond jobs and wages, directly impacting the amenities and quality of life in these areas for both college and non-college graduates. The broad changes in these cities are reflected in their shares of college graduates, as Boston's share of college graduates grew by 30 percent more than Detroit's from 1980 to 2000.

Increasing a city's share of college graduates also leads to local productivity increases for both college and non-college workers, driving up all workers' wages (Diamond 2013). For example, increased physical proximity of educated workers may lead to better sharing of ideas, faster innovation (Berry and Glaeser 2005), or faster technology adoption (Acemoglu 2002; Beaudry, Doms, and Lewis 2010), all of which drive up the wages of college graduates. Further, low-skill workers' wages can also benefit as the increased college share drives demand for local goods and services, creating jobs and increasing wages for low-skill workers (Autor and Dorn 2013). Autor and Dorn (2013) find that between 1985 and 2005, the share of hours worked by low-skill workers in service occupations increased by 50 percent and real hourly wages for these workers increased by 11 percentage points, more than the wage growth in other low-skill occupations. The rising employment and wages in low-skill service occupations reflect the increased demand from high-skill workers for these services that cannot be easily substituted and require co-location of the demanders and providers of the services in the same metropolitan areas.

The combination of desirable wages and amenities in these increasingly high-skill cities makes them attractive places to live for both college and non-college workers, which leads to sharp increases in housing prices as a result of supply constraints. However, housing price increases limit the in-migration of low-skill workers much more than that of high-skill workers. Diamond (2013) finds that while both college educated and non-college educated workers prefer cities with high wages, low housing costs, and high levels of amenities, college graduates place much more weight on the quality of amenities, while non-college graduates make their choices based on affordability. The higher price elasticity of housing demand found among lower-skill workers can be explained by their lower wages, resulting in their having a higher marginal benefit from an additional dollar of savings.

Handbury's (2013) study of households' demand for grocery products across cities finds similar results. Her work finds that cities with higher incomes per capita have better quality and a larger variety of grocery products (an amenity), but also higher prices for these products. Richer, more educated individuals prefer expensive cities with a high-quality selection, while poorer, less-educated individuals locate in more affordable cities with a lower quality and more limited variety of products.

The high housing costs in skilled cities is a strong component of what keeps these cities disproportionally high skill. Diamond (2013) finds that cities with less elastic supply of housing experienced larger housing price and college share increases. If the housing supply were to suddenly increase in a high-skill city, housing prices would fall. The resulting in-migration would disproportionately be low-skill workers, as these workers would find the newfound affordability of these cities particularly desirable. Thus, inelastic housing supply helps high-skill, high-quality cities remain this way, with the cost that the benefits of these cities (access to high-wage labor markets as well as an array of more desirable amenities) disproportionately accrue to the highly skilled.

Economic Well-Being Inequality: The Importance of Considering Amenities

If college educated and non-college educated workers primarily elect where to live based on local wages and housing costs, then the welfare analysis need only to account for those factors. In fact, amenities should also be taken into account.

Moretti (2013) finds that high-skill workers have experienced a larger increase in housing costs than low-skill workers due to their concentration in high housing cost cities. Controlling for differences in the changes in housing costs for low- and high-skill workers, he estimates that while the nominal wage premium between college and high school graduates increased by 50 percent from 1980 to 2000, the wage premium *net of housing costs* increased by 20 percent less. If the only forces influencing these workers' location choices were wages and housing costs, this would suggest that the increase in wage inequality overstates the true increase in consumption inequality. Essentially, this would mean that the differences in consumption growth from 1980 to 2000 between college graduates in New York and high school graduates living in Cleveland aren't actually as large as the differences in the growth in their incomes suggest. The New York college graduates are not actually getting that much "bang for their buck."

However, Diamond (2013) finds that the desirability of amenities in high-skill cities is an important reason college graduates are willing to pay such high housing costs to live in these expensive, high-wage cities. A substantial part of the reason the college graduate living in New York City is willing to pay such high housing prices to live in New York City is to enjoy the many amenities available there. Thus, even though the New Yorker must pay significantly more for housing in New York City than he would in Cleveland, he is not only getting housing for his money. He is enjoying the benefits of New York City, and this should be taken into account when considering the inequality effects of spatial skill segregation.

The increase in spatial sorting of college and non-college workers into very different cities raises the question of whether the large increases in wage inequality over the past three decades truly represents a similar increase in economic well-being inequality or whether, if the quality of location (as well as the cost of location) is taken into account the actual increases in wage inequality are larger than those that have been so far identified. Since housing costs are much higher in cities where more college graduates live than in those where more lower-skill workers live, it is possible that high local house prices diminish the overall consumption benefits college workers receive from their high wages. For example, in 2013 the median studio in San Francisco sold for $863,000 while the median four-bedroom house could be purchased in Las Vegas for only $220,100.[7] Since college graduates live in areas where one gets much less house for the money, their high wages may not translate into nearly as much consumption as the wage figures alone imply.

On the other hand, high-skill cities offer inhabitants access to high-wage labor markets as well as an array of more desirable amenities. If the economic value of living in a high-amenity city more than compensates college graduates for high housing prices, the growth in wage inequality would *understate* the increase in economic well-being inequality. The welfare implications of the increase in the wage gap and in geographic sorting between high-skill and low-skill workers might therefore be more pronounced than the differences in nominal wages or real wages would suggest.

Diamond (2013) finds that the utility college graduates gain from having access to a variety of desirable local amenities outweighs the negative effects of high housing costs. Since such large numbers of college graduates chose to migrate to high housing cost cities, the draw of the local amenities must have compensated them for the high housing costs. The size of the actual well-being gap is estimated: the 50 percent increase in the wage gap between high school and college graduates from 1980 to 2000 understates by at least 30 percent the true increases in economic well-being inequality due to changes in wages, housing costs, and endogenous local amenities.

These dynamics can be thought of as a nationwide "gentrification effect." Initially, changes in firms' demands for college educated and non-college educated workers increased the college share in high-skill cities. This initial spark then amplified as the presence of college workers in the city made it a more desirable, but also a more expensive place to live. As a result of increasing wage inequality due to the selective demand for high-skill workers in these cities, lower-skill workers were unable to pay the high prices that allowed access to cities with better quality amenities, which led them to relocate to more affordable areas with lower quality amenities. So, while low-skill workers would gain from locating in high-amenity cities they are increasingly crowded out by higher housing costs, resulting in magnifying welfare inequalities between low- and high-skill workers.

In addition, and, perhaps most important, the increasing spatial sorting of low- and high-skill workers across labor and housing markets that results from these dynamics has potentially negative effects on intergenerational social mobility if children of low-skill workers are less likely to access the amenities that will ensure their ability to develop skills and social capital (good quality schools, cultural institutions). See Chetty (this volume) for a discussion of intergenerational social mobility.

Policy Implications of Spatial Sorting by Skills

These dynamics of spatial skill-sorting inform policy in a number of ways. First, from the perspective of these results, policies that attract college graduates can have large spillovers: improving the local productivity of firms in the city and creating desirable amenities, which further attract additional college graduates. Examples of policies that could achieve this include offering technical assistance to firms employing high-skill workers (see Bartik, this volume, for a discussion of the role of cities in providing specialty services for new or relocating firms), or funding improvement in the quality of public amenities through policies to reduce crime or to improve the quality of local schools.

While policies that attract college graduates may improve local economic conditions and quality of life within the city for both college educated and non-college educated residents, they also have the potential to drive away the less educated and lower-income inhabitants to the extent that they drive up housing prices. As a result, the high-skill city can be an attractive and productive city, but lower-income and less educated may no longer find the area affordable and lose access to the improved city.

A possible policy tool to help less skilled or lower-income households remain in high-skill, prosperous cities is to expand affordable housing programs. New York City mayor Bill de Blasio has made this a top priority by unveiling a plan to create 200,000 units of affordable housing in New York City over the next ten years. San Francisco mayor Ed Lee is also prioritizing the expansion of affordable housing with a goal of increasing the affordable housing stock by 30,000 units by 2020.

These dynamics are also important to keep in mind in order to understand the welfare effects of local land-use regulations that restrict the elasticity of housing supply. Restricting local land use and preventing real estate development in areas with high demand for housing leads to rising house prices. This, then, has the indirect effect of increasing the share of college-educated workers living in the city, as rising house prices disproportionately discourage lower-skill workers from living in the area. The rising share of college educated workers then endogenously improves local amenities and productivity, creating a more desirable city, which benefits the college-educated at the expense of lower-skill workers who were forced to relocate.

This relates to the broader point that, from a social perspective, it is not clear what the optimal allocation of college graduates across cities should be. One local government may attract college graduates, but this will come at a cost to another city, which loses college educated residents. For the federal government to implement socially optimal polices that incentivize college graduates to locate in certain types of cities, the government would need to know what type of cities gain the most in terms of increased productivity and local quality of life from additional college workers (Glaeser and Gottlieb 2009) and whether there is an optimal distribution of low- and high-skilled workers nationally from an economic productivity and social welfare perspective to ensure that policy incentives to attract college workers do not result in a zero sum game. As shown by Glaeser and Gottlieb (2009), while the theoretical foundations of urban growth and decline are well established, additional evidence on optimal spatial forms, agglomeration economies, and skill sharing are needed to guide national policy on these issues.

A key way to improve the share of college graduates across all cities is the implementation of policies that incentivize more students to attend and graduate from college. These policies likely are best funded by the federal government, as opposed to state and local governments, since, when local governments subsidize higher education they pay the full cost of the subsidy but face the risk that another city or state will receive the benefits if the college student migrates after graduation (Kline and Moretti 2013).

Conclusion

The divergence in the location choices of college graduates and less skilled workers from 1980 to 2000 was fundamentally caused by a divergence in the labor demand of local firms for high- and low-skill labor. The cities that attracted a higher share of college graduates then endogenously became more desirable places to live, as increases in a city's population share of college graduates led to improvements in the quality and variety of local retail markets, improved air quality, and less crime. Notably, increases in a city's college share also improved the productivity and wages of both college educated and noncollege educated workers employed within the city.

The desirable wage and amenity growth in high-skill cities were desirable to both high- and low-skill workers. College educated workers are particularly attracted by desirable amenities, while low-skill workers are particularly attracted by desirable wages. The increase in population in high college share cities leads to large housing price increases. Since low-skill workers are more sensitive to affordability, the rise in housing costs disproportionately discourages low-skill workers from living in these high-wage, high-amenity cities. Thus, in equilibrium, college workers sort into high-wage, high-rent, high-amenity cities. Lower-skill workers are not willing to accept a lower local real wage to live in high-amenity cities, which leads them to choose more affordable, low-amenity cities.

The net welfare impacts of the changes in wages, rents, and endogenous amenities across cities from 1980 to 2000 led to an increase in economic well-being inequality between college and high school graduates of at least 30 percent more than the increase in the wage gap between college and high school graduates alone. The additional utility college workers gained from enjoying more desirable amenities, despite the high housing local prices, increased college workers' well-being, relative to high school graduates.

PART II

How to Encourage Growth
and Expand Opportunity

CHAPTER 5

Building Shared Prosperity Through Place-Conscious Strategies That Reweave the Goals of Fair Housing and Community Development

Margery Austin Turner

A future of shared prosperity requires serious attention to the intersecting challenges of poverty, place, and race in metropolitan America, because neighborhood exclusion and distress undermine the well-being and long-term life chances of low-income families, and especially people of color. Past efforts have mostly addressed the problems of neighborhood exclusion and neighborhood distress separately, and although both fair housing and community development practitioners have achieved significant gains, tensions between their goals and strategies arise often. Looking ahead, demographic changes promise to transform housing markets and communities in metro areas across the country, and demand a next generation of strategies that both revitalize distressed neighborhoods and remove the barriers that exclude people from opportunity-rich communities.

This chapter offers principles to guide a shared framework for holistic "place-conscious" strategies to accomplish these joint goals. These principles recognize the importance of place in the lives of families and explicitly address the particular challenges of distressed neighborhoods. But they look beyond narrowly defined neighborhood boundaries to address market-wide opportunities and barriers, the role of residential mobility, and alternative models of how neighborhoods can function for their residents. The sections that follow review the history and context of place-conscious strategies and introduce the proposed principles.

Poverty, Place, and Race in Metropolitan America

Neighborhood Exclusion and Distress
Undermine Families' Well-Being

Historically, high housing costs have intersected with discriminatory market practices and exclusionary land-use policies to block low-income families and people of color from communities that offer safety, good schools, a healthy environment, and access to jobs. At the same time, as Jargowsky (this volume) discusses, many low-income neighborhoods—where homes and apartments are more affordable—have been the victims of disinvestment and neglect, leaving them with failing schools, inadequate services, physical and environmental blight, and high levels of crime and violence. Higher-income households have understandably fled from these neighborhoods, further raising their poverty rates and accelerating the cycle of disinvestment and distress.[1]

These long-standing dynamics—which are seen by some as intractable or inevitable—have serious consequences, because where we live matters to the well-being of our families. Most importantly, conditions in severely distressed neighborhoods have been shown to undermine both the quality of daily life and the long-term life chances of parents and children (Ellen and Turner 1997; Ellen et al. 2001; Turner and Rawlings 2009; Santiago et al. 2011; and Barrington et al. 2014). For example, studies have found that preschool children living in low-income neighborhoods exhibit more aggressive behavior when interacting with others. Young people from high-poverty neighborhoods are less successful in school than their counterparts from more affluent communities. They earn lower grades, are more likely to drop out, and less likely to go on to college, in an era when post-secondary education is increasingly essential to economic success (see Carnevale and Smith, this volume). Neighborhood environments influence teens' sexual activity and the likelihood that girls will become pregnant during their teen years. Young people who live in high crime areas are more likely to commit crimes themselves, other things being equal. Exposure to crime and violence has far-reaching consequences, including persistent anxiety and emotional trauma that undermine children's physical and mental health. And living in disadvantaged neighborhoods significantly increases the risk of disease and mortality among both children and adults.

Moreover, as Chetty (this volume) shows, evidence suggests that living in a high-poverty area undermines some outcomes not just for one generation, but across generations. Children whose parents grew up in poor neighborhoods score dramatically worse on reading and problem-solving tests than those whose parents grew up in nonpoor neighborhoods, other things being equal (Sharkey 2013).

Decades of rigorous research have documented the high costs of racially and economically segregated residential patterns, not only for individual families but for our society as a whole (see Carr and Kutty 2008; Turner and Rawlings 2009). The persistence of neighborhood exclusion and distress ultimately hurts all of us by depressing residential property values and hence property tax revenues, raising the costs of delivering public services, reducing government spending on productive public goods, undermining the competitiveness of the nation's workforce, and sustaining racial stereotypes and social polarization. Neighborhood disparities exacerbate racial inequality and constrain the vitality and economic performance of metropolitan regions by sustaining pockets of poverty and distress, thereby fueling flight and sprawling residential development, which raise commuting times and traffic congestion. Thus, as the chapters in Part I show, neighborhood distress and regional disparities contribute to the persistence of poverty across generations.

Past Efforts Have Mostly Addressed the Problems of Neighborhood Exclusion and Distress Separately

For decades, policy makers, advocates, and on-the-ground practitioners have worked to tackle the intertwined challenges of neighborhood exclusion and neighborhood distress. But too often, the goals of inclusion (aka fair housing) and community development (including affordable housing development) have been pursued separately, with a different set of public agencies, advocates, and practitioners devoted to each. And tensions between these goals and their respective constituencies arise often—in decisions about whether to invest in the preservation of affordable housing located in distressed or marginal neighborhoods, about whether to help low-income families move to nonpoor neighborhoods or prioritize the redevelopment of neighborhoods where they are currently concentrated, and about how much income-mixing is desirable (or feasible) in housing developments and neighborhoods.

The fair housing movement has focused primarily on breaking down the barriers that exclude people of color from predominantly white neighborhoods (where, for the most part, the schools perform effectively, the streets and parks are safe, and the environment is healthy). They have worked to combat discrimination against minority homeseekers by real estate agents, landlords, and mortgage lenders and to reform suburban zoning and land-use regulations that block the development of more affordable housing. They argue for allocating federal housing subsidies (including public housing and low income housing tax credits) to produce and preserve subsidized rental housing in higher income and majority white communities rather than in poor communities of color. And they promote the use of housing choice vouchers—accompanied by search assistance and counseling—to expand poor families' access to opportunity-rich communities.

In contrast, community development advocates and practitioners have focused on changing conditions *within the boundaries* of distressed neighborhoods by building and rehabilitating housing, improving community amenities, delivering needed services, and expanding jobs within the neighborhood. These place-based efforts have made important contributions to the well-being of inner-city neighborhoods, in particular by increasing the availability of decent, affordable housing. To date, however, few have achieved their larger goal of sustainable neighborhood transformation—reversing the effects of disinvestment and distress and effectively connecting low-income residents with the economic mainstream (Kubisch et al. 2010).[2]

As Jargowsky (this volume) points out, although blacks and other minorities are less starkly segregated from whites than in the past, racial and ethnic segregation interacts with rising income inequality and high housing costs to sustain neighborhoods of concentrated poverty and distress. During the 1990s, we saw a welcome decline in the share of poor people living in high-poverty neighborhoods, but that trend reversed between 2000 and 2010. And although a rapidly growing share of poor people—including poor people of color—now live in suburban communities, almost all the neighborhoods suffering from concentrated poverty and severe distress are located in central cities.

Moreover, as Diamond (this volume) points out, the larger forces that exclude low-income people from communities of opportunity and undermine conditions in distressed urban neighborhoods have, if anything, intensified over recent decades. The economy has seen manufacturing jobs give way to globalization and technology, replaced by low-wage jobs that have left as much as a third of the population a paycheck away from poverty. Income inequality is intensifying, and the purchasing power of wages is dwindling for a large segment of the income distribution. In most metropolitan areas, rents have risen faster than wages for low- and middle-skill workers, pushing housing costs out of reach for a growing share of households. During the Great Recession, home values plummeted, leaving many homeowners underwater. But this decline had little impact on housing cost burdens for low- and moderate-income households, in part because rents have risen in many markets, but also because tighter mortgage lending standards prevent households with low wealth or blemished credit from buying.

Demographic Change Brings New Challenges and Opportunities

Looking ahead, sweeping demographic trends are underway that will almost certainly transform both housing markets and communities. Over the next three to four decades, members of the baby boom generation will hand off their housing to a dramatically more diverse and less wealthy cohort of newly forming households. This handoff is already happening as the leading edge of the baby boom generation reaches retirement and begins moving to smaller housing units and warmer climates, but it will accelerate in the decades ahead as more baby boomers retire, downsize their housing, and die. These trends could intensify existing neighborhood disparities or tip more neighborhoods into a downward spiral of disinvestment and distress. But they also have the potential to open up opportunities for greater inclusion and diversity.

This demographic transition is likely to play out in dramatically different ways in different parts of the country, and is already contributing to a divergence of city and metropolitan futures. Some metros are experiencing robust population growth—along with rising housing costs and intensifying affordability challenges, while others are losing population and face rising housing vacancies and even abandonment. In some places (notably San

Francisco, Washington, D.C., and New York, for example) affluent house-holds (including both millennials and empty nesters) are increasingly choosing city locations, fueling a welcome resurgence of urban vitality (and considerable racial and ethnic diversity) but also pushing housing costs beyond the reach of low-, moderate-, and even middle-income households. The residents of many other cities (with Detroit at the extreme) face the opposite challenge of declining property values, abandonment, and a reduction in ethnic and socioeconomic diversity.

These evolving and divergent urban futures call for a next generation of strategies that *both* revitalize distressed communities *and* remove the barriers that exclude (or displace) people from thriving, opportunity-rich communities. Instead of battling over the allocation of scarce resources, advocates for fair and open housing and advocates for community revitalization should be collaborating to craft larger strategies that advance both goals. The specifics of these strategies have to be hammered out at the metropolitan scale in response to local conditions, history, trends, and institutional capacities. But these local strategies can be informed by lessons learned from past successes (and disappointments) in both community development and fair housing.

Today, I see innovative practitioners, scholars, and advocates beginning to craft a next generation of strategies that can best be described as "place-conscious" rather than "place-based." I use this term intentionally to highlight opportunities to move beyond old battles pitting "place-based" versus "people-based" policies, and between neighborhood reinvestment versus mobility strategies. Place-conscious encompasses work that explicitly recognizes the importance of place and focuses on the particular challenges of distressed neighborhoods, but is less constrained by narrowly defined neighborhood boundaries than traditional community development work, more attuned to region-wide perspectives and trends, and aimed both at improving people's quality of life and at expanding access to opportunities for families.

Six Principles to Guide a Shared Framework
of "Place-Conscious" Strategies

Here I offer six principles that define this "place-conscious" approach. These principles integrate the goals of community development with those of fair housing. They look beyond narrowly defined neighborhood boundaries to address market-wide opportunities and barriers, the role of residential mobility, and alternative models of how neighborhoods can function for their residents.

The Optimal Geographic Scale for Tackling Problems of Place Varies Across Policy Domains

Although the evidence that "place" matters is compelling, neither research nor practice has given sufficient attention to defining the scale at which particular conditions affect outcomes for people. In some cases, interventions can have the greatest impact by focusing at the block level. In others, it makes more sense to intervene across a larger geography, or even at a citywide or regional scale. For example, a child's exposure to crime and violence may be determined by conditions on the blocks immediately surrounding his or her home, so a violence-prevention intervention that targets a small subneighborhood might be essential to improve that child's life chances. In contrast, ensuring that the child has access to adequate healthcare, or that his or her parents can buy healthy foods may call for larger-scale interventions (building a community clinic or affordable grocery stores within walking distance, for example). And improving the quality of a child's education requires action at the scale of an elementary school enrollment zone, or possibly the school district as a whole.

Correspondingly, while some neighborhood challenges can be effectively addressed through work by and with residents and community-based institutions, many require action at higher levels of governance. For example, see Bartik (this volume) for a discussion of the incentives and services cities and states can provide to create jobs and expand economic opportunities. Severe distress within a neighborhood ultimately stems from the interaction between market forces and public policies at city, metropolitan, and state levels that constrain opportunities for poor people and disinvest from the neighborhoods where they live. Therefore, the levers for addressing the many challenges facing these neighborhoods are not all contained within the boundaries of the neighborhood itself. The potential impact of initiatives focused solely on local collaboration can be limited because they are likely to have difficulty gaining access to resources at different levels of the political system and building the broader capacity necessary to sustain change (Weir, Rongerude, and Ansell 2011). Sustainable changes in neighborhood conditions are more likely to be achieved when all levers are activated—when place-conscious efforts reform policies and mobilize resources at city, state, and federal levels in addition to breaking out of conventional programmatic and institutional boundaries at the neighborhood level.

Moreover, meaningful inclusion of low-income families and people of color does not require income-mixing in every housing development or on every block. The key is to ensure that low-income people have access to opportunity-enhancing amenities and opportunities, which requires attention to the scale at which these opportunities are delivered. This means that in a new housing development at the heart of a poor neighborhood, it makes sense to incorporate features with potential to attract and serve residents with a mix of income levels, in hopes of catalyzing new demand and attracting private sector investment. But in a higher-income community, a new rental housing development designed to serve only low-income households would effectively advance the goal of access and inclusion. For example, Douglas Massey's research on a subsidized housing project in the affluent town of Mt. Laurel, New Jersey, finds that low-income families reap huge benefits from living in a safe, opportunity-rich community, even though their housing development does not itself include a mix of income levels (Massey et al. 2013).[3] Massey's Mt. Laurel study also confirms other research showing that the introduction of a low-income housing development does not undermine property values, safety, or quality of life in an affluent neighborhood, despite the fears often expressed by long-time residents.

Some Neighborhoods May Function as "Launch Pads" for Low-Income Residents

Traditionally, place-based community revitalization initiatives have reflected an implicit vision that a neighborhood should function as an incubator for its residents—especially its low-income or otherwise vulnerable residents (Coulton, Theodos, and Turner 2009). The theory of change underlying this approach is that investments in neighborhood programs and services provide the supports that low-income families need to thrive as well as the amenities that make them want to remain in the neighborhood as their circumstances improve. Simultaneous investments in community building strengthen social capital and civic capacity, further enhancing the well-being of individual residents and the vitality of the neighborhood. Over time, gradual improvements in well-being among residents reduce overall neighborhood poverty and distress levels (without displacement).

This is an admirable aspiration, but it is not the only possible vision for neighborhood success. Some neighborhoods may more effectively serve as launch pads for their residents, instead of incubators (Coulton, Theodos, and Turner 2009). Like an incubator neighborhood, a launch pad offers needed services and supports, enabling residents to advance economically. But as residents achieve greater economic security, they move on to more desirable neighborhoods, continuously replaced by new cohorts of needy households. Launch pad neighborhoods would experience high mobility, and, even though many residents were making significant individual progress, the neighborhood as a whole might not show any improvement on indicators such as employment, income, or wealth. Past research suggests that neighborhoods that serve as entry points for successive waves of immigrants may function this way (Borjas 1998). And it may be fruitful to see these as highly successful neighborhoods, even though they remain very poor over time.

A city- or region-wide strategy for helping low-income families gain access to opportunities might identify some neighborhoods that already function as launch pads—or have the potential to do so, and others that can become incubators. Then, neighborhood-level investments could be tailored to strengthen their performance, with an emphasis on improving outcomes for low-income families, whether they stay in place or move. This kind of strategy calls for the development of new indicators of success, because simply measuring changes in the poverty rate or the unemployment rate within a neighborhood's boundaries does not effectively capture outcomes for the families that have moved. For its Making Connections Initiative, the Annie E. Casey Foundation repeatedly surveyed neighborhood residents, including those that moved out between survey waves (Coulton, Theodos, and Turner 2009), providing rich information about outcomes for both neighborhoods and families. But this approach is costly, and we need to craft more economical data collection strategies going forward.

Place-Conscious Strategies Should Connect People and Neighborhoods to City and Regional Opportunities

Many of the services and opportunities families need are located outside the neighborhoods in which they live, and interventions that connect them to these opportunities may be more effective than interventions that try to create them within every neighborhood. The best example is employment. Few people work in the neighborhoods where they live. Rather, they commute to jobs in other parts of their metropolitan region. The primary employment challenge facing residents of distressed urban neighborhoods is not a lack of jobs within their neighborhoods but barriers to accessing job opportunities in the larger region. They may not know about those opportunities; they may not have the skills or credentials necessary to qualify for them; or the time and cost of commuting may be too high.

Expanding access to regional employment opportunities means helping residents enroll in a city- or region-wide training and placement program with a strong track record, helping them learn about and apply for jobs in unfamiliar locations, and overcoming transportation barriers. Over the past several decades, jobs have become increasingly dispersed across the metropolitan landscape. And for people who rely on public transportation, commuting from inner-city neighborhoods to suburban jobs can be tremendously time consuming and costly. So attention to public transit routes, costs, and schedules plays a critical role in a place-conscious, opportunity-enhancing strategy. One approach for tackling the problem of transit access is to provide special-purpose vans or buses that transport workers from low-income neighborhoods to outlying employment centers. This approach has generally produced quite disappointing results, because job locations are widely dispersed, and work schedules vary, making the services costly for providers and inconvenient for riders.[4]

An alternative approach is to help low-income people buy (and maintain) cars. A growing body of research finds a positive relationship between automobile access and employment rates among the poor. Studies that directly compare the relative benefits of cars and public transit find that automobiles are far more powerful determinants of job acquisition and job retention than is public transit (Pendall et al. 2014). Nonprofit organizations in cities across the country operate programs that distribute cars directly to families, make low-interest loans for car purchases, or facilitate matched savings for car down payments and purchases. In addition, car-sharing services, like Zipcar and car2go, may offer the potential to address the transportation needs for some low-income people, although at present, these services typically target higher-income people and neighborhoods.

Interventions that expand access to quality schools may also offer solutions to the profound education challenges facing children who live in distressed neighborhoods. In many low-income neighborhoods, the public schools perform very poorly, with undermaintained facilities, inadequate supplies, ineffective teachers, chaotic classrooms, and high rates of truancy and dropouts. Efforts are underway at local, state, and federal levels to improve the schools that serve low-income neighborhoods and these unquestionably merit continued attention and support. However, some children may benefit from strategies that offer access to high-performing schools outside their immediate neighborhoods. Research evidence strongly suggests that the challenges to effective teaching and learning are substantial when a large share of students in a classroom are poor (Kahlenberg 2001), and a recent study found that low-income students who were randomly assigned to attend low-poverty schools scored higher on math and reading exams than those assigned to higher-poverty schools, despite the county's policy to direct extra resources to higher-poverty schools for full-day kindergarten, smaller class sizes, teachers' professional development, and special instruction for students with special needs (Schwartz 2010). Interventions that can give poor children access to nonpoor schools include public school choice programs, charter schools, and school vouchers (Greene et al. 2010). A number of urban school districts are currently implementing at least some programs of this type, including Washington, D.C., New Orleans, and New York City. Significant questions remain, however, about whether low-income children are able to take full advantage of the opportunities these programs create and about how to combine them with initiatives that strengthen neighborhood schools (rather than pitting these approaches against one another). See Jargowsky et al. (this volume) for a comprehensive discussion of the portfolio of tools cities and states can deploy to expand poor children's access to high-quality schools.

Place-Conscious Interventions Should Be Tailored to Respond to Metro-Level Conditions and Trends

A growing understanding of how city and regional dynamics influence neighborhood outcomes is leading to the recognition that a single approach to place-conscious work will not be equally effective everywhere. Many of today's best-known neighborhood revitalization initiatives evolved in the big cities of the Northeast and Midwest, where the legacy of racial segregation and poverty concentration has isolated and "trapped" residents in high-poverty neighborhoods—blocking their access to opportunities in the larger metro region. In other metropolitan areas, the geographic patterns and opportunity structures are different. For example, in some of the fast-growing metros of the South and Southwest, poor neighborhoods may not be as isolated, and a booming regional economy may be creating more opportunities for employment and earnings.

Practitioners in these metro areas are developing and testing strategies for connecting poor people to opportunities that reflect the realities of their geography, demographics, and economy. These strategies are regional in scope, though also focused on the distressed neighborhoods where large numbers of poor people live. The communities within which they work are loosely defined and dynamic and they generally do not aspire to transform poor neighborhoods into mixed-income communities, but rather to strengthen social supports within the neighborhoods and linkages to larger regional opportunities.

Although it is critical to recognize that "one size does not fit all," every region should not have to invent an entirely unique strategy for tackling the challenges of poverty and place. Instead, research is needed to identify key differentiators between regions and assess the effectiveness of different approaches in specific contexts. Then policy makers and practitioners in metros that share key characteristics can begin learning from each other's experience and developing models that work for particular types of metros.[5]

Place-Conscious Strategies Plan for Residential Mobility

Place-conscious practitioners increasingly recognize that residential mobility plays a critical—and complicating—role in the effectiveness of their work. Neighborhood distress is a dynamic process, sustained by the inflow of poor people (who have few alternatives for where to live) and the outflow of non-poor people seeking better environments. About 12 percent of the U.S. population moves to a new address each year and mobility rates are even higher among low-income households and renters. As a result, distressed neighborhoods frequently experience rates of mobility that exceed the national average.

Residential mobility can be a symptom (and a source) of instability and insecurity, with many low-income households making short-distance moves because of problems with landlords, creditors, housing conditions, or in response to family violence or conflict. But mobility can also reflect positive changes in a family's circumstances, such as buying a home for the first time, moving to be close to a new job, or trading up to a larger or better-quality house or apartment. Similarly, staying in place sometimes reflects a family's stability, security, and satisfaction with its home and neighborhood surroundings, but in other cases it may mean that a family lacks the resources to move to better housing or to a preferred neighborhood (see Coulton, Theodos, and Turner 2009).

High levels of mobility complicate the intended mechanisms of many neighborhood change strategies if substantial numbers of families leave before they have had time to benefit fully from enhanced services and supports or if they are crowded out by rising rents in a revitalizing neighborhood. One way to address these challenges is to try to reduce involuntary mobility among families living in a neighborhood who want to stay there. Indeed, helping families avoid unplanned or disruptive moves can play a critical role in their well-being and in the success of a neighborhood change strategy.

In addition, however, place-conscious policies can and should offer an assisted housing mobility option, giving low-income families the option of moving to more desirable neighborhoods that offer safety, effective schools, decent services, and amenities. These programs (which have been the focus of considerable federal attention and experimentation over the last two decades) typically provide families with a portable housing voucher funded through the federal Section 8 program, along with help searching for and moving to a better neighborhood (Scott et al. 2013).

The best-known assisted housing mobility program is the Moving to Opportunity (MTO) demonstration, conducted by the Department of Housing and Urban Development (HUD) in five metropolitan areas to evaluate the impact of relocation for poor families and their children (Briggs, Popkin, and Goering 2010). The evaluation concluded that, as a group, the MTO experimental families do enjoy significantly lower crime rates, improved housing, and better mental health than the control group but not higher employment, incomes, or educational attainment (Sanbonmatsu et al. 2011). The health gains enjoyed by MTO's experimental families are hugely important. High rates of obesity, anxiety, and depression severely degrade a person's quality of life, employability, and parenting abilities. However, one reason that MTO gains were limited to health outcomes is that the special mobility assistance provided by the demonstration did not enable the experimental families to gain and sustain access to high-opportunity neighborhoods. Experimental families moved to better-quality housing and safer neighborhoods but few spent more than a year or two in low-poverty neighborhoods. New analysis finds that the MTO families that lived for longer periods in neighborhoods with lower poverty did achieve better outcomes in work and school, as well as in health (Turner, Nichols, and Comey 2012).

These findings argue for investments in programs that help low-income families find and afford housing in well-resourced neighborhoods, including housing vouchers (accompanied by mobility assistance and incentives), but also (as Massey argues in this volume) targeted housing acquisition and construction programs to expand the availability of moderately priced rental housing in nonpoor neighborhoods. Such investments should be seen, not as a rebuke to ongoing efforts to revitalize and strengthen poor neighborhoods, but as a complementary approach that recognizes the power of place and helps remedy spatial inequities.

Private-Sector Housing Development Plays a Critical Role

Most of the attention and debate around expanding the availability of affordable housing in vibrant communities focuses on the allocation of federal subsidy resources. And the allocation of these resources does play an important role. But across the country, the gap between the number of low-income households and the number of housing units they can reasonably afford has widened steadily, and public programs to close the gap meet only a small fraction of the need. Sadly, it is unrealistic to expect housing subsidies to expand significantly in the foreseeable future, so advocates and practitioners have to look beyond housing units and developments that are publicly subsidized to find ways to expand the production, financing, and operation of moderately priced housing by the private sector.

Expanding affordable housing options in vibrant communities often requires changes to local zoning and land-use regulations to encourage higher-density development (including multifamily rental properties), and inclusionary zoning provisions that mandate the inclusion of some affordable units into every new subdivision. Other strategies might include changes to local occupancy codes to allow developers and homeowners in high-cost communities to experiment with lower-cost housing models, like microunits and auxiliary housing units (garage apartments and granny flats). And these reforms can be accelerated by state policies that establish and oversee "fair share" requirements that every jurisdiction accommodate a portion of its region's projected housing needs. In some areas where housing supply is constrained and demand pressures are high, simply allowing more production to occur may help ameliorate affordability problems. Even if the new units are for the most part quite costly, they may accommodate middle- or high-income households who would otherwise bid up the price (or rent) of older units.

Federal Government Initiatives

In recent years, the federal government has absorbed lessons from the history of place-based work and is contributing to the evolution of more place-conscious strategies. The Obama administration has launched two important new programs: Choice Neighborhoods (led by HUD) and the Promise Neighborhoods Initiative (led by the Department of Education). The administration has also sought to align targeted investments like Choice and Promise with other (preexisting) federal programs to ensure that resources from the departments of Agriculture, Education, Housing and Urban Development, and Justice can be effectively mobilized by local efforts to turn around high-poverty communities across the country.[6] The Federal Transit Administration has announced that it will include zoning for affordable housing as a factor in its scoring process for allocating grants in support of new rail lines (Hickey 2014). And HUD's emerging approach to fair housing challenges (broadly defined) may offer an opening for on-the-ground practitioners to further develop and advance place-conscious strategies.

The Federal Government's Choice and Promise Programs Offer
Opportunities to Implement Place-Conscious Principles

The Choice Neighborhoods program builds on experience from the HOPE VI program, which sought to revitalize or replace severely distressed public housing developments. Like HOPE VI, Choice is centered on the redevelopment of distressed subsidized housing projects, and aspires to create vibrant mixed-income neighborhoods with high-quality public and private sector amenities. However, the Choice program places much greater emphasis on the preservation of affordable housing options for low-income families and on improving essential non-housing assets like public schools, parks, and community services. The expectation is that the revitalized neighborhood will attract more middle- and upper-income residents without displacing low-income families who rely upon subsidized housing. Achieving this vision requires partnerships and investments that extend beyond a housing development and its immediate neighborhood, to connect with larger city and even regional initiatives.

The Promise Neighborhoods Initiative was inspired by the accomplishments of the Harlem Children's Zone (led by Geoffrey Canada), which focuses on the well-being of a neighborhood's children from "cradle-to-career" rather than on physical redevelopment or income mixing. Over several decades, the Harlem Children's Zone (HCZ) has systematically expanded and improved the services and supports children in the neighborhood need, building an impressive continuum from prenatal services to safe after-school activities to college counseling (see Tough 2008). The vision for Promise Neighborhoods is to replicate this model in more places, providing all children in targeted low-income neighborhoods with "access to effective schools and strong systems of family and community support that will prepare them to attain an excellent education and successfully transition to college and career" (U.S. Department of Education 2013). In their chapter in this volume, Jargowsky et al. analyze HCZ to provide a deeper understanding of this model's efficacy.

New Fair-Housing Rules May Open a Window of Opportunity to Craft More Holistic Place-Conscious Strategies

The Department of Housing and Urban Development (HUD) has a longstanding, statutory mandate to "affirmatively further fair housing,"[7] which requires the department (and the federal government more generally) to do more than combat discrimination but to actively promote more fair and open housing options for all Americans (see National Commission on Fair Housing and Equal Opportunity 2008). State and local governments that receive federal funding through HUD's various housing and community development programs have also been obligated (in principle) to "affirmatively further" the purposes of the federal Fair Housing Act. But to date, efforts to enforce this obligation have achieved only limited success.

Regulations recently issued[8] by HUD to more effectively advance the affirmatively furthering fair housing (AFFH) mandate create a point of leverage for place-conscious advocates, policy makers, and housing providers at the local, regional, and state levels. Under the new regulations, HUD will provide data and a template that states and localities must use to complete a formal, evidence-based assessment of fair housing. These assessments will identify the primary factors affecting fair housing outcomes and set goals for mitigating or addressing them. Then subsequent state and local plans for using federal housing and community development funding must link to this assessment and include investments and actions that affirmatively further fair housing.

HUD's guidance for local assessments of fair housing focuses on four primary goals that implicitly connect the work of community development and revitalization with that of combatting discrimination and segregation. Specifically, the new rules define what it means to affirmatively further fair housing to encompass: 1) overcoming historic patterns of residential segregation promoting more integrated neighborhoods; 2) reducing concentrations of minority poverty; 3) narrowing disparities (based on race, ethnicity, and other protected characteristics) in access to community assets (education, transit access, and employment) and in exposure to environmental hazards; and 4) responding to the disproportionate housing needs of racial and ethnic minorities and other protected groups.[9] Advancing these four goals clearly calls for place-conscious interventions that tackle both residential exclusion and neighborhood distress.

If these regulations are effectively implemented, jurisdictions across the country will be held accountable for identifying and addressing the barriers that exclude and isolate lower-income households and people of color and that undermine the well-being of the neighborhoods in which they live. Advocates will have standing to challenge local zoning, land-use, and occupancy policies, as well as the allocations of federal housing and community development resources. Nonprofit housing developers will be looking for models of how to produce affordable housing in communities that have previously seemed off-limits. And investments that focus on the revitalization of particular neighborhoods will be evaluated in the larger context of opportunities and disparities in the city or region as a whole.

There is no guarantee, of course, that HUD will implement its new regulations effectively or that they will survive a change in administration. But they create an important opening and impetus for fair housing and community development advocates and practitioners to join forces around a shared framework of place-conscious actions and investments that integrates their fundamental objectives.

Conclusion

Looking ahead, the success or failure of efforts to overcome the challenges of neighborhood exclusion and distress will help determine the kind of country we become. Already, alarms are sounding about worsening inequality and low levels of upward economic mobility. Raj Chetty and his colleagues (Chetty, Hendren, Kline, and Saez 2014) have assembled new evidence showing that few children born to low-income parents achieve high incomes as adults (see Chetty, this volume, for a discussion of this evidence). But their analysis also reveals quite dramatic differences across metro areas in intergenerational mobility, and neighborhood patterns appear to explain part of the variation. Children growing up in metros with higher racial and ethnic segregation and greater poverty concentration are less likely to advance economically over the life-course.

This new evidence strengthens the case that a future of shared prosperity requires serious attention to the intersection of poverty, place, and race in metropolitan America. Changing these stubborn spatial patterns requires strategies that tackle both the disinvestment and distress plaguing high-poverty neighborhoods and the barriers that exclude low-income people and people of color from neighborhoods of opportunity. We cannot afford to think of these as competing goals when in fact they are interdependent and mutually reinforcing.

CHAPTER 6

Confronting the Legacy
of American Apartheid

Douglas S. Massey

Rapid industrialization during the late nineteenth and early twentieth centuries dramatically increased the size and density of cities and differentiated urban land use by social status and function to create an ecological structure ripe for ethnic and racial segregation compared to preindustrial cities. As a result, Southern and Eastern European immigrants who arrived in America during the 1880s and 1890s experienced much higher levels of segregation than did the German and Irish immigrants who arrived in American cities during the 1840s and 1850s (Hershberg et al. 1981). The degree of residential segregation between two groups is most commonly measured by the Index of Dissimilarity, which ranges from 0 to 1 in fractional terms or 0 to 100 in percentage terms. Here we use the percentage form so that the index varies from 0 (when the groups are evenly distributed across neighborhoods) and 100 (when the groups share no neighborhood in common). When compared to native whites of native parentage, persons of Irish and German origin displayed dissimilarity indices in the range of 30 to 50 prior to the Civil War. Four decades later, however, Polish, Italian, and Jewish immigrants displayed values in the range of 55–65 (Lieberson 1963).

In the end, segregation levels for European immigrant origins rarely rose above 65 and dissimilarity values tended to fall across the generations and with rising socioeconomic status. Although ethnic segregation persisted at relatively high levels into the 1920s, with the cessation of mass European immigration in 1929, levels of European ethnic segregation steadily fell over the ensuing decades until by 1970 formerly segregated groups such as Italians and Poles were largely integrated into the residential fabric of the nation (Lieberson 1980) and experiencing the "twilight of ethnicity" (Alba 1985, 1992).

As mass European migration peaked and drew to a close, however, the Great Black Migration of African Americans out of the rural South was just taking off. The outflow began in the 1890s, accelerated during the First World War, continued through the 1920s and Great Depression, and accelerated again during the Second World War. Mass black migration continued apace during the postwar era and finally came to an end around 1970. Virtually all black migration was directed to urban areas, especially to industrial cities of the West, Midwest, and Northeast. In 1900 some 90 percent of all black Americans lived in the South, whereas the figure stood at just 53 percent in 1970. During the first two-thirds of the twentieth century, the Great Black Migration transformed race from a regional to a national issue.

Like their European counterparts, black migrants who arrived in the booming industrial cities of the early twentieth century experienced relatively high levels of residential segregation. Rather than peaking with dissimilarity values in the range of 55 to 65, however, black segregation levels continued to move upward. As urban black populations expanded, ever higher levels of segregation were imposed on African Americans in a way that set them distinctly apart from contemporaneous European immigrant groups (Lieberson 1980). By 1920 the black ghetto had become a characteristic feature of urban America and black-white dissimilarity levels varied from 75 to 95 (Massey and Denton 1993). No racial or ethnic group in the United States, at any time before or since, has experienced such intense spatial segregation.

Initially black segregation was enforced by vigilante and communal violence perpetrated by whites (Massey and Denton 1993), but levels of violence dissipated during the 1920s and 1930s as racial discrimination was institutionalized in the real estate and banking industries (Helper 1969). However, when the suburban boom of the 1950s and 1960s caused a massive exodus of whites from cities and the rapid expansion of black neighborhoods threatened elite white districts and institutions, federal and state governments stepped in to buttress the walls of the ghetto through urban renewal projects and public housing construction (Hirsch 1983; Jackson 1985). As a result, in 1970 the large majority of urban African Americans lived under conditions of hypersegregation, a uniquely intense form of segregation that isolates African Americans on multiple geographic dimensions simultaneously (Massey and Denton 1989).

Segregation in America Today

Residential segregation was the last issue to be addressed by civil rights legislation, and very imperfectly at that. The Civil Rights Revolution began with the *Brown* decision of 1954 and reached high tide with the passage of the 1964 Civil Rights Act and the 1965 Voting Rights Act. The former outlawed racial discrimination in education, services, accommodations, sales, and hiring while the latter prohibited discrimination in voting. Both acts established strong federal enforcement mechanisms to achieve compliance. The 1964 act authorized the attorney general to take action to promote school desegregation, ultimately leading to the widespread use of busing to achieve progress toward integration (Aretha 2001). The 1964 act also established the Equal Employment Opportunity Commission, which eventually developed a new policy of "affirmative action" to promote desegregation in labor markets (Skrentny 1996). The Voting Rights Act empowered federal authorities to regulate voting in districts with a history of racial discrimination and low rates of black participation. In the wake of these measures, racial segregation by occupation fell (Jackson 1982), black employment and earnings rose (Heckman and Payner 1989), and black voting rates mushroomed (Davidson and Grofman 1994).

Although housing and lending markets were covered in the original version of the 1964 Civil Rights Act, these economic sectors were dropped from coverage in the final bill as a concession to achieve passage. Despite being reintroduced in successive congressional sessions, fair housing legislation was repeatedly blocked by southern legislators. The Fair Housing Act would probably not have passed at all were it not for the assassination of Martin Luther King in April 1968, which spurred a wave of race riots across urban America and compelled Congress to address the deterioration of black inner cities, if only symbolically because the act contained weak enforcement provisions. In a compromise to secure the law's passage, federal enforcement authorizations were gutted from the bill, placing the burden of enforcement on individual victims of discrimination to sue in federal court to secure their rights. Federal prohibitions on lending discrimination took even longer to enact. It was only in 1974 that the Equal Credit Opportunity Act was passed to ban discrimination against black borrowers and 1977 when the Community Reinvestment Act was enacted to prohibit discrimination against black neighborhoods.

The legal underpinnings of residential segregation thus persisted well into 1970s so it was not surprising that when Massey and Denton (1993) undertook their systematic analysis of 1980 Census data, they found little progress toward black-white integration across metropolitan areas. Since 1980 some progress has been made, but the pace of desegregation has been slow and highly uneven across regions. Significant shifts toward black-white integration have occurred principally in newer metropolitan areas with small black populations, a strong black middle class, a significant military presence, and well-developed systems of higher education (Farley and W. Frey 1994; Jargowsky, this volume). Unfortunately most African Americans do not live in such areas, and most large, older metropolitan areas where African Americans disproportionately live remain highly segregated (Wilkes and Iceland 2004; Jargowsky, this volume).

Although intense levels of black segregation may no longer characterize all metropolitan areas in the United States, research shows that black segregation continues to be perpetuated in large areas by ongoing racial prejudice, lagging black economic progress, and exclusionary zoning policies in suburbs (Rugh and Massey 2014). Although the *average* black-white dissimilarity index fell from 78 to 60 between 1970 and 2010, among hypersegregated areas the decline was only from 81 to 67; and in the five most segregated areas (New York, Newark, Gary, Detroit, and Milwaukee) there was no decline at all, with dissimilarities clustered tightly around an index value of 80 in 2010 (Rugh and Massey 2014). As a result, roughly half of all black urban dwellers continue to live under conditions of hypersegregation and two-thirds live in areas of high segregation, with a dissimilarity index of 60 or greater (Massey 2004).

Owing to the revival of mass immigration to the United States, the racial and ethnic composition of metropolitan America was radically altered in the last third of the twentieth century. From 1970 to 2010 Hispanics grew from 5 percent to 13 percent of the total population while Asians rose from 0.8 percent to 5 percent. Although dissimilarity levels for Asians generally fall in the low to moderate range (averaging around 40 in 2010 with little change over time), levels of Hispanic segregation slowly rose to reach an average of 50 in 2010 (Rugh and Massey 2014). Although Hispanics were not hypersegregated in any metropolitan area in 1980 (Massey and Denton 1989), by 2000 hypersegregation had emerged for Hispanics in New York and Los Angeles, America's two largest Latino communities (Wilkes and Iceland 2004). Hispanic segregation is especially high in new destination areas and in metro areas where a large share of Latinos are undocumented (Park and Iceland 2011; Hall and Stringfield 2014). With respect to residential segregation and neighborhood isolation, the circumstances of blacks and Hispanics appear to be converging at a relatively high level.

As Hispanic segregation has risen and black hypersegregation has continued in large metropolitan areas, class segregation has emerged as a new axis of urban spatial differentiation in urban America, in part because of the huge increase in inequality itself (Piketty 2014). Massey and Fischer (2003) found that dissimilarity between affluent and poor families rose from 29 to 37 in sixty metropolitan areas between 1970 and 2000, an increase of 28 percent. Using a different measure of segregation (the H Index), Bischoff and Reardon (2013) found family income segregation rose 29 percent between 1970 and 2010, but increased much more sharply among African Americans, essentially doubling over the forty-year period. They found that income segregation also increased rapidly among Hispanics, rising by 38 percent between 1980 and 2010. As a result, in the second decade of the twenty-first century the geography of metropolitan America is quite fragmented by race and class.

The Consequences of Class and Racial Segregation

The social ecology of the United States is thus characterized by a growing interaction between race and class that leaves different race-class groups at the top and bottom of the neighborhood pecking order (Massey and Brodmann 2014). At the bottom of the socioeconomic and spatial hierarchy are poor African Americans and increasingly poor Hispanics. These subgroups are concentrated in racially isolated, disadvantaged neighborhoods characterized by very high rates of poverty. The average poor black family inhabits a neighborhood that is 34 percent poor while the typical poor Hispanic family lives in a neighborhood that is 29 percent poor. At the top of the social and spatial ladder are affluent whites and Asians who increasingly are concentrated in affluent white neighborhoods. The average affluent Asian lives in a neighborhood that is 49 percent affluent, and the average affluent white lives in a neighborhood that is 44 percent affluent (Massey and Rugh 2014).

Residential segregation has been called the "structural linchpin" of racial stratification in the United States (Pettigrew 1979; Bobo 1989; Massey and Denton 1993) because geographic segregation of racial and ethnic minorities greatly facilitates exploitation and opportunity hoarding, the fundamental processes of stratification, rendering them easier and more efficient (Massey and Denton 1993; Massey 2007). Persistent residential segregation among blacks and rising segregation among Hispanics, when combined with rising inequality and growing spatial separation by income and wealth, guarantees that a large share of America's two largest minority groups will live under conditions of geographically concentrated poverty (Quillian 2012).

Recent research confirms the existence of a strong ecological connection between neighborhood racial segregation and a host of maladies, including concentrated deprivation, low collective efficacy, social isolation, limited trust, poor physical and mental health, high rates of family disruption, elevated levels of crime and violence, pervasive joblessness, social disorganization, and low levels of educational attainment (Sampson 2012a; Chetty, this volume). As a result, poor African Americans and increasingly poor Latinos are trapped in a self-perpetuating cycle of poverty that is largely transmitted through the intergenerational inheritance of neighborhood disadvantage (Sharkey 2013). Living in a segregated, high-poverty neighborhood dramatically reduces the likelihood of socioeconomic achievement and upward mobility and is a prime factor explaining the lack of progress toward racial equality. Whereas before the civil rights era intergenerational poverty was transmitted on the basis of race (O. Duncan 1969), today it is transmitted more on the basis of place (Sharkey 2013; Cashin 2014).

Undoing American Apartheid

As noted earlier, the Fair Housing Act's prohibitions of discrimination have never been seriously enforced by federal authorities, or by state and local authorities for that matter—despite clear evidence that subtle but powerful practices of public and private discrimination continue to segment housing markets along the lines of race and class (Blank, Dabady, and Citro 2004; Sampson 2012a; Massey and Brodmann 2014). In lending and insurance markets as well, studies indicate that racial discrimination persists (Ross and Yinger 2002; Squires and Chadwick 2006). To date, the only tool available to combat this discrimination has been for private individuals, often backed by a nonprofit fair housing group, to file civil suits in federal court to demonstrate bias and then collect damages and fines from discriminatory agents, a piecemeal approach that has had little deterrent effect over the years and rarely brings perpetrators of discrimination to justice (Massey and Denton 1993).

One obvious way to push the nation toward racial integration would be to amend existing laws so that federal authorities can operate to detect and prosecute discrimination in housing and lending markets using audit studies. Comparable teams of white and black auditors would be sent out to pose as customers seeking homes, apartments, or mortgages and their treatment at the hands of real estate and lending agents would be recorded and analyzed to detect systematic bias (Massey and Blank 2006). These methods could assess the level of discrimination prevailing in different metropolitan areas and then target those areas where levels of discrimination are high for a second round of audits that would identify specific agents to prosecute, compelling them to go to court or plead guilty and pay a fine, with the size of the penalty rising for repeated violations (Massey 2011).

It is hard to know the degree to which vigorous prosecution of illegal discrimination in housing and lending markets would shift America toward greater residential integration. It certainly couldn't hurt. A more certain policy is the expansion of residential mobility programs that enable poor families to leave distressed neighborhoods and move into affordable housing units dispersed throughout middle- and upper-class white communities. According to estimates by Rusk (2011), such policies hold considerable potential to achieve residential desegregation by race and class. Residential mobility programs are structured in three basic ways: by giving vouchers to low-income families that enable their movement into advantaged, integrated neighborhoods; by requiring set-asides of affordable units in new market rate projects erected by developers; and by the construction of 100 percent affordable housing projects at scattered sites within affluent communities located throughout the metropolitan landscape.

Although the use of vouchers in the Gautreaux demonstration project permitted many former residents of Chicago Housing Authority projects to move into white suburban neighborhoods and achieve impressive rates of upward socioeconomic mobility (Rubinowitz and Rosenbaum 2000; Polikoff 2006), results from the Moving to Opportunity project, which sought to test Gautreaux's results experimentally across a wider set of metropolitan areas, proved disappointing and generally failed to observe the upward economic trajectories seen earlier (Briggs, Popkin, and Goering 2010; Ludwig et al. 2013).

This failure to replicate occurred for a variety of reasons: only half those offered housing vouchers accepted them and moved to a low-poverty neighborhood; the vast majority of moves were to other black neighborhoods with lower poverty rates but still inside the ghetto and often in the same school catchment area; after a year there was selective migration back to high-poverty areas (Clampet-Lundquist and Massey 2008). Absent strong interventions to counsel participants in the operation of rental markets and provide information about the availability of housing in advantaged neighborhoods, voucher holders enter housing markets that are strongly segmented by race and class and tend to simply replicate the status quo of racial and class segregation (Sampson and Sharkey 2008) yielding a "neighborhood glass ceiling" that poor African Americans find difficult to overcome (Sampson 2012b). When vouchers are accompanied by support and counseling in the housing search process, however, assisted mobility programs have shown considerable success in promoting desegregation (DeLuca and Rosenblatt 2011; Darrah and DeLuca 2014).

Local measures to require set-asides of affordable units in market rate developments have also shown great promise in promoting desegregation and have been successfully implemented in a variety of locations, including New Jersey (Bush-Baskette, Robinson, and Simmons 2011), Massachusetts (DeGenova et al. 2009), and Maryland (Schwartz 2011). In return for the right to profit from the construction of market rate housing, developers are required to set aside a small share (generally 10 to 15 percent) of new housing units for low and moderate income households. Studies show that such set-aside programs not only promote racial and class integration, but constitute an effective means of enhancing the social welfare of families, the economic mobility of adults, and the academic achievement of children (Schwartz et al. 2012). Set-aside programs have the additional advantage of making affordable housing less visible because they are embedded within larger market-rate developments, and thus less likely to become targets of political resistance by community residents and local officials before the fact and less likely to be stigmatizing to residents after the fact.

The final approach to fomenting residential mobility is to construct 100 percent affordable housing developments at scattered sites in affluent neighborhoods throughout the metropolitan landscape and make them available to poor residents of distressed, low-income neighborhoods. Often such developments are financed through the Low Income Housing Tax Credit program established by the Tax Reform Act of 1986, and research suggests that increases in the use of these tax credits are associated with declines in racial segregation across metropolitan areas (Horn and O'Regan 2011).

Aside from funding, the principal barrier to the construction of affordable housing developments in advantaged, affluent communities is exclusionary zoning, which limits the density of residential construction and thereby reduces the supply of housing to increase its cost (Pendall 2000). Studies show that restrictive density zoning regimes that commonly prevail in suburban areas throughout the nation have a powerful effect in promoting segregation on the basis of both race (Rothwell and Massey 2009) and class (Rothwell and Massey 2010). Thus the wider implementation of residential mobility programs ultimately rests on zoning reform to ease the density restrictions that presently characterize many affluent suburbs.

In New Jersey, affordable housing advocates were successful in challenging the use of restrictive zoning in the affluent Philadelphia suburb of Mount Laurel, N.J. (Kirp, Dwyer, and Rosenthal 1995). After the local planning board denied permits for the construction of an affordable housing project sponsored by local black residents, litigants took the case to the New Jersey Supreme Court. Not only did the high court agree that municipalities could not constitutionally write zoning regulations to preclude the construction of affordable housing, but it held that every municipality in the state had an *affirmative obligation* to allow for the construction of its "fair share" of the regional need for affordable housing.

In late 2000 a residential complex of 140 fully affordable housing units finally opened in Mount Laurel, despite vociferous protestations from many community residents who argued that the project would inevitably lower property values, raise crime rates, and increase taxes. However, a systematic analysis of the project's effect on the host community and adjacent neighborhoods could detect no detrimental effects with respect to any of these outcomes, showing it was indeed possible to locate an affordable development in an affluent white suburb without imposing negative externalities on the surrounding community (Massey et al. 2013).

The study also revealed great benefits for the low-income families who were fortunate enough to move into the development. In order to assess the effect of moving into an affluent white neighborhood, the study team developed a series of indices to measure advantaged and disadvantaged outcomes, computing them for residents of the affordable housing complex as well as

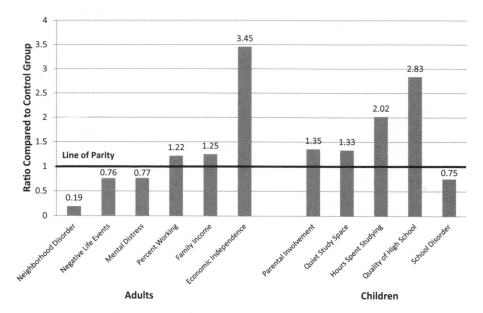

Figure 6.1. Benefits experienced by affordable housing residents compared to control group. Massey et al. 2013.

for a control group of people who had applied for affordable units but were still on the waiting list at the time of the study, thus controlling for self-selection bias. Figure 6.1 presents a bar chart showing ratios of index values for project residents and persons in the control group. A ratio of 1.0 would indicate no difference between the two groups and thus no benefit to the move into affordable housing (indicated in the figure by the solid line of parity). Ratios for adults are shown to the left of the chart and those for children to the right.

As can be seen, in no case do the bars approach a value of 1.0 and rigorous analyses performed by the investigators reveal all of the departures from parity to be statistically significant (Massey et al. 2013). Thus adult affordable housing residents experienced an 81 percent reduction in exposure to neighborhood disorder and violence compared to persons in the control group, as well as a 24 percent reduction in negative life events and a 23 percent reduction in symptoms of mental distress. At the same time they experienced a 22 percent increase in employment and a 25 percent increase in family income. In the end, residents increased their overall economic independence by three and a half times. Children who moved into the complex likewise experienced a 25 percent reduction in exposure to disorder and violence at school and school quality improved by a factor of 2.8. At home, they experienced a 33 percent increase in access to a quiet place to study and doubled the time they spent studying, and their parents were 35 percent more involved in education and enrichment activities. Finally, although most children had moved from a very uncompetitive to a very competitive school district, grades did not suffer. Children earned the same grades they would have in their old schools, but received a much higher quality education.

In the end, combining greater enforcement of fair housing and fair lending laws with a wider implementation of residential mobility programs for the urban poor would go a long way toward desegregating American society by race and class. Whether mobility were to be achieved through an assisted voucher program, affordable set-asides within market rate developments, or construction of fully affordable projects using housing tax credits, research to date indicates that properly designed and well-managed residential mobility programs are effective in promoting the twin goals of desegregation and poverty reduction.

As always, the barriers to greater use of residential mobility programs are political more than practical. Rather than opposing such developments, residents and officials in affluent communities should push for their proper design and implementation, looking to the examples cited above for guides on how to proceed and thereby create a win-win situation for all concerned: a lack of negative consequences for host communities, a path out of poverty and into the middle class for aspiring poor families, and the transformation of formerly maligned dependents into respected taxpaying citizens.

CHAPTER 7

Expanding Educational Opportunity in Urban School Districts

Paul A. Jargowsky, Zachary D. Wood, J. Cameron Anglum,
and David N. Karp

Inequality in educational outcomes in the United States has grown over time, both because income inequality has increased in recent decades and because a historically polarized urban-suburban public school system has led to stark differences in school quality. This divide is driven in part by entrenched geographic segregation (along race and income lines) and the resulting underfunding of urban school systems (where the municipal tax bases have shrunk). Residential segregation translates to segregation within schools, causing children of low-income families to be increasingly likely to attend schools serving other children from a similar sociodemographic background. These low-income children are also more likely to attend lower performing schools in high-poverty areas, leading to a widening achievement gap across socioeconomic lines (Reardon 2011). Moreover, the consequences of gaps in educational quality are compounded as innovations in modern technologies and an increasingly global economy continue to put high-paying jobs out of reach of the underskilled and undercredentialed. As a result, education (at all levels) is increasingly critical to a child's life chances, career opportunities, and lifetime earnings. In a labor market characterized by increasing returns to skill and higher levels of global competition, it is essential that all children have access to quality education to ensure the economic mobility of the nation's most disadvantaged children.

The problem is clear: the nation's public school system is disproportionately failing its most disadvantaged students, those who stand to gain the most. The problem has a well-defined spatial dimension, given that poor students are clustered in poor school districts, particularly in the inner cities of large metropolitan areas. Not surprisingly, therefore, the central question of how to fix failing urban schools has dominated educational policy discussions for decades. Nor will the question be going away any time soon: the number of people living in high-poverty neighborhoods—census tracts with poverty rates that are 40 percent or more—increased 72 percent since 2000 (Jargowsky 2013, this volume). Schools in segregated high-poverty neighborhoods are characterized by high teacher turnover, low academic achievement, and high dropout rates (Leventhal and Brooks-Gunn 2000; Burdick-Will et al. 2011; G. Duncan and Murnane 2011). These disparities make it far more difficult for poor children to succeed academically, thus reducing social mobility and contributing to widening income inequality. Many programs and policies have been proposed to address the problem of poor quality inner-city schools. The latest generation of such programs is epitomized by the Harlem Children's Zone (HCZ), which embeds whole school reforms within a framework of programs to support and strengthen students' families and the community generally. The promise shown by the HCZ model has led the Obama administration to create the Promise Neighborhood program, which essentially seeks to replicate the HCZ model in poor urban neighborhoods in twenty states and the District of Columbia (U.S. Department of Education 2013a).

The trials and tribulations of high-poverty schools have been exhaustively documented. The starting point for understanding why inner-city schools so often fail is that family socioeconomic status is itself a more powerful predictor of academic performance than school characteristics (Coleman et al. 1966; Ladd 2012). Many schools in the central cities of metropolitan areas are located in poor neighborhoods and therefore have high concentrations of poor students; 40 percent of students in urban areas attended schools where almost half of their classmates were eligible for free and reduced-price lunch, compared to 10 percent in suburban areas (Lippman, Burns, and McArthur 1996: 7). These two facts together would be sufficient to ensure that high-poverty schools in urban areas performed worse than their better-endowed suburban counterparts solely due to the socioeconomic composition of the student body.

The problem of inner-city education is far worse than that, however, because the school performance of a student of a given socioeconomic level is heavily influenced by the academic level of his peers (Hanushek et al. 2003; Zimmer and Toma 2000) and the level of poverty in the neighborhood (Brooks-Gunn, G. Duncan, and Aber 1997; Jargowsky and El Komi 2011; A. Summers and Wolfe 1977). This effect is so strong that a nonpoor student attending a high-poverty school is more likely to fall behind than a poor student attending a low-poverty school (Kennedy 1986: 22). As a result, students in high-poverty schools perform worse on average than students in low-poverty schools on reading and mathematics, even after controlling for family background and socioeconomic status (J. Anderson, Hollinger, and Conaty 1992).

Students attending schools in high-poverty areas are also more likely to drop out of high school, even after controlling for family background (Brooks-Gunn et al. 1993; Jencks and Mayer 1990). Indeed, high schools in high-poverty neighborhoods have been called "drop out factories" (Balfanz and Legters 2004). Central city school districts, which house nearly all high-poverty census tracts, have far higher dropout rates than suburban school districts. The average 2005 dropout rate for urban districts in the nation's forty-one largest metropolitan areas was 40.7 percent, compared to 22.7 percent for suburban districts in the same metro areas (Swanson 2009: 17). The largest urban-suburban gap in dropout rates was 42.6 percentage points in the Cleveland metropolitan area, where 62 percent of students in the urban school district dropped out compared to 19.5 percent in suburban districts. On average, the gap was 18 percentage points in the district-wide averages, but this does not reflect the full extent of the problem in high-poverty neighborhoods. The gap is far greater when comparing schools in the poorest neighborhoods to wealthy neighborhoods even within urban school districts.

Understanding and addressing the racial and socioeconomic achievement gaps in public schools has been a goal of researchers, policy makers, educators, and practitioners alike for years. These gaps are likely to persist as long as racial and economic segregation combine to concentrate poor students in high-poverty areas, as Jargowsky argues in Chapter 2. In the short run, however, poor neighborhoods will continue to contribute to educational failure, and therefore interventions are needed that have the prospect of improving urban schools despite unhelpful neighborhood contexts.

There have been a number of innovative interventions that have attempted to achieve improvements in the efficacy of schools in high-poverty neighborhoods, and these interventions have taken a multitude of shapes: from individual school interventions, entire district interventions, and interventions that are tied to community-focused wraparound programs. However, definitive measures of the impacts of these interventions have proven to be considerably more elusive. Here we focus on examples that appear to be successful models for achieving the kinds of improvements desired for high-poverty neighborhoods and traditionally low-performing urban schools. We use as exemplars initiatives at all stages of education, including early childhood education, high school based interventions, pathways to college, and comprehensive community-based programs that have served as a model for the Promise Initiative (see Turner, this volume). Each program is either community-wide or citywide and thus serves as a potential model for improving neighborhood and citywide educational outcomes. The importance of such initiatives for life chances of poor children is clear. Here we consider what is to be learned from each for replication to solve the broader issue of unequal access to high-quality education.

Well-structured and well-designed school-based and community-based interventions have the potential to increase educational and social outcomes. Short- and long-term effects of interventions in early education and K-12 schooling have been observed to increase test scores, competency in various disciplines, retention and graduation rates, college attendance rates, and adult earnings. While many of these programs and initiatives are too new to conduct full, comprehensive evaluations, assessment of the most promising interventions have been conducted at various points in the educational process: early education, elementary, secondary, and postsecondary—all with the aim of improving educational outcomes and narrowing the achievement gap.

In this chapter, we analyze promising case studies of school systems that significantly increase educational success for less advantaged students in disadvantaged urban environments, reducing the gaps in achievement between low-income students and their more advantaged peers. These city-led and community-led interventions demonstrate that local government can play a role in developing effective policy to increase access to quality education and increase performance of low-income students. By engaging in partnerships with schools, using data-driven methods, and through the use of directed incentives, policy makers and community stakeholders can restructure K-12 education to provide all low-income children with high-quality educational experiences. This chapter reviews a comprehensive, portfolio approach to reform, highlighting policy initiatives that aim to alleviate the challenges high-poverty schools face in preparing students, from the start, for higher-skilled jobs in the future.

Early Education

Early childhood education is critical for development and long-term achievement in terms of academic performance as well as the increased life chances and future employment and earning opportunities that are associated with a quality education, and proper social and cognitive development (Heckman 2006; Knudsen et al. 2006). Efforts to address achievement gaps between children from low- and middle-income families have focused on establishing pre-K programs in many high-poverty and urban areas. These programs, dating back to those started in the early 1970s, have aimed to provide better preparation for entry into kindergarten. Through highly structured curricula that teach children language skills and improve cognitive and socioemotional development, these programs aim to equip students with the necessary aptitude to perform in K-12, and beyond. Students that enter K-12 with a proper set of skills will be more prepared to take advantage of the instruction (G. Duncan and Murnane 2014). This has been precisely the focus of much research in the area of evaluation: *does the impact of early education programs have long-term effects that follow students through elementary school, high school, and on to college?*

Results from a study of Kalamazoo County's Ready 4s program—based on kindergarten entrance assessments—showed that the math and vocabulary test scores improved for pre-K program participants, while not having significant effects on letter-word identification or behavior (Bartik 2013). A study of Tulsa's universal pre-K program estimated effects associated with future adult earnings—both half-day and full-day programs were observed to have positive benefit-to-cost ratios of 3 or 4 to 1 (Bartik, Gormley, and Adelstein 2012). Similar state programs in Georgia and Oklahoma that have increased preschool enrollment rates in both lower- and higher-income families have shown increased testing performance through the eighth grade, in addition to other positive social benefits to the family, particularly for low-income families (i.e., ability to work) (Cascio and Schanzenbach 2013). Statewide early childhood education initiatives in North Carolina have had positive effects on third-grade reading and math test scores; these programs include improving childcare services for children under five, as well as funding to enroll disadvantaged four-year-olds in preschool (Ladd, Muschkin, and Dodge 2014). Boston's publicly funded pre-K program has been shown to have positive effects on participating students' language, literacy, numeracy and mathematics skills, as well as on executive functioning (Weiland and Yoshikawa 2013). Chicago's Child-Parent Center Education Program has been studied to look at indicators of well-being, with findings to suggest that school-based early education can have a positive impact on educational and socio-economic outcomes, sustained through to adulthood (Reynolds et al. 2011).

Well-known examples of targeted early interventions are two well-studied cases, the Perry Preschool Project and the Carolina Abecedarian Project. These highly structured programs enrolled children from low-income families to provide free pre-K education. Although these programs were small—with 123 children and 111 infants, respectively—they were resource rich, intensive, and employed a true experimental design. The success of these programs is well documented to show effects that carried through into K-12 and beyond (M. Anderson 2008; Campbell et al. 2002; Heckman et al. 2010b; Schweinhart et al. 2005). The ability to replicate these programs has been questioned, both in terms of scale and cost. Most efforts to deliver similar programs to high-poverty areas across the country—most notably through the federally funded Head Start program—have returned mixed results, mainly due to great variability in quality, curricula, teacher training, resources, and non-standardized implementation. Though evidence has shown that Head Start participants have performed better than nonparticipating siblings, effects have not been as long lasting, with achievement boosts less widespread, and not observed beyond the first grade (G. Duncan and Murnane 2014: chap. 5).

The fact that enrollment in early education programs remains lower for children from lower-income families, compared to those from families of higher incomes, has led a number of states and local municipalities to take action to address the effects that result in long-run achievement gaps (i.e., sociodemographic disparities among high school graduation rates, college attendance and completion rates, career and lifetime earnings opportunities).

A handful of state- and city-run programs have begun to implement pre-K schooling aimed at replicating the successes and improvements in educational outcomes achieved through quality programs like Perry and Abecedarian, yet on a wider scale. In the 2012–2013 school year, forty states, plus the District of Columbia, enrolled 1.1 million four-year-olds in publicly funded pre-K programs. This amounts to 28 percent of the nation's four-year-olds, which has continued to climb from 14 percent starting in 2002. In

2012–2013 another 10 percent were enrolled in Head Start programs (Barnett et al. 2013).

Boston Public Schools (BPS), the city's school district, runs a full-day pre-K program aimed at narrowing the performance and graduation rate gap between students of low-income and middle-income families. Issuing a lottery enrollment beginning in 2004, BPS established the program to provide free schooling to four-year-olds. The program included standardized instruction materials and curricula, corresponding training manuals for teachers, and coaching and ongoing support for teachers to ensure quality instruction. The program gives primary attention to the training of teachers to ensure proper delivery of well-designed material. Assessments of program quality and evaluation of impact on student achievement find that Boston's pre-K program has had positive effects, evidenced from studies that have looked at ongoing achievement outcomes. Test scores in the third grade improved for pre-K participants compared to students that did not go through the program. Additionally, the achievement gap between black and white students was one-third smaller among program participants compared to nonparticipants (G. Duncan and Murnane 2014: chap. 5).

The Harlem Children's Zone

The Obama administration's push for Promise Neighborhoods is a direct replication attempt of Geoffrey Canada's Harlem Children's Zone (HCZ) in New York City, which has been praised and hailed as the kind of comprehensive, holistic approach needed to truly reverse poverty and its impacts in distressed communities. HCZ has been the darling of the media and the focus of a best-selling book, *Whatever It Takes* (Tough 2008). If indeed the replication of this model is the next big push in education reform, with a substantial investment from the federal government, a deep and clear understanding of the efficacy of the model is essential. The question remains: does a community-focused intervention lead to better results of student academic achievement than a schools-only intervention model?

The Harlem Children's Zone model was designed under the assumption that schools alone could not sufficiently combat the multitude of barriers that students in high-poverty neighborhoods face, especially when many of those barriers originate outside the school itself, such as socioeconomic and family-environment factors. Therefore a push to address aspects of poverty, health, and family conditions figured to open the door for better environments for students to learn within schools (Tough 2009). The model called for the creation of new public-charter schools to cover a 97-block area of Harlem, in which wraparound services would support the work done in the schools, such as parenting classes, community health programs, tutoring, crime, and foster care prevention programs, and even financial and tax assistance. School admissions are based on a lottery system.

Understanding the true efficacy of Harlem Children's Zone is somewhat complicated due to the relative newness of the model. It is possible that not enough time has passed to get a true sense of how the model is performing. HCZ holds its dramatic test score improvements and extremely high college placement numbers (approximately 90 percent according to HCZ's website) as the key measure of its success in dramatically diminishing the achievement gap. A recent examination of HCZ has had a slightly different take. Dobbie and Fryer (2009, 2011) explored the improved test scores of HCZ and also designed a model that would allow them to simulate a randomized experiment for the purposes of measuring the impact of the community-program aspect of the model. Their results indicate that enrollment in HCZ schools did dramatically improve test scores and even shrank the achievement gaps considerably, even "enough to close the black-white achievement gap in mathematics" for middle-school students (Dobbie and Fryer 2011: 158). However, they also found that the community programs were neither necessary nor sufficient to produce test score gains, which were driven entirely by the improvement in school quality.

The student achievement gains reported by the HCZ are impressive; yet the gains reported are broadly consistent with other high-performing charter schools-only interventions (Angrist et al. 2010a). However, the question remains about whether the community-focused interventions of HCZ produce a more substantial impact on student academic achievement than the schools-only models. Dobbie and Fryer create a model to explore this question by using students of HCZ schools that live within range of the additional community programming and those that that do not, and find that the community-based support programs have little to no effect on academic achievement outcomes (Angrist et al. 2010b).

Whitehurst and Croft (2010) are more critical. They highlight the importance of the difference between HCZ being effective and being "effective as advertised" (2010: 2). Whitehurst and Croft developed a new model of analysis to explore this and found that indeed HCZ schools trend well in the improvement of test scores compared to other charter schools in NYC that utilize a schools-only approach. Their results indicate that while test scores did improve at HCZ schools, they did so either less than or equal to schools that do not have community programming, which leads them to infer, similar to Dobbie and Fryer, that resource-heavy community programming efforts seem to have no impact and therefore may not be the best use of precious federal resources. Certainly, if dramatic improvements in student academic achievement can be gained for less financial investment, that situation would likely be preferred; and if federal education reform initiatives will be largely based on a holistic model such as HCZ, it becomes even more essential to have a clear understanding of how goals, success, and measures of that success will be defined.

As government funding sources, most notably the federal Department of Education, have increased attention to the replicability and scalability of the education interventions they research and fund, it is important to closely examine the ways in which the HCZ differs from its local education counterparts. Despite its open lottery system of attracting local students, a New York City requirement stipulating that oversubscribed public charter school seats be filled by open lotteries, schools in the HCZ are often criticized for educating a population of students that are not truly fully representative of their surrounding neighborhood schools and for reporting their successes based on this skewed sample (Whitehurst and Croft 2010). For example, in an oft-cited example of charter school enrollment criticism, the HCZ Promise Academy expelled an entire grade of eighth graders in 2007 due to poor performance (Dobbie and Fryer 2009). Collectively, charter schools are accused of overaggressive expulsion patterns that skew their standardized test scores (Ravitch 2010). Traditional public schools are equipped with much more limited means to treat difficult students, let alone students that simply may negatively impact school test scores. Finally, to determine causal inference of the HCZ student-level effects compared to other local schools or other charter schools across New York, Dobbie and Fryer would need to conduct a fully randomized control trial, not a more limited comparison of students to rejected lottery entrants that does not capture all observed and unobserved characteristics of sample members (Whitehurst and Croft 2010).

Similar critiques of the HCZ model focus on the financial prowess amassed by the organization and their per-pupil spending rates, both drastically higher than local counterparts. The HCZ boasts an endowment of over $200 million, a figure that rivals many institutions of higher education, funded in part through so-called "venture philanthropists" including billionaire board members Stanley Druckenmiller and Kenneth Langone. In fact, the financial institution Goldman Sachs donated $20 million for a new school facility, a luxury few schools and their students enjoy (Otterman 2010). In total, HCZ has attracted over $100 million in private philanthropic contributions, an amount many states would envy (Whitehurst and Croft 2010). This financial fortitude translates to per-student funding of roughly $21,000 including additional time in school and other neighborhood support measures, an amount that is over 45 percent higher than local New York City public schools (Hanson 2013). Despite some encouraging initial results, issues pertaining to student push-out and financial expenditures remain and threaten the replicability and scalability of the HCZ in the form of Neighborhood Promise Zones across the nation.

NYC Small School-High School Initiative

The New Century High Schools initiative, supported by the Carnegie Corporation, the Gates Foundation, and the Open Society Institute, was established in the 1990s to facilitate the creation of "New Century Schools" that could establish positive community-school partnerships and collaborations, including funding to community partners to support planning efforts. Between 2002 and 2003, thirty small New Century High Schools were opened in New York City, in Brooklyn and the Bronx (G. Duncan and Murnane 2014: chap. 7). Importantly, the opening of many of these small high schools was targeted to cater to graduates from other local elementary schools. These inter-school linkages were key to various aspects of high school prep, continuity, and community-specific curriculum design. Sponsored by the New Century Initiative, the opening of these small schools, while independently planned, was universally guided by the principles set out in the proposal and development process: rigorous instruction, individualized attention to students, performance tracking, ties to the community for expanded engagement, and opportunities for student and parent feedback and input.

New York City School Chancellor Joel Klein vastly expanded the autonomy and potential of these small schools, in exchange for making schools accountable for performance, by linking funding to demonstrated reading and math test scores. This effort was paired with a system-wide school report card system, as well as the New York City Leadership Academy, which serves to recruit and train teachers and school administrators to work in high-poverty schools. Other policies were renegotiated with the city's teacher union to give the school more control over hiring practices. Nonprofit School Support Organizations (SSOs) were also created to provide additional administrative support (logistical and instructional) to schools on an individual basis (G. Duncan and Murnane 2014: chap. 7).

Beginning in 2002, the NYC Department of Education (NYCDOE) closed thirty-one large, low-performance high schools and created more than 200 new small secondary schools. Over half the new schools (123 of them) are located in the same high-poverty neighborhoods where large failing schools were closed, aiming to serve students of these disadvantaged communities. Called Small Schools of Choice (SSCs), these new schools emphasize strong, sustained relationships between students and faculty. The SSCs were designed to have three common characteristics: (1) academic rigor, (2) personalization, and (3) community partnerships to offer learning opportunities outside the classroom. NYC eighth graders have to rank up to twelve high schools that they want to attend, but when an SSC has more applicants than spaces, the district uses a randomized process to assign students to the SSC (Bloom and Unterman 2013). The total number of small high schools expanded in the last two decades to more than 200, paralleling simultaneous efforts to close large, underperforming schools. Key components of the development and success of these schools include a competitive design process; emphasis on best practices; engagement with community partners; student selection process (lottery); performance based accountability; and third-party resources for logistical, instructional, and administrative support (G. Duncan and Murnane 2014: chap. 7).

New York's small high schools across the city have proven able to provide the necessary structure and individual-level attention to students—many from disadvantaged backgrounds—needed to achieve significant increases in retention and graduation rates, as well as improved academic performance. A rigorous evaluation was conducted by the Manpower Development Research Corporation (MDRC), a nonprofit education and social policy research organization, which tracked 12,130 students in SSCs and large, control-group high schools in NYC. [1] The result has been a 7 percentage point increase in graduation rates, relative to the students who were not admitted through the lottery, corresponding to a 10 percent increase in the overall graduation rate. Test results were also shown to improve, with students who attended an SSC being more likely to score 10 percentage points above the minimum passing score for the Regents English Examination (G. Duncan and Murnane 2014). Between 2004 and 2007, the four-year graduation rate was higher for SSC students, an average of 70.4 percent, compared to 60.9 percent in large high schools with comparable students. Low-income students had a graduation rate of 68.6 percent in SSCs and only 57.4 percent in large schools. Students who entered high school performing below grade level, graduated at a higher rate from SSCs compared to large schools. Of students that only partially met eighth grade proficiency standards, graduation rates were of 68.1 percent in SSCs compared to 58.3 percent in large schools, and 68.1 percent in SSCs and 56.3 percent in large schools, for reading and math, respectively. Relative to the control group, graduation rates were higher for all demographic subgroups, including black and Hispanic male and female students (Bloom and Unterman 2013).

These figures indicate that the SSCs reduced achievement gaps, although substantial gaps remain. Moreover, the move to smaller schools involves substantial additional costs in terms of administration and infrastructure. New York City, aided by large philanthropic gifts, has been able to make these investments for the benefit of their students. Poorer cities, however, such as Philadelphia and Detroit, currently lack the resources to reduce school size (or, for that matter, to guarantee pre-K education or college tuition). While these models prove that inner-city schools can be improved, the ability to replicate these models in many struggling communities that lack New York's vibrant economy and strong civic culture is still an open question.

Kalamazoo Promise

The Kalamazoo Promise, another innovative privately established solution to low-performing schools, was established in 2005 as a means to bolster student achievement as well as to motivate and encourage students to attend college. This scholarship program offers anywhere from 65 to 100 percent of tuition and fees for up to four years of college at any of the forty-four public colleges or universities for students who graduate from Kalamazoo Public Schools. Eligible students must have been continuously enrolled in Kalamazoo Public Schools for at least four years prior to graduation. By making all children eligible, part of the idea was to change the prevailing attitude in the community about the accessibility of higher education. By making higher education attainable, the program seeks to counter the lack of role models in the community and provide an incentive for students to resist the temptations of drugs, gangs, and the underground economy.

Early indicators point to the Kalamazoo Promise having a positive impact in a number of intended areas. As Bartik, Eberts, and Huang (2010) point out, Kalamazoo Public Schools has seen increases in enrollment (largely due to declining dropout rates), stabilization of racial and ethnic enrollment percentages, and increases in test scores across the board. Bartik and Lachowska (2013) find that the Kalamazoo Promise appears to have increased the average number of credits earned and significant reductions in the number of suspensions. In African American students, Bartik and Lachowska found an increase in average GPA, although they found little evidence of GPA increases in the full sample. Additionally, Andrews, DesJardins, and Ranchhod (2010) found the Kalamazoo Promise seems to lead more students to consider public colleges and universities in Michigan, especially those families with an annual household income under $50,000.

Similar to Harlem Children's Zone, this program is in relative infancy so while the trends seem encouraging in terms of student achievement marks, the true long-term effects likely will not be known for some time. Also similar to Harlem Children's Zone, the Kalamazoo Promise is privately funded, and therefore potentially challenging to replicate; however, promising results could drive more public investment in this direction.

What is interesting about the Kalamazoo Promise is that if the trends and early indicators are true, the simple offer of opportunity to students in high-poverty neighborhoods may improve student achievement. In these neighborhoods, the connection to higher education and individual expectation and opportunity to attend may be weaker. It is certainly possible that a scholarship program such as this opens the door for students who otherwise may not have felt college was an option for them, connecting the dots for students between their own school performance and future opportunity.

Other Interventions

There are other interventions that have been discussed and examined for their potential for closing the achievement gap in high-poverty neighborhoods. Early intervention programs such as Head Start and Nurse-Family Partnership have been shown to improve school readiness in young children, but their results seem to have a fading effect in the long run (Currie and

D. Thomas 1995; Olds 2006). Moving to Opportunity utilized the approach of relocating individuals from high-poverty to low-poverty neighborhoods, and research has shown that its effects were either null or negative for student achievement (Sanbonmatsu et al. 2006), although positive benefits in health and subjective well-being were achieved. Angrist and his colleagues explored the effects of schools-only charter models in Boston, which display test score improvements similar to those in HCZ, further supporting the conclusion that community programming has little effect on student achievement (Angrist et al. 2010a).

Other research has focused on internal factors that improve schools in high-poverty neighborhoods, and the results are considerably mixed. Some have argued that reductions in class size are the key to closing the achievement gap (Finn and Achilles 1999; Finn, Gerber, and Boyd-Zaharias 2005), while others argue that leadership, teacher quality, and community engagement are the key characteristics of successful interventions (Desforges and Abouchaar 2003; McGee 2004). Research findings on these programs and policies often lead to contradictory conclusions, leaving a complicated and confusing picture; however, a number of these characteristics are incorporated into the more comprehensive interventions such as HCZ that can be examined as the effects of those models are tested.

Discussion and Implications

The evidence on the efficacy of interventions to improve schools in high-poverty neighborhoods, while mixed, does seem to indicate that such schools can be improved, especially with a substantial influx of new resources. The Harlem Children's Zone, the New York City Small School Initiative, and the Kalamazoo Promise were all based on substantial infusions of resources from foundations, philanthropists, and governments at different levels. These resources helped to offset the lack of resources in high-poverty neighborhoods and the greater cost of educating students from disadvantaged environments.

The community-focused approach of programs like Harlem Children's Zone has performed well at improving the academic achievement of its students, but as Whitehurst and Croft (2010) point out, perhaps not as advertised. The HCZ model's key claim is that the schools-only approach is simply not enough to comprehensively address the barriers to achievement that high-poverty students face. Evidence seems to indicate that while HCZ schools have strong improvements in academic achievement, it is not greater than those of similar schools-only interventions, calling into question the need for funding for the wraparound community services. This may simply be a question of goals. For instance, if the goal is improved academic achievement in high-poverty neighborhoods, then we see some solid models in both the community-focused interventions and the schools-only interventions. However, if the goal is a deeper and more complex attempt to reduce neighborhood poverty, as indicated in much of the Obama administration campaign and policy rhetoric (Darling-Hammond 2009), then improved test scores may not be the most appropriate measure of success. Results of this type of impact may only reveal themselves in longer-term studies. As White-hurst and Croft (2010) point out, these goals may be excellent, necessary, and even an effective use of resources; however, they are not education reform and therefore should not be measured as such. They are, in fact, policies to improve neighborhoods from within an educational policy. We argue that it would be far more effective to improve neighborhoods from within housing and community development policy.

There are a number of questions that remain unanswered in the assessments of interventions for improving academic achievement that must be addressed before a truly clear picture can take shape. We still need to understand the validity of standardized test scores as the appropriate measure overall, and the potential impact "teaching for the test" may have on overall learning. Is it possible our measures are not sufficient for the success we hope for? Chetty and his colleagues explored this question and found that test scores were decent measures of short-term successes, but that the factors that make up the quality of a classroom were much better predictors of future earnings, college enrollment, and even retirement savings (Chetty et al. 2011).

We also do not know whether community-focused approaches, like HCZ and Obama's Promise Neighborhoods, are more likely to show extended results and neighborhood improvements over time that simply won't be captured within short-term examinations of test scores. These approaches take a more holistic view of intervention and the approach is to embed into a culture that, it could be argued, would show more significant results on the broader neighborhood environment over time. Tied to this is a question about whether it is appropriate to assume that improved schools and test scores will lead to better life chances, which in turn will improve the overall poverty of an area. Certainly it may not be that direct a causal line, which again calls for clarity on goals and how the measures of success line up with those goals.

Each of these questions is an essential aspect to examine as the shifts in policy and resource allocation are being decided. Significant federal resources are being called for to initiate the replication of the holistic model seen in the Harlem Children's Zone into Promise Neighborhoods across the United States and abroad. It is essential to truly understand whether the model works as it has been touted, and especially whether the additional resources for wraparound community programming will lead to additional increases in academic achievement in high-poverty schools. The evidence seems to indicate that it may not.

All the programs described above share one central characteristic: they attempt to ameliorate the negative effects of high-poverty neighborhoods on school quality. These policies and programs have shown that dramatic improvements in student outcomes are possible, but only with sustained capital investments. Moreover, as high-poverty neighborhoods continue to proliferate, the social disorganization and severe economic distress of these neighborhoods serve to undermine even the most well-intended reforms. Unless and until cities and metropolitan areas develop in a more equitable pattern, with fewer high-poverty ghettos and barrios, fixing failing inner-city schools will continue to be a daunting challenge. Patterns of segregation by race and concentration of poverty create formidable obstacles to providing equality of educational opportunity. Efforts to improve inner-city schools must continue, but in parallel with those efforts we must also begin to address the root causes of the existence of high-poverty neighborhoods. As Schwartz (2010) noted, "housing policy is school policy."

CHAPTER 8

Preparing Today's Youth for Tomorrow's Jobs

Anthony P. Carnevale and Nicole Smith

Postsecondary education is an important tool to expand opportunity and promote economic prosperity. However, many American youth do not have access to the education they need to attain a middle-class lifestyle. In fact, access to higher education is increasingly stratified across socioeconomic lines. In today's job market, a high school diploma is no longer a reliable ticket to the middle class. While there is wide variation in earnings within educational attainment levels, the odds of climbing the socioeconomic ladder without some postsecondary training are decreasing. For several decades, the demand for high-skilled workers has been increasing, and this is expected to continue to the point where most jobs will require postsecondary education in the coming decades. The challenge is to address the increasing stratification of higher education opportunity, as well as the growing gap between the supply of and demand for college-educated workers. Initiatives to accomplish this are at the intersection of education, training, and workforce development.

The evidence for "skill-biased technological change" is clear: the revolution in technology favors high-skilled workers, whose jobs for the most part cannot be automated as easily as those of their relatively lower-skilled counterparts. The result has been a significant and steady rise in the "wage premium" that one can earn by attaining a higher level of education. Recent estimates indicate that the average family of college graduates earns $58,000 more than high school graduates (Autor 2014). Over a lifetime the median worker can expect net returns of $300,000 from a four-year college degree that will cost them $80,000 (Carnevale, Smith, and Strohl 2013). These net returns have grown and upper-income youth college attendance and graduation rates have grown as well. Between 1960 and 1980, college graduation rates rose from 40 percent to 55 percent among affluent households. However, for students from the bottom quartile of the income distribution this rate remained at single digits, growing only from 5 to 10 percent for girls and decreasing for boys (Bailey and Dynarski 2011). Moreover, in the thirty-seven-year period from 1970 to 2007, the share of people with graduate degrees in the middle class declined from 46 percent to 30 percent—a decrease of 16 percentage points. People leaving the middle class with graduate degrees were leaving for higher wages, as the share of people with graduate degrees in the top three income deciles increased from 41 to 61 percent (Carnevale, Smith, and Strohl 2013).

These statistics point to the depth of the nation's educational deficit. While the payoff from a college degree is almost twice as big as it was in 1979, a growing fragment of the nation's youth has not been able to benefit from the potential of these returns to investment in human capital.

The Great Recession exacerbated the nation's education deficit. Low-skilled workers are usually the hardest hit by recessions and this episode was no exception. While the increase in unemployment has been largely cyclical, rising across the board for all levels of education, workers with only a high school diploma face the highest rates of unemployment—and the greatest risk of permanent job loss. Nearly four out of five jobs lost were held by those with no formal education beyond high school. At the other end of the spectrum, workers who had completed a four-year college degree or higher were largely protected against job losses during the recession, and high-education fields had job gains. Since the end of the recession, two of three new job openings have been for those with postsecondary education and training beyond high school.

Many of America's youth are ill prepared for these opportunities. While the demand for college-educated workers has been growing at a stable rate of 3.6 percent for the past five decades, the supply of college education in the workforce has grown at 2.5 percent in the 1980s, 2 percent in the 1990s, and only 1 percent in the 2000s. Hence the rising wage premium, with employers paying more to attract an increasingly inadequate supply of high-skilled workers to fill the job openings.

An explanation that puts sole responsibility on the workers themselves for acquiring necessary training misses the deeply embedded inequalities of opportunity in the educational system. The fact is that many American youth do not have access to the education they need to attain a middle-class life-style. In many ways, the disparity in education is not so much an *explanation* for income inequality as it is a *manifestation* of it, sorting students according to the opportunities they were given before they ever entered a college admissions office. This phenomenon is evidenced by patterns of college application and attendance, with low-income students tending to attend less selective colleges, even when they have equal or higher test scores than their more advantaged peers (Carnevale and Strohl 2013). Only half of low-income students enroll in college, compared to 80 percent of high-income students (Porter 2014). And, as noted above, only 9 percent of low-income students *graduate* from college, compared to 55 percent of high-income students (Bailey and Dynarski 2011).

Moving forward from this point, the inequality deepens, as more-educated workers receive jobs that give them more training, while less-educated workers remain stuck in routine jobs with little room for advancement. For high-skilled workers, technology is complementary, increasing their labor value; for low-skilled workers, it is often a substitute.

This chapter examines the bifurcated job market, the skill competencies required to be successful in twenty-first-century jobs, and the means to develop these competencies. We document the industries and occupations where job openings are to be found, and we project where the job openings will be in the coming decade. We find that this job growth will contribute to the rising demand for postsecondary education and training in two ways. First, the fastest-growing industries—such as computer and data processing services—require workers with disproportionately higher education levels. Second, over time, occupations as a whole are steadily requiring more education. In the next section, we examine the role of career competencies in the occupational landscape, and in the following section propose policy solutions to give Americans the opportunity to develop these competencies.

Need for Postsecondary Credentials by 2020

While we often think of postsecondary education as colleges and universities, the reality is that they represent only 35 percent of the system. The rest consists of formal and informal training programs that are equally important for the pursuit of shared prosperity and opportunity for all (Carnevale, Smith, and Strohl 2013). Nondegreed learning systems are also important to

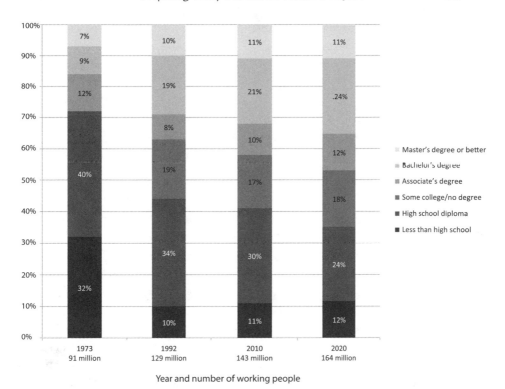

Figure 8.1. By 2020, 65 percent of jobs will require postsecondary education and training, up from 28 percent in 1973.

access and success in the workforce. These postsecondary training programs that result in certificates, test-based licenses and certifications are important for access to technical jobs that lead to further human capital improvements from on-the-job training. Jobs today require not only knowledge to complete tasks, but the interaction of a sophisticated set of core work competencies for success in the workplace.

We estimate that by 2020, 65 percent of all jobs in the economy will require at least some postsecondary education and training beyond high school. Some 35 percent will require a bachelor's degree or higher, while 30 percent will require middle skills—an associate's degree (12 percent) or some college (18 percent), the latter of which can run the gamut from a few highly selected college courses to a postsecondary vocational certificate or test-based industry credential. That is a full 6 percentage points higher than the current need

Table 8.1. By 2020, We Will Fail to Meet the Demand for Postsecondary
Talent by 11 Million

	Demand	Supply	Shortage
Middle skills: Certificates, some college, Associate's degrees	15.3	11.1	4.3
BA underproduction	17.7	8.2	6.8
BA under-credentialed		2.7	
Total	**33**	**22**	**11.1**

Georgetown University Center on Education on the Workforce, Analysis of Current
Population Survey data, various years; U.S. Department of Education, National Center for
Education Statistics, various years, American Community Survey data, various years.

for postsecondary education at 59 percent. Currently, 17 percent need some
college, 10 percent an associate's degree, and 32 percent a bachelor's degree
or higher (Carnevale, Smith, and Strohl 2013).

Between 2014 and 2020, the U.S. economy will produce 22 million new
postsecondary graduates as part of the active labor supply (Carnevale, Smith,
and Strohl 2013). The economy will, however, demand 33 million workers
with postsecondary education and training. This means that the economy
will need an additional 11 million workers with postsecondary education and
training.[1]

We estimate that there will be 55 million job openings in the economy
through 2020: 24 million from newly created jobs and 31 million due to
baby boomer retirement (Carnevale, Smith, and Strohl 2010, 2013).[2] By educational attainment of the additional 33 million needed, we estimate that
the jobs will require credentials as follows:[3] 15.3 million jobs for holders of
postsecondary vocational certificates, associate's degrees, or some college,
and 17.7 million jobs for workers with a bachelor's degree or higher (see
Table 8.1).

The shortage of bachelor and associate degrees consists of *underproduction*—the inability of institutions to keep up with the rising demand
for talent—as well as *undercredentialing* and the upskilling of undercredentialed workers[4] currently employed in bachelor and associate degree jobs,
but with only some college credits and not with degrees or the skills that come
with the completed education.

Carnevale, Rose, and Fasules (CRF 2015) demonstrate, using Current
Population Survey (CPS) data, that close to 21 percent of workers without

bachelor's degrees are also working in jobs more suited to someone with a bachelor's degree and the associated additional training.[5] Not only has supply failed to keep up with demand for college-educated workers, but many workers are also performing in jobs for which they are insufficiently credentialed. Undercredentialed workers tend to make less than their more credentialed peers and have relatively lower opportunities for training and upskilling.[6] Using the work of CRF (2014), we estimate the number of undercredentialed workers that also contribute to the shortage of postsecondary trained workers. Thus the true measure of the skills shortage for credentialed workers between 2014 and 2020 amounts to the sum of existing shortages that arise from current trends in underproduction in the system plus the undercredentialed workers who could increase their productivity and wages through increasing education.

Extending the assumptions used by CRF, we estimate that 2.7 million additional undercredentialed workers are available for upskilling with a bachelor's degree through 2020. Added to estimations of underproduction of postsecondary talent, we find a total shortage of 11 million workers with postsecondary education and training through 2020, 6.8 million bachelor's degrees and 4.3 million postsecondary certificates.

Employers pay more for the college degree—a symbol of a worker's attainment of the knowledge, skills, and abilities that improve productivity. The persistence of the college wage premium sends a clear message: through booms and slumps, rising and falling unemployment, job creation and job loss, workers with postsecondary education earn 74 percent more than workers with a high school diploma or less. Among those with full-time, full-year jobs, the wage premium rises to 84 percent. Given these trends, we estimate that 6.8 million additional bachelor's degrees and 4.3 million middle-skill workers with some college credit and associate's degrees will be required to match the demand for credentials through 2020 (see Table 8.1).

Wages do signal the need for workforce skills in response to shortages. For example, Goldin and Katz (2008) track the rising demand in the American economy for more highly educated workers over the past ninety years. They find very different wage outcomes depending on the relative demand and supply for education. When the relative supply of education outpaced demand—as occurred during the movement toward compulsory education and GI bill education benefits—relative wages for postsecondary workers fell. However, since the 1980s, the demand for postsecondary education and training has risen at a far greater pace than the ability of postsecondary institutions to supply fresh credentials. As a result, during the period 1980 to 2005, Goldin and Katz find that the wage premium for holders of bachelor's degrees over high school-educated workers rose significantly. By 2007, that difference had reached 81 percent for men, compared to 37 percent in 1967. The story was similar for women, with the college wage premium rising from 54 to 81 percent over that time. The wage premium for postsecondary education and training has remained strong, even during the worse months of the recession when all wages tapered off.

Although wage premiums do provide signals on needed job skills, the supply response to this wage signal needs to involve institutions as well as individual decisions. Connecting the information on skills needed for jobs and specific wage premiums to students' potential is not automatic. Many credentials may seem to meet a certain level of educational attainment, but they may in fact fail to do so because they do not connect the credential holder with lucrative career pathways, marketable job-market competency, or skill that is transferable to other occupations (Carnevale, Strohl, and Melton 2011). The problem is connecting the information on skills needed to educational programs that are appropriate and likely to reward the individual's and society's investment in time and money. In the following we propose policy initiatives to address barriers that prevent this potential return on investment from being realized.

Policy Recommendations

Students need to know what steps to take to advance their career prospects. In its current form, the educational system falls short of this vision. Indeed, less advantaged students rarely receive information such as what majors, courses, and other decisions are more likely to result in stable, high-wage jobs with opportunities for advancement. If these students are to play the same "game" as their more advantaged peers, they must be informed of the same "rules" to success.

The first recommendation is for postsecondary educational institutions to link students more directly with the types of opportunities that will benefit them financially in the future. Especially at the local labor market level, information on the availability of high-paying jobs, commuting distance to these jobs, education and training requirements, as well as location of postsecondary institutions offering the required credentials are necessary to the development of a learning-labor exchange. Such an exchange would facilitate students being better informed of the career earnings available in each occupation through the better use of census demographic data, unemployment-insurance wage record data, postsecondary transcript data, and internet jobs postings.

The U.S. Department of Education has recently taken a step in this direction by tying student-loan eligibility to students' employability and earnings after graduating from for-profit and community colleges. The proposed regulation addresses concerns about the high levels of for-profit student loan debt for some of these programs by specifically targeting (with the objective of eliminating) the most egregious of these programs.[7] This incentive should be extended to other postsecondary institutions, encouraging them to educate students on what kinds of majors and other training the economy is demanding. One way schools can do this is by matching job openings to available courses offered at their institution and informing students of the connection in their online job-search engines. State government agencies can encourage this kind of innovation by releasing the necessary data, namely the employment outcomes that are associated with different school majors and courses in the real world. This kind of database can be constructed from unemployment insurance records and school transcripts. In addition, government standards need to be established to eliminate predatory practices, to regulate for-profit universities and encourage accountability in their performance. The U.S. Department of Education has taken steps in this direction with its new "gainful employment" rule, which aims to tie program performance, measured by employability and earnings, to Title IV student-loan eligibility. This development indicates the movement—although painfully slow—of the nation's higher postsecondary education system toward greater accountability with the objective of better aligning postsecondary education programs with employment opportunities.

Second, students who cannot attend college can still receive postsecondary training through a variety of (currently underfunded) programs. Back in the 1970s, the federal government began administering the Comprehensive Employment and Training Act (CETA) to address this need, but its funding waned in the 1980s. Today, a similar program, the Workforce Investment Act (WIA), receives approximately $3 to $4 billion on an annual basis. If it were funded at the level of CETA, adjusting for inflation, it would receive $25 billion in real terms (Carnevale, Smith, and Strohl 2010).

Third, less advantaged students can be given better access to postsecondary education. Carnevale, Rose, and Strohl (2014) use simulations to demonstrate how colleges can ensure greater admission rates for minorities without the use of "race alone" by adjusting a candidate's test scores according to their socioeconomic status. Giving more disadvantaged students a slightly higher position in the queue despite slightly lower test scores would control for the inequality of opportunity that preceded the admission process and more accurately reflect inborn ability. Governments can encourage these sorts of innovations by requiring a minimum percentage of Pell grant recipients for a college to receive funding. They can also target their funding toward community colleges that serve disadvantaged youth and adults, bringing them closer to the funding levels of four-year colleges.

Fourth, both governments and educational institutions should be adopting more apprenticeships, paid internships, work-study programs, industry-based certifications, and online learning, all of which create pathways directly from high school to jobs that require more than a high school degree. We can and we must build new bridges that workers can cross from the former world to the latter, for it is only in the world of postsecondary education that Americans can reliably find the opportunities they desire and deserve.

And last, in addition to the focus on providing access to postsecondary education and training, and guiding/linking students to gainful employment, there must also be a comparable effort at the high school level, to provide adequate counseling, and guidance that aims to connect and get students on track to become high-performing college students. Several community colleges have created "high school to college" transition programs that target students while still in high school for college level programs. Students enrolled in these programs are allowed to complete up to an associate degree or take a test-based licensure exam while still in high school to strengthen the preparedness levels of the new high school grads for college and/or careers.

Conclusion

Since the 1980s, there has been a fundamental shift in the structure of the economy toward a more intensive use of education and skills in the production process. The increasing entry-level skill requirements for work have made postsecondary education the gatekeeper for access to training on the job and state of the art technology at work. Postsecondary education has led to a consistent earnings advantage for over a generation. By obtaining a bachelor's degree, a worker contributes the greatest percentage jump to his or her earning power—84 percent over high school graduates. Despite this increasing link between economic prosperity and education, the supply of college-educated workers has not kept up with demand since the 1980s.

Not only has supply failed to keep pace with the growing demand for high-skilled, college-educated workers, but the problem is worsened by the fact that a large portion of existing positions are currently staffed by under-credentialed workers. If we include the 2.7 million workers that are under-credentialed, our true estimate of the credentialed labor shortage would be eleven million postsecondary educated workers between 2014 and 2020, (6.8 million bachelor's degrees [including 2.7 million undercredentialed baccalaureates available for upskilling], and 4.3 million Associate's degrees and postsecondary certificates).

With a commitment to policies that reduce the inequality of access to postsecondary education and direct workers toward the competencies and occupations that are necessary for socioeconomic advancement, we can both respond to this potential national deficit in education and mitigate the inequality of opportunity that is in part responsible for this outcome.

There is a clear need for policy to minimize the achievement gap through programs and initiatives that equip current students, while in school, with the guidance and directive needed to most efficiently obtain the skills and training needed to enter the workforce. In addition, postsecondary educational institutions must link students more directly with the types of opportunities that will benefit them financially in the future, through education planning database tools and career counseling. Government standards need to be established to eliminate predatory practices, and to regulate for-profit universities to be accountable for their performance. Less advantaged students can be given better access to postsecondary education, by ensuring greater admission rates for minorities by adjusting a candidate's test scores according to their socioeconomic status. Students who cannot attend college can still receive postsecondary training through a variety of programs, although this may require additional federal funding. Governments and educational institutions should establish and expand apprenticeships, paid internships, work-study programs, and other opportunities for industry-specific training experience.

This set of recommendations aims to address the various points of intervention where policy can have an impact on the factors that are failing the postsecondary education system. The challenge of addressing the increasing stratification of higher education across socioeconomic lines, as well as the growing gap between the supply and demand of college educated workers, poses significant constraints on the growth outlook and economic prospects for the nation, as well as its implications for increasing broad social disparities and reductions in upward mobility and overall life chances. It is at the intersection of education, training, and workforce development that this labor shortage can be overcome and income and education gaps narrowed.

CHAPTER 9

Labor-Demand-Side Economic Development Incentives and Urban Opportunity

Timothy J. Bartik

This chapter focuses on "labor-demand-side" economic development policies that target specific firms or relatively narrowly defined groups of firms. The central focus: how such policies might broaden urban opportunities.

The "labor-demand-side" economic development policies analyzed in this chapter are targeted government subsidies to firms, intended to affect labor demand. The targeting means that government either chooses which specific firms get subsidies, or which groups of firms undertaking the desired actions get subsidies. Subsidies may be financial; for example, consider a property tax abatement to reduce a firm's property taxes below their usual level, which may be offered to entice a new branch plant to locate in a particular local area. Subsidies may be customized services; as part of an economic development deal, a new or expanding firm may be offered a free training package from a local community college, which will train workers for that specific firm's needs.

In the United States, these subsidies are mostly financed and run by state and local governments, sometimes with federal help. These subsidies' central goal is typically to increase the quantity and quality of local jobs in a local labor market, such as a metro area or a state.

Some subsidies go beyond promoting overall job growth for the metro area or state to promoting more specific forms of economic development. For example, some subsidies also aim to help employ the disadvantaged. Such subsidies include tax credits or cash payments that are conditioned on employers hiring the long-term unemployed, or welfare recipients, or other needy groups. Other subsidies aim at redeveloping specific neighborhoods or land parcels within metro areas. These subsidies include enterprise zone programs for distressed neighborhoods, and brownfield development policies.

Labor-demand-side incentives for firms are not the only way to promote state or local economic development. The quantity or quality of local jobs may also be increased by other policies. For example, local labor supply policies may increase the numbers or wages of local jobs by attracting new workers to the local area, or by improving local workers' education. Other state and local policies may affect labor demand, for example local labor demand will be affected by overall state and local taxes and spending.

But targeting specific firms or groups of firms for incentives is more politically controversial. The immediate benefits of such incentives go to firms. Are there broader benefits for local residents, which might justify incentives' costs for local taxpayers? Furthermore, there is the important issue of fairness across different firms. Under incentive programs, either individual firms are chosen to receive incentives, or groups of firms receive special tax breaks or services because they invest in a narrowly defined area or hire certain workers. Other firms do not receive these incentives. Are there sufficient social benefits from this assistance to specific firms or specific groups of firms that might justify this differential treatment?

This chapter focuses on how such labor-demand-side incentives might broaden economic opportunities, particularly for urban residents. The chapter identifies "leakages" that impede subsidies to firms from expanding opportunities. Leakages include subsidizing jobs that would have been created anyway, subsidizing jobs that substitute for other jobs (both within a local area, and across the entire United States), and creating jobs for persons who otherwise would have found similar jobs. The chapter also discusses "multiplier" effects beyond the subsidized firms. Multipliers include increased demand for local suppliers to the subsidized firms, increased local consumption spending by workers in the subsidized firms, and technology spillovers from subsidized firms to other local firms. For incentives to have higher ratios of benefits to costs, policy makers must better target such subsidies, both to increase multipliers and to reduce leakages. State and local governments have some reasons to better target incentives, but federal policy may also be needed, particularly when a state's subsidies produce negative spillovers, for example by reducing jobs in other states.

This chapter's empirical findings conclude that labor-demand-side economic development incentives are most effective if provided in the form of customized services. These customized services provide information or job training that is in short supply to many small and medium-sized businesses, and that can provide a high bang for the economic development buck. Tax incentives for economic development can work, but only if carefully targeted at high-wage firms with high local multipliers in the local export-base sector. For hiring subsidies for the disadvantaged, the available evidence is that such tax or other cash incentives are more effective if combined with screening and training services that help assure firms that these hires will be productive. For neighborhood development subsidies for distressed neighborhoods, the evidence suggests that tax incentives for firm location or expansion are more effective if combined with support for neighborhood services that will make the neighborhood more productive for business. When there are real barriers to using some factor of production, whether it is disadvantaged workers or distressed neighborhoods, cash alone as an incentive for such utilization is more effective if combined with services that help overcome the real barriers to employing these workers or utilizing this land.

The next section further describes economic development subsidies. After that, a logic model will be presented for understanding subsidy effects. Evidence on subsidy effects will then be summarized. This theory and evidence lead to policy recommendations.

The Varieties of Economic Development Subsidies

Although all state and local policies affect local jobs, "labor-demand-side" economic development incentives are distinguished by being targeted with discretion at specific firms or at groups of firms that invest in specific areas or hire specific workers. This targeting allows greater flexibility in achieving policy goals, while also allowing a greater chance for costs to escape accountability.

Economic development subsidies include financial subsidies and customized services. Either of these types may be further targeted at hiring specific types of workers, or targeted at specific geographic areas within the local area. Both financial subsidies and customized services may sometimes be combined to encourage economic development. For example, the federal Empowerment Zone program of the 1990s, to be discussed further below,

combined both tax incentives and subsidies for services in encouraging redevelopment of distressed neighborhoods. As another example, Minnesota's
MEED program of the 1980s, also to be discussed further below, combined
cash incentives for firms hiring the long-term unemployed with screening
and training services.

Financial subsidies include tax incentives. For example, property tax
abatements reduce a new or expanding firm's tax rate. Firms may also be provided with free land, grants for research and development, or loans at below-
market interest rates.

These subsidies also include customized services. A frequently provided
customized service is free or subsidized job training customized to the individual firm's needs. This may include job training for new hires in expanding firms, or job training for new hires or incumbent workers in firms facing
competitive threats. Such subsidized or free job training is most commonly
provided by local community colleges.

Other customized services address a firm's specific infrastructure needs.
Access roads may be provided on an expedited basis to a firm's new site.
Infrastructure may be paid for by tax increment financing, in which the
property tax increment from new development within a specified area is
devoted to infrastructure within that area.

Many customized services are informational. Economic developers help
individual firms to deal with regulations and government programs. Entrepreneurs and new firms may be provided with entrepreneurial training and
advice. Manufacturing extension services may help small or medium-size
manufacturers with advice on upgrading the firm's technology, human resources, marketing, or products.

As will be reviewed below, the empirical evidence suggests that customized services are frequently more cost-effective, compared to tax incentives
or other financial incentives, in achieving economic development goals. Why
this is so will be clearer as we discuss the logic of economic development and
the evidence.

Financial subsidies and customized services are often specific to particular firm types. Firms targeted by economic developers are usually "export-
base": businesses that sell most of their goods or services outside the state or
local economy. (See below for why such targeting makes sense from a state
or local perspective.) Targeted firms may be required to pay a "living wage."
Informational services often specialize in particular business types, such as

start-ups, small business, manufacturing, or high technology. High-tech clusters are often given special attention.

Some subsidies are tied to hiring from disadvantaged groups. Hiring incentives may be provided by tax credits. Hiring incentives are sometimes provided not as tax incentives but as explicit cash spending supported by the spending of local workforce agencies, tied to hiring the disadvantaged workers who are trained or screened by these agencies' programs. Some regular tax incentives for economic development purposes are transformed in part into hiring incentives by being tied to "first source agreements." Under such agreements, a firm can only receive an economic development tax incentive (e.g., a property tax abatement) if the firm agrees to make a good faith attempt to use local workforce agencies as a "first source" for entry-level hires (Bartik 2001; Molina 1998). As will be reviewed below, the empirical evidence suggests that tax credits or other financial incentives for hiring the disadvantaged are more effective if tied to workforce services that help assure firms of these workers' productivity.

Although most subsidies aim at job growth for an overall metro area, some subsidies may promote development only for smaller areas. One example is enterprise zones, in which firms in some neighborhood are made eligible for subsidies. Another example is brownfield programs, which promote the redevelopment of contaminated land. These neighborhood and land development subsidies vary in whether they exclusively rely on tax incentives and other financial services, or whether they also include services. For example, most state enterprise zone programs rely exclusively on tax incentives for redeveloping targeted distressed neighborhoods. In contrast, the federal Empowerment Zone program of the 1990s expanded on the enterprise zone concept by combining tax incentives with considerable funds for expanding services in distressed neighborhoods. As will be reviewed below, the empirical evidence suggests that adding services to tax incentives is more effective in redeveloping neighborhoods with significant development barriers.

Despite this variety, the bulk of economic development subsidies are tax incentives. For example, in one study of Michigan, about two-thirds of economic development subsidies are tax incentives (Bartik 2011).

Most economic development subsidies are financed by state and local government. However, the federal government has provided subsidies for neighborhood development (e.g., Empowerment Zones), hiring the disadvantaged (e.g., Work Opportunity Tax Credits), small businesses (Small

Business Development Centers), and manufacturers (Manufacturing Extension Partnership).

Economic development incentives for firms may total $40 billion a year (Bartik 2001). Total incentives are higher if we include "tax expenditures" that entitle all businesses meeting the law's criteria to a tax break. For example, journalist Louise Story of the *New York Times* concluded that economic development subsidies were $80 billion/year nationally, but $50 billion was due to state tax laws exempting interbusiness sales from the sales tax (Story 2012; K. Thomas 2012). Kenneth Thomas (2010) estimates that annual economic development subsidies are $70 billion, but his total includes tax expenditures. Distinguishing incentives that target specific types of firm behavior, from more general tax provisions that define business tax bases, is not always straightforward.

This dizzying array of highly varied economic development financial subsidies and services for firms poses a challenge for policy evaluation. How are we to understand these programs' effects? To do so requires a specific model for evaluating the benefits and costs of such assistance to firms, which will be developed in the next section. The model used here focuses on how much incentives cost per net job created, and what benefits jobs created provide in higher earnings per capita. The model used here will consider such costs and benefits both from a local perspective and a national perspective. The local perspective generates such questions as these: how many jobs at what cost does this program create in this state or metro area? How do such jobs affect state or metro area earnings per capita? The national perspective generates such questions as these: how many jobs at what cost does this program create on net in the nation? How do such jobs affect national earnings per capita? The two perspectives differ because jobs and earnings created in one local area may come at the expense of other local areas.

As will be explored in the empirical section, the evidence suggests that customized services to firms, compared to financial subsidies for firms, are not only more effective from a local perspective, but from a national perspective, in increasing earnings per capita. From a national perspective, boosting productivity, which customized services can do, is more economically efficient than simply providing financial subsidies that alter business location patterns. In addition, combining services with cash subsidies, rather than cash subsidies alone, to redevelop distressed neighborhoods, or to encourage hiring of the disadvantaged, is more effective in boosting earnings per capita not only from a local perspective but also from a national perspective.

Overcoming the real barriers to employing the disadvantaged, or to utilizing distressed land, enlarges both local and national economic output.

A Logic Model for Effects of Economic Development Incentives

This chapter now turns to outlining a "logic model" for how economic development incentives for firms affect earnings per capita. The model begins by considering effects for local earnings per capita, before going on to consider national earnings per capita.

Earnings per capita is the focus because it is the most important benefit of local job growth. For example, one study found that increases in earnings per capita from local job growth were at least four times the annual equivalent value of increases in land values, and at least five times the increase in fiscal benefits for state and local governments (Bartik 2005).[1]

What factors alter the "bang for the buck" of incentives in boosting earnings per capita? Figure 9.1 outlines a logic model for how incentives increase earnings per capita, identifying leakages that reduce the bang for the buck, and multipliers that increase it.

The first leakage is that only some proportion of the incentives actually changes firms' behavior. Economic developers may claim that tax incentives are costless because no tax revenue would have been created without the new plant. But this claim assumes that 100 percent of the incented business activity is due to the incentive, which is false.

A second leakage occurs if the incented business does change its behavior, but this business activity directly substitutes for some other business activity. For example, if the incented business was attracted by a vacant site or available labor, this site or labor might have attracted some other firm.

A third leakage occurs if the incentive goes to a locally oriented firm selling to a local market. If so, then the expansion of the incented business reduces local markets available to other local firms, thereby reducing their activity. In contrast, if incentives go to businesses that are "export-base"—businesses that sell their goods and services outside the local area—then the incented business brings new money into the metro economy.

One multiplier effect is the traditional Keynesian multiplier at the local level. The incented business will use local suppliers, increasing their jobs. The workers in both the incented business and local suppliers will spend some

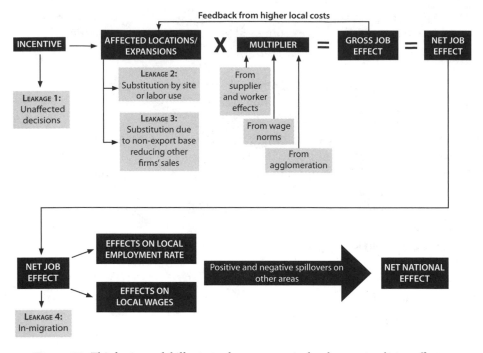

Figure 9.1. This logic model illustrates how economic development policies affect earnings per capita.

wages on locally produced goods and services. These multiplier effects depend on the incented business's local supplier network, which is more extensive in larger metro areas. Multiplier effects will also be larger if workers in incented businesses or suppliers are paid more. Multiplier effects are larger if more consumption goods are produced locally, which is higher in larger metropolitan areas.

Another multiplier is wage norm effects if the business pays wages above or below normal wages for workers of that skill level. Evidence suggests that when the local industry mix shifts to high-wage industries, local wages go up by about twice what would be expected based on direct effects (Bartik 1993).

Another type of multiplier is "agglomeration economies" due to either greater overall local activity or a larger industry cluster. Agglomeration effects are cost savings associated with higher industry concentrations of employment or greater urban size. These agglomeration economies may be based on having thicker markets for workers and suppliers, which allow economies of scale that make it easier locally to access more specialized suppliers and workers. Agglomeration economies may also be due to sharing of innovative ideas within or across metro industries. Agglomeration economies exist (Moretti 2010; Greenstone et al. 2010), but it is unknown whether they are subject to threshold effects. Therefore, it is unclear whether adding a specific firm to a metro area will add to agglomeration economies, which is what is relevant in evaluating incentive impacts. Overall multipliers, including agglomeration economies, may be greater for high-tech industries (Moretti 2010).

A negative feedback effect occurs due to greater local business activity pushing up local prices and wages. These increased local costs will reduce the attractiveness of the area for other business expansions. These negative feedback effects depend in part on how elastically the area supplies housing, which will depend on state and local housing regulations (Glaeser, Gyourko, and Saks 2006).

A labor market leakage is that only a portion of the net new jobs created will increase the local employment rate. An increase in local jobs must in the end result in a combination of some reduction in local unemployment, some increase in local labor force participation, and some increase in local population. Even if some of a new or expanding firm's hires are already employed, such hires create local vacancies. The chain of vacancies must ultimately result in either increases in local employment rates or the local population to match the increased local employment. The percentage increase in local employment must be approximately equal to the sum of the percentage increase in the local employment rate plus the percentage increase in the local population:[2]

(Eq. 1)   % change in $E \approx$ % change in (E/P) + % change in P.

In this equation, E is employment, and P is population.

In the short run, 40 to 80 percent of all jobs go to local residents, and the remainder go to persons who otherwise would have lived elsewhere. In the longer run, the percentage of new jobs that go to local residents is only 20 percent, under normal labor market conditions (Bartik 1991, 2015).

The persistence of local employment rate effects must reflect some enduring changes in local workers' productivity in response to short-run labor demand increases. One plausible explanation is the better skills due to short-run job experience (Phelps 1972; Bartik 2015).

Earnings effects are augmented by increases in local wages. The increase in local wages will be related to how much labor supply responds to the increase in local demand.

How labor demand shocks affect local employment rates and wages will depend on who gets the jobs in the short run (Persky et al. 2004). Who gets the jobs will depend on how well the newly created jobs match local skills. Who is hired also depends on institutional details, such as whether incented businesses work with workforce agencies to hire local residents.

An additional issue is what proportion of earnings increases go to workers at the bottom of the income distribution. The evidence suggests that local growth shocks are modestly progressive: the percentage change in earnings is greater for low-income groups, but not the dollar change in earnings. The earnings effects of local labor demand increases are distributed as follows: for every dollar in increased earnings of the lowest-income quintile, about $2 goes to the middle-income quintile, and $3 goes to the highest-income quintile (Bartik 2011). But earnings effects as a percent of income for the lowest-income quintile are about twice those of the middle-income quintile, and about five times the percentage effects for the highest-income quintile.

All of these effects are for a metropolitan area. From a national perspective, when jobs expand in one metropolitan area, this reduces markets for firms in other metro areas. This zero-sum game aspect of local development is reduced if the policy does not simply induce job growth, but also increases productivity, which enlarges the national economic pie. Productivity is enhanced when firms use resources more productively than they otherwise would be used, which may occur due to better worker skills or firm information, or by firms utilizing land and labor that otherwise would be underutilized.

Empirical Evidence

This section considers empirical evidence for financial subsidies and customized services, before considering the special issues of hiring incentives and neighborhood incentives.

To focus ideas, the preceding section can be summarized by some simplified equations for the annual costs and benefits per job created by an economic development policy. Because the total additional jobs created in some geographic area will equal the jobs directly created by the policy, times the multiplier effect of those jobs, the cost per additional job will go up with a higher cost per directly induced job, and will go down with a higher multiplier:

(Eq. 2)   Costs/additional job = Costs/ (directly-induced job*multiplier)
                    = (Costs per directly-induced job) times
                    (1/multiplier).

The benefits for the residents of some geographic area of creating jobs will go up with higher earnings of those jobs. The benefits will also go up with a higher fraction k of those jobs' earnings that benefit the residents of that geographic area, either by increasing the employment rates of local residents, or increasing their real wages:

(Eq. 3)   Benefits per additional job = (fraction k) times (average
                    earnings per additional job).

In these equations, all elements are affected by the factors discussed in the preceding section.[3] What does the empirical evidence show?

Financial Subsidies

For tax incentives, the empirical evidence suggests that from a state and local perspective, net benefits are closely balanced, and sensitive to plausible variations in effectiveness and multipliers. Net national benefits are unlikely.

Empirical findings for tax incentives are based on how state and local business activity responds to state and local business taxes. Economists describe this sensitivity by the "elasticity" of state and local business activity with respect to state and local taxes, where "elasticity" is defined as the ratio of the percentage change in local business activity to the percentage change in state and local business taxes. We would expect this ratio to be negative, as we would expect lower (higher) business taxes to induce more (less) local business activity. This research literature suggests a long-run elasticity of state and local business activity with respect to state and local business taxes of somewhere between −0.05 and −0.6, with a central value of −0.2 (Bartik 1991;

Wasylenko 1997). This central value of −0.2 means that if all state and local business taxes were reduced by 10 percent, we would expect that an area's business activity would in the long run increase by 2 percent. Direct evidence on incentives is consistent with this estimated sensitivity to costs (Bartik and Hollenbeck 2012; Moretti and Wilson 2014).

At a −0.2 elasticity, the incentive costs per induced job would be $30,000/year. This is the annual cost to induce one additional local job.[4] This incentive cost can be expressed as the probability that a typical incentive package, which averages $1,300 annually per job, would tip a location decision. This typical package would tip the location decisions of 4.3 percent of all jobs provided incentives. If the cost of inducing a new job is $30,000, then an incentive package of $1,300 annually, to be equally cost-effective, will induce only 1,300/30,000 = 4.3 percent of all incented decisions.[5] Without incentives, at least nineteen of twenty firms would have chosen the same location.

But because the research is consistent with a range of elasticities, there is also a large range of incentive costs. If the elasticity of business activity with respect to costs is only −0.05, then the incentive costs per directly induced job would be $121,000 annually per job and the typical incentive package would only tip 1.1 percent of all jobs incented. At a −0.6 elasticity, the annual costs per directly induced job would be only $10,000 and the typical incentive package would tip 13 percent of all location decisions.

These costs per directly incented job must be combined with net multiplier effects, as shown above in equation (2). For example, if one-third of the jobs go to export-base jobs, and the multiplier for export-base jobs is two, the net multiplier is 0.67. As equation (2) shows, the cost per net additional job is equal to the cost per directly induced job, divided by the multiplier. With a net multiplier of 0.67, the cost per net additional job will be 150 percent of the costs per directly induced job.

Benefits will depend on how well these jobs pay, what fraction of these jobs go to the unemployed and those out of the labor force, and the extent to which the jobs increase wages. Empirical estimates suggest that on average, a new job will yield long-run increases in earnings per capita of about 40 percent of the new job's earnings, half due to higher employment rates, and half due to higher real wages (Bartik 1991). If we assume that any leisure loss due to higher employment is offset by reduced stigma effects of unemployment (Bartik 2015), then all of the earnings increase due to higher employment should be counted as benefits. If we adopt a local perspective, or a worker perspective, the increased earnings due to higher wages should also be counted as social benefits (most of the profit reduction due to higher wages will affect absentee owners of capital). If we count all earnings benefits as social benefits, and if new jobs had average gross compensation of $50,000, then the social benefits of each new local job would be $20,000.

Whether or not business tax incentives pay off depends critically on the elasticity of business location decisions, and the multiplier. If one assumes a high elasticity and high multiplier, then business tax incentives are frequently likely to pay off from a state and local perspective. With a more conservative elasticity and a low multiplier, business tax incentives are highly unlikely to pay off. If the elasticity is close to -0.2, with a modest multiplier, then incentive costs and benefits from a state and local perspective will be closely balanced. For example, with a multiplier of 1.5, costs of job creation will be around $20,000 per job, and if the jobs pay around $50,000 on average, the social benefit per job created will also be about $20,000.

Empirical research on specific tax incentives finds wide variation in local benefit-cost ratios. For example, one study of a Michigan tax incentive program found that the program likely had high local benefits relative to costs, because it was tightly targeted on high-wage export-base businesses with extensive local supplier networks and high multipliers (Bartik and Erickcek 2014). A study of a state of Washington tax incentive program found that the program was less likely to pass a local benefit-cost test, because many incentives went to non-export base businesses or subsidized firm activities that would have occurred anyway (Bartik and Hollenbeck 2012).

From a national perspective, however, it is highly unlikely that discretionary tax incentives pay off, at least at times when macroeconomic authorities are managing the economy to maintain full employment. From a national perspective, the jobs created in this state or metropolitan area will be mostly offset by jobs destroyed in other areas.[6]

An exception might be incentives that encourage innovative high-tech industries, which might boost national productivity. But this depends on whether the incentives induce additional innovative activity, rather than simply relocations. Large effects on innovation might require larger government intervention than typical state and local tax incentives (Mazzucato 2013).

Another exception might be job creation incentives when national unemployment is high (Bartik and Bishop 2009). But such incentives are more effective if deficit financed, and are more efficient if applied to all job creation, rather than job creation in firms chosen by local policy makers.

Customized Services

For customized business services, the sparse evidence suggests that some types of services may be far more efficient than financial incentives. The evidence is strongest for customized job training and manufacturing extension services. A quasi-experimental study of firms with different access to customized job training suggests that such job training has productivity benefits that in just one year are about 1.8 times these programs' costs (Holzer et al. 1993; Bartik 2010). A quasi-experimental study of firms with different access to manufacturing extension services suggests that manufacturing extension has productivity benefits that in just one year are about 2.1 times program costs (Jarmin 1998, 1999; Bartik 2010).

The benefit/cost ratios for these services depend upon how long productivity effects persist. The Holzer et al. (1993) estimates suggest persistence, whereas Jarmin (1998) finds some depreciation. But even with considerable depreciation, these productivity benefits imply local employment effects that would be large compared to costs. Local employment effects would occur because higher productivity will lower local costs, increasing the attractiveness of local expansion. Suppose the productivity benefits of customized job training depreciate by 25 percent annually, that business location decisions have the cost sensitivity implied by a −0.2 business tax elasticity, and that the social discount rate is 3 percent. (The social discount rate is the annual interest rate that helps translate between future annual flows of benefits or costs, measured in dollar terms, and today's dollars.) Then the annual equivalent cost per job created of customized job training would be $1,600 per job created.[7] Under similar assumptions, the annual equivalent cost per job created of manufacturing extension would be $1,300 per job created.

Other evidence finds slightly higher costs per job created for customized services, but still much lower costs than for business tax incentives. Hollenbeck (2008) uses surveys of firms to find that customized training grants induce one direct new job for every $23,000 in one-time grants. Ehlen (2001) uses surveys of firms to find that manufacturing extension services induce one direct new job for every $18,000 in services. Suppose the jobs created depreciate at the rate of 25 percent per year, and the social discount rate is

3 percent. Then the Hollenbeck survey implies an annual cost per job created of $6,000 for customized job training, and the Ehlen survey implies an annual cost per job created of $5,000 for manufacturing extension.[8] These costs are somewhat higher than the previous estimates, but much lower than the annual costs of $20,000 per job created that might be found for business tax incentives.

Why might manufacturing extension and customized job training be more effective than business tax incentives? Manufacturing extension services are providing information to firms. Information is cheap to provide, yet can be quite valuable.

For customized job training, such services will mostly be used by firms that value such training, whereas any firm will want the cash from tax incentives. Hiring workers requires large up-front costs for screening and training, and new hires frequently do not work out. In small and medium-sized firms, "after six months on the job, more than one-quarter of new hires were producing less than 75 percent of what was anticipated when they were hired" (Bishop 1993: 336). A public program that screens and trains new hires to meet productivity standards will produce large immediate benefits. Community colleges have comparative advantages in providing training, which makes it plausible that the value of training will significantly exceed costs.

For both manufacturing extension and customized job training, the benefits for firms are front-loaded. Firms immediately benefit from savings on hiring costs and in productivity improvements. Because firms have large real discount rates in making decisions (a 12 percent annual rate estimated by L. Summers and Poterba 1994), and social discount rates are lower (a typical social discount rate ranges from 2 to 5 percent—Bartik 2011, Moore et al. 2004), there are social gains to providing benefits up front.[9]

A social benefit of customized training is that such training may encourage hiring of disadvantaged workers. To do so, customized training programs must seek such workers, and devote extra efforts to screen and train these workers up to job standards. Case studies suggest that some customized training programs are successful in involving disadvantaged workers (Batt and Osterman 1993). But there is little aggregate evidence on how the average customized training program affects who is hired.

From a national perspective, manufacturing extension and customized job training are more likely to increase overall national output than are tax incentives that only relocate economic activity. Customized services also lead to relocation of economic activity, but this relocation allocates economic activity to more productive locations, which is efficient.

Other customized services also have some evidence of effectiveness. A randomized experiment found that entrepreneurship training increases business start-ups (Benus, Wood, and Grover 1994). Survey evidence of client firms, and before and after comparisons, indicate that firms that receive more intensive assistance from Small Business Development Centers (funded by the U.S. Small Business Administration, along with state and local governments) tend to be more successful (Chrisman et al. 2005; Chrisman 2002; Seo et al. 2012). Business incubators also have supportive evidence from client firm surveys, and before and after comparisons of client firms (Molnar et al. 1997; Amezcua et al. 2013).

The overall research evidence for customized business services is favorable but sparse. Much evidence is from surveys, or before and after comparisons. Only a few studies are quasi-experimental or experimental, which provide stronger evidence.

Hiring Subsidies

Subsidies for hiring the disadvantaged that only provide tax credits or cash are ineffective. If workers advertise their eligibility to be subsidized as disadvantaged, they are less likely to be hired, because of stigma effects (Burtless 1985). Businesses are reluctant to use such subsidies to hire the disadvantaged. Many businesses do not bother to claim such subsidies, and if they do, claims are made after the hiring, for hiring that would have occurred anyway (Hamersma 2003, 2008).

A better design combines hiring subsidies with screening and job training that provides firms with more assurance that hires will meet skills standards. Such programs were run with some popularity with both businesses and social welfare groups in Minnesota in the 1980s, and as part of the stimulus package for welfare recipients during the current recession. For example, Minnesota's MEED program provided generous six-month wage subsidies for hiring the long-term unemployed for newly created jobs (Bartik 2001). However, rather than being run as a tax incentive, the program was run through local workforce agencies, which combined the wage subsidies with screening and training of eligible workers for interested businesses.

Although hiring subsidies combined with screening and training services is a promising design, it is lacking in strong evidence. Firms report in surveys that such programs affect both jobs created and who is hired (Rode 1988). Empirical evidence suggests that recent wage subsidy and screening programs for hiring TANF recipients increased earnings, but this evidence does not come from studies with a strong experimental or quasi-experimental design (Roder and Elliott 2013).

From a national perspective, if hiring subsidies lead to more employment for the hard-to-employ, these programs offer national benefits. By increasing the employability of a group that otherwise would be less productive, such programs enlarge the national economy. Hiring subsidies for the disadvantaged at one location may lead to fewer jobs in the short run for more advantaged workers at other locations, but the greater availability of employable labor should boost overall job creation.

Neighborhood Development Subsidies

For neighborhood development subsidies, the strongest evidence is for enterprise zones. The empirical evidence on state and local enterprise zones is mixed. Many studies indicate no significant effects (Elvery 2009; Greenbaum and Landers 2009; Neumark and Kolko 2010). Other studies suggest some significant effects (Ham et al. 2011; Freedman 2013).

Effects are greater for one variant of the enterprise zone concept, the federal Empowerment Zone program (Busso, Gregory, and Kline 2013; Ham et al. 2011). The difference may be that Empowerment Zones combined subsidies for firms in designated neighborhoods with neighborhood services. These neighborhood services help the designated neighborhoods to overcome the barriers to redevelopment, which are not overcome through simply providing new or expanding firms with cash subsidies.

The Busso et al. evidence uses a quasi-experimental methodology, which compares Empowerment Zone grantees to rejected applicants and future successful applicants. Their methodology suggests that these Empowerment Zones created about 78,000 jobs at a cost of $1.7 billion, or $22,000 per job.[10] If we assume that the jobs created depreciate at 25 percent per year, and that the appropriate social discount rate is 3 percent, then the effective annual cost per permanent job equivalent would be $6,200.[11]

Economic development subsidies also sometimes target brownfields with tax subsidies and cleanup, or target downtowns or other areas with special services through tax increment financing districts. Before and after comparisons suggest that such services are effective in spurring development in the targeted neighborhoods (De Sousa 2013; Weber 2013; Dye and Merriman 2003).

But what about the rest of the metro area? Nearby neighborhoods do not seem to suffer negative spillovers in most studies; some studies find positive spillovers (De Sousa 2013). However, beyond nearby neighborhoods, we might be concerned that subsidies to locally oriented businesses in target neighborhoods might reduce market shares of local businesses elsewhere in the metro area. Tax increment financing districts (TIFs) produce more favorable effects on overall area development if TIFs target industrial rather than commercial development (Dye and Merriman 2003). We might also expect that if neighborhood subsidies lead to usage of land that otherwise would be undeveloped, area output would be more likely to expand, due to expansion of the effective land supply. However, there is no good empirical evidence on this hypothesis.

From a national perspective, we would expect much of the increased activity in some communities to be offset by the loss of jobs in other communities, due to competition in the national market. However, if redeveloping distressed neighborhoods leads to greater use of land or labor that otherwise would be unemployed, these subsidies are more likely to expand overall national economic output.

Conclusion: Some Policy Recommendations

Based on this discussion, what policy advice seems warranted? First, state and local governments should rely less on business tax incentives. These seem less effective than customized services, even from a state and local perspective.

One way to restrict tax incentives is to incorporate them into the state and local tax system. Discretionary tax incentives tend to gradually expand from their original targets. Governors and mayors find it difficult to "just say no." In contrast, if a legislature incorporates an incentive into the tax code, this requires consideration of costs.

But state and local leaders are unlikely to accept this advice. Discretionary incentives allow political leaders to claim credit for new business. With an optimistic interpretation of the research, discretionary tax incentives can be argued to pay off from a state and local perspective.

Because tax incentives lack a national payoff, they should be subject to federal regulation. One model is the incentive regulations of the European Union (Sinnaeve 2007). In the EU, business incentives are illegal except under special circumstances: EU-designated distressed regions, high-tech industries, small business, and job training.

For customized business services, no special restrictions are needed, as such incentives are more likely to pay off from both a local and national perspective. But we need more research on these services' effectiveness. This should include experiments randomly assigning businesses to be eligible for services, and quasi-experiments comparing businesses across location or size classes that trigger eligibility for services.

Incentives that target otherwise unemployed labor or land also need further experimentation. We should consider experiments that randomly assign distressed neighborhoods to special incentives and services, or randomly assign hiring incentives and screening and training services for the disadvantaged to both workers and firms.

For firm-specific incentives to be more cost-effective in broadening urban opportunities, we need to better target such policies. This requires rigorous research to see which combinations of cash and services will provide the most effective targeting.

The inefficiencies of many currently popular incentive programs also should encourage state and local policy makers to explore alternatives to incentives. For example, local labor supply policies, such as high-quality universal pre-K, can be viewed as a state or local economic development program. In the case of universal pre-K, empirical research suggests that the benefits in higher future local earnings per capita, per dollar of program cost, may be better than many tax incentive programs (Bartik 2011). Policy makers should enlarge their thinking about how best to promote local economic development. Wise local economic development policy will evaluate many types of programs for promoting broadly shared local growth.

PART III

Shared Prosperity: Perspectives
on Equitable and Inclusive Growth

CHAPTER 10
══════

Equitable and Inclusive Growth Strategies for American Cities

Victor Rubin, Angela Glover Blackwell, and Chris Schildt

America's growing racial and ethnic diversity calls for an inclusive, equitable model for growth, not only in the name of justice and fairness, but as an economically smart strategy. Strategies which ensure that all Americans can have genuine opportunities to succeed and contribute will not only reduce inequality but will spur economic expansion and the revitalization of our cities. In many cities, ranging from those that have seen the most severe disinvestment to those with the hottest markets for talent, work space, and housing, leaders from a range of sectors are constructing creative and potentially powerful policies and programs for equity and racial inclusion. Their concerns range from the high-tech, high-growth innovation economy to the most basic neighborhood-level service businesses. Their approaches represent new ways to train and hire local residents, help them to start or grow firms, and tie their business plans to more comprehensive community building strategies. Across the various strategies there is a strong sense of local pride, building on home-grown assets, and holding local institutions accountable. Many of the new policies emerged through the work of community leaders and residents, often in partnership with philanthropy, business, and public agencies. And, in many cases, the agenda for equitable growth has moved beyond the inner city to also be a priority for regional sustainability plans. In this chapter, we examine a set of equitable growth policies and strategies, first providing a framework of four broad categories, and then through examples from across the United States. Throughout the chapter, we will return to how the strategies are being adopted in three cities reflective of very different economic circumstances: Detroit, Baltimore, and San Francisco.

A Framework for Equitable Urban Growth Policies

Even before the Great Recession, it was becoming clear that the implicit model for growth in American cities was badly flawed. Even as gross job creation numbers have started to rebound from the Recession, large numbers of people who are working are not earning enough to stay out of poverty. In 2013, in a preliminary assessment of strategies for creating good jobs and making them more accessible to low-income communities of color, we described the context as follows:

> The bubble economy masked patterns of slow and unequal growth set in place decades before the recent crisis. Policies emphasizing deregulation, privatization, a shrunken safety net, and weakened labor laws led to slow job growth, stagnant wages, increasing racial and income inequality and a withering middle class. Policy choices, globalization, and technological change have worked in concert to drive away many of the blue- and white-collar jobs that provided pathways to the middle class. This left the nation with a polarized economic structure that has a burgeoning low-wage sector and growing high-wage sector, but a hollowed-out middle. (Treuhaft and Rubin 2013: 2)

Fortunately, though, many leaders and advocates of all kinds are not waiting around for one big solution, nor are they seeking their economic salvation in "smokestack chasing" or other traditional forms of ineffective subsidies for dubious megaprojects. Instead, they are developing strategies that build on one's own local and regional assets, placing increasing value on multiple small endeavors rather than just a few big ones, and above all, on the importance of creating opportunities for people and communities who were previously left outside the mainstream. There are still big public investments to be made, of course, in infrastructure in particular, but this economic development framework is aimed directly at inclusion and participation.

These urban policies and strategies intended to advance inclusion and opportunity frequently have a number of general goals in common:

- They are aiming to create or sustain "good quality jobs," and while that can have a number of meanings, it most often refers to living wages, at the minimum enough to meet basic needs. This job quality also often refers to employee benefits, stability and security, opportunities for career advancement, and other features often associated with unionized workplaces.
- They are supportive of locally owned and operated businesses, with a focus on opening up opportunities for women and people of color. This can involve directing public spending toward such firms or supporting them in other ways that increase their competitive positions in private markets.
- While neighborhood commercial revitalization is very important, they seek to move beyond just that type of community development and increase the presence and impact of diverse entrepreneurs in the larger economy: the growing "export" sectors of a given region, and, in general, untapped markets for goods and services both near and far.
- They are building on local assets and talents, and serving unmet local needs, by enabling new enterprises, whether they are for-profit companies or social ventures, to fill gaps left by the standard private marketplace and to enable local residents and workers to accrue wealth, not just income.
- They include strategies that cover, and plan for, whole metropolitan areas. Regions, more than cities, are the relevant scale of economic development, and regional planning needs to incorporate values and priorities of equity as well as sustainability. Networks of equity advocates and organizers in many regions have become influential in transportation, land use, environmental and economic planning processes. They recognize that the distribution of affordable housing, and fair access to housing in general, will determine access to good jobs. The blueprints produced in many regions have led to new incentives for where job centers are built, how well they are connected to affordable housing by transit, and whether the targeted sectors for development are likely to produce good jobs.
- They reflect an understanding not only of the competitive advantages for individual firms of having a diverse workforce and leadership cadre, but, more fundamentally, that the competitiveness of cities and regions depends on people of all races and backgrounds

having a legitimate opportunity to thrive. That requires making full, productive use of the increasingly diverse workforce.

This last goal, a broad commitment to racial inclusion, and the recognition that it is of paramount importance for economic growth as well as being morally necessary, undergirds all of the recent work of PolicyLink and a growing number of allies. Demographic trends in most parts of the country are leading to the workforce becoming a majority of people of color now or in the near future. The significantly younger age profile of nonwhite populations means that increasingly, the nation's workers, professionals, entrepreneurs, and business leaders will be drawn from this diverse pool, and that the nation's economic competitiveness depends on maximizing their talents and potential (Cárdenas and Treuhaft 2013).

State and local strategies for responding to demographic change and promoting inclusive economic development have been emerging in scores of cities and have become the subject of numerous regional and national conferences and publications. There is an important national dialogue emerging about the reasons why, and the ways in which, "equity is the superior growth model." From among the myriad policies, initiatives, and programs being put forward to meet these goals, four categories are worth examining to capture a range of issues, scales of operation, organizational players, and economic impacts.

- **Entrepreneurship: Promoting racial and ethnic diversity in the creation of new firms and the expansion of existing ones, from neighborhood small businesses and business services to innovative technology start-ups.** The last several years have seen a flowering of new and creative ways to help small firms and social ventures in older core cities. The various stages of start-up and expansion require different types of capital, and distinct forms of technical assistance. While entrepreneurs may be notoriously independent, they are also often seeking collaborators, partners, spaces in which to grow, and local networks. In many cities, an "ecosystem" is being consciously formed to knit together the support organizations and increase the odds of the individual and collective success of local entrepreneurs.
- **Anchor Institutions: Increasing the positive local economic and social impact of universities, medical centers, and other large or-**

ganizations that are permanently based in the city. These entities have enormous economic and social impact, which can be guided through authentic community partnerships and explicit commitments to equity and inclusion. Traditionally the power and privilege of these institutions led to inequitable outcomes in development, but over the past two decades a new, more reciprocal and enlightened field of anchor practices and public policies has gradually been emerging. Local residents and communities can benefit from anchor-motivated development if it is done the right way.

- **Maximizing Jobs and Local Employment Through Public Investment: Implementing more effective and equitable practices for hiring, workforce development, contracting, and procurement tied to public spending and investment.** Government spending and investment remain among the most important drivers of local economies and are necessary components of most large development projects. The jobs and contracts for small- and medium-sized firms that result from those investments are the ones most within the control of government officials. Cities have found many creative ways to nurture local enterprises and prepare a home-grown workforce in order to generate and keep as much employment local as possible.

- **Sustainable Development, Good Jobs, and Equity: Developing local and regional plans and policies that align equity, environmental sustainability, and economic development.** Local and regional plans for sustainability set priorities to guide housing, transportation, and land use planning that can advance equitable economic development. A growing number of communities have incorporated into these plans and related legislation priorities that should help connect low-wage workers to good job opportunities and promote development patterns that invest in low-income communities without displacing existing residents.

The broad goals of inclusion that these categories represent may be universally relevant across the country, but context matters a great deal, so it will be useful to look at some cities and regions with sharply contrasting rates of growth and different challenges. After a brief introduction to these places, the domains of strategy listed above will be examined in turn, first through several brief examples from diverse communities, including Cleveland,

St. Paul, Philadelphia, New Orleans, and Portland, and then an episode or two drawn from the authors' experiences in Detroit, Baltimore, and San Francisco.

Exploring Economic Inclusion in Three Contrasting Cities

The specific form taken by strategies for economic inclusion depends a great deal on local conditions. Every city needs to create a system of supports for greater diversity in entrepreneurship, for example, but doing that in a severely disinvested city is different than in a very hot market. Each city has anchor institutions whose engagement with the community can be guided by principles of equity and inclusion, but the programs and projects will vary with economic and political circumstances. Detroit, Baltimore, and San Francisco represent different points on the spectrum of disinvestment and revitalization, and thereby provide some useful contrasts as well as common themes.

Detroit has, by most measures, suffered the greatest decline of any large American city, with the loss of more than half its peak population, from nearly two million down to 700,000, and the abandonment of not only scores of thousands of homes but also numerous office buildings, factories of all sizes, public facilities, and neighborhood commercial properties (Sugrue 2005, 2011). Job losses and the decline of the big three carmakers were not limited to the city, of course: manufacturing jobs in Michigan declined by 50 percent between 2000 and 2010 (Scorsone and Zin 2010) and the state has had one of the slowest rates of growth or recovery, showing losses of population in some recent periods. While many of Detroit's first-ring suburbs are experiencing some of the same problems as the city, there remains a great deal of wealth in the region, much of it concentrated in a tier of suburban cities and counties that are more self-contained, racially segregated, and, in many respects, more cut off from the central city than any metro area in America (Galster 2012; J. Thomas 2013; Farley, Danziger, and Holzer 2000).

That is not the only Detroit narrative, however. Detroit is simultaneously undergoing a different process of change, one that has important prospects for economic revitalization. There is a climate of entrepreneurship being deliberately cultivated, with areas of emphasis ranging from advanced manufacturing to software development to food, and a robust effort to energize and support "the entrepreneurial ecosystem." Its success depends on generating firms and jobs not only in the high-growth innovation sectors but also in conventional business-to-business vending and contracting, and in the city's challenged neighborhoods.

Baltimore was never as thoroughly devastated by disinvestment and industrial decline as Detroit, but it has had its share of debilitating job losses, poverty, population loss, high crime, and structural shortcomings of its public services and schools. Even as the city's Inner Harbor was turned into a showcase and various waterfront neighborhoods became fashionable and economically reenergized, large areas of the city remained severely distressed, with significant proportions of abandoned housing, and large proportions of the population with little or no connection to the workforce. In these lowest-income, largely African American communities, there were few investments locally and few bridges to the opportunities offered by job growth at local hospitals, in the downtown, or in the suburbs. The poverty rate among African American residents of Baltimore was 24 percent in 2010, and the average household income $33,260, compared to 14.6 percent and $54,531 for white residents (Annie E. Casey Foundation 2015).

Baltimore has always had hospitals as one of the anchors of its local employment, and the broader health and biotechnology sectors are now the largest drivers of its regional economy. Responding to these sectors at the regional and local levels has provided opportunities to enact policies intended to promote greater economic inclusion. Expansion of the Johns Hopkins medical center and transformation of the surrounding East Baltimore neighborhood has been one such long-term strategy, complemented by region-wide efforts to prepare the workforce for health and biotech jobs.

San Francisco, always an attractive city in one way or another, is one of the hottest of hot real estate and employment markets in 2014. The city is in the midst of a boom in the technology sector which is both regional and local, and has driven up the cost of office space and housing, and driven the overall unemployment rate down to about 4 percent. Thousands of tech professionals whose jobs are in San Francisco are seeking to live near their work. So many other people who work in the tech corporate campuses in Silicon Valley, thirty miles to the south, are choosing to live in San Francisco that there is an inversion of typical regional housing and job patterns, with so-called "Google buses" shuttling city residents to suburban offices. The pressure of more, mostly younger people with money chasing scarce units has been transforming San Francisco neighborhoods more rapidly than during the previous "dotcom" boom (Metcalf 2013). The proportion of the population made up of families with children, already the lowest of any major U.S.

city, continues to drop. The African American population fell from 10.9 percent of the population in 1990 to 6.5 percent just fifteen years later, and was projected by the state's demographers to fall farther to 3.2 percent by 2050 (San Francisco Mayor's Office 2009).

The images and indicators of gentrification and displacement may draw the most headlines, but they are not the whole story pertaining to equity and inclusion. The San Francisco Bay Area, so often at the cutting edge of new trends, has been in the vanguard of increasing income inequality, as growth in both high-wage jobs in technology and information and low-wage service sector jobs has greatly outpaced openings in middle-wage positions, not just in San Francisco but throughout the Bay Area (Terplan and Bhatti 2013). The responses to that trend have generated some innovative plans and legislation.

Support for Entrepreneurship and Small Business

An Equity Agenda for High-Growth and High-Tech Sectors

The knowledge-based "innovation economy" may be globally interconnected in many respects, but local development leaders necessarily have more parochial objectives. The goal of local entrepreneurship support systems is to ensure that the area's research and development entities and independent creators generate commercially viable intellectual property which translates into start-up firms and, eventually, services and manufacturing that stay around and generate local jobs. The equity challenge in this sector is to connect black and Latino businesspeople, designers, and technologists to the mainstream institutions, companies, social networks, and sources of financing in meaningful ways. Entrepreneurs and would-be entrepreneurs from communities of color, regardless of their qualifications and experience, face historic and current barriers not normally encountered by white businesspeople in the high-tech and high-growth sectors, and the process of overcoming those barriers in the high-growth sectors is underway in a number of places.

Perhaps no region has generated more extensive efforts to diversify the innovation economy than greater Cleveland, where at least half a dozen organizations provide guidance to firms. In northeast Ohio, African and Latino Americans make up only 2 percent of business owners in tech-based growth industries (NorTech 2012). "Northeast Ohio is the first region in the country where partner organizations in the innovation ecosystem—Bio-Enterprise, JumpStart, MAGNET, NorTech, and Team NEO—and the Fund for Our Economic Future have united to measure the competitiveness of African and Latino Americans in regional innovation clusters and commit to a common framework for collective action. The effort will be focused on four main areas: employment, entrepreneurship, engagement, [and] education" (Holifield, Kamins, and Lynch 2012). MainStreet Inclusion Advisors, also based in Cleveland but working nationally, makes the tangible connections that will increase diversity in the high-growth sectors by facilitating new relationships between "mainstream" entrepreneurial organizations and networks of minority technical and professional associations. All these organizations in northeast Ohio have assisted hundreds of high-growth firms in the region overall, but this kind of outreach and engagement for diversity has only been fully underway for a couple of years, so systematic evidence of its impact has yet to be assembled.

In Detroit, an array of foundations, nonprofit organizations, and university, healthcare, and business leaders are actively seeking a similar local impact from new technologically based firms or new areas of business for existing firms. The challenge is for the technology-based enterprises to become more racially diverse at all levels, and a variety of groups are working in Detroit to build bridges between the mainstream institutions and minority professional and business groups. Detroit, with its industrial legacy, has a plethora of engineers and designers looking for the next big opportunity to restart advanced manufacturing in whatever form that will take. Given that the auto industry had developed a robust system of minority suppliers, there is a precedent for diversifying certain sectors, but the new environment is substantially different and will require a new approach.

One strategy for increasing the number, and enhancing the prospects, for entrepreneurs who are people of color and women is to provide an accelerator designed for their needs and interests. One such accelerator is NewME, based in San Francisco and established in 2011, a company with an intensive twelve-week residential program to help founders and CEOs hone their business plans and perfect the all-important pitch. The eight participants in each residential cycle live and work together, receive one-on-one mentorship from industry veterans and, most critically, connections to a network of technology players—lack of access being perhaps the greatest barrier to entrepreneurs of color. As of June 2014, 60 percent of NewME graduates had attracted $16.9 million of seed funding, and 75 percent of companies started by NewME graduates were still operating. NewME has also produced "pop-up" one-time accelerator workshops in a number of other cities, including Detroit (Policy-Link 2013b; www.newmeaccelerator.com).

Neighborhood-Level Business Revitalization

At the other end of the spectrum from the high profile and novelty of technological innovation, the familiar business of every city, even disinvested ones, goes on in its neighborhood commercial districts and in countless small service and manufacturing firms. Community-level enterprises, usually run by people of color and often by recent immigrants, can, cumulatively, be a tremendous opportunity for inclusive job creation. "Because entrepreneurs of color are more likely than other firms to hire people of color [Bates 2009] and locate their firms in communities of color [EuQuant 2007], their growth leads directly to more job opportunities for the group that need them the most" (Treuhaft and Rubin 2013). But for significant employment to be generated, the firms have to grow and be sustained, which is where the newer generation of small business support programs have been making an impact.

The Neighborhood Development Center (NDC) in St. Paul, Minnesota, helps emerging entrepreneurs from a wide range of cultures start their businesses and thereby contribute to the revitalization of their neighborhoods. A key principle of NDC's approach is provide instruction and guidance in the basics of starting and running a business in the language, and in a setting, familiar to the participants, many of whom are recent immigrants. Participants have included Somali, Oromo, Hmong, and Latin American immigrants as well as Native Americans and African Americans. The introductory training is followed up with start-up and expansion capital, ongoing technical assistance, and, where needed, space in an incubator or *mercado*. As of 2013, more than 4,000 residents—90 percent low income people of color— had completed the training, with 500 of their businesses employing 2,200 people. The NDC-spawned enterprises return $73 million to their communities in payroll, rent, and taxes annually (Schauben 2013).

Detroit is becoming fertile ground for the creation of a more inclusive revitalization strategy. Very small businesses abound, but many are too small to survive long and lack the tools and access to markets which they will need in order to reach the level where they have employees and growth potential. Every city has this challenge, but it is hardest where property values are so low, population densities have dropped, and city services and safety are often inadequate. But the entrepreneurial energy in these neighborhoods remains quite high, and a host of innovative providers of support and financing have recently emerged serving very diverse populations with roots not only in the African American community but among residents from the Middle East, Bangladesh, Mexico and other countries in Latin America, Korea, and other parts of the world. The key to equity as a goal for entrepreneurship support in the neighborhood sector is connecting accessible financial tools with appropriate mentorship and smart business planning. ProsperUS is a new collaboration among community-based organizations, adapting the model of NDC in the Twin Cities, to provide culturally specific training and support to people starting new neighborhood-level businesses. In their first year, they trained over sixty residents, the majority of whom are African American (Policy-Link 2013e). The Growth Center at ACCESS, a multifaceted human services agency supporting the region's Middle Eastern community, a population estimated as high as 400,000 in the three core counties of the Detroit metro area (Arab American Institute Foundation 2011), has also created training courses for new and growing enterprises. A newly launched microlending collaborative is composed of three microlenders who came together with an initial $5 million investment to support Detroit-based small business. They also work closely with a local business support group to mentor new entrepreneurs, prepare them to apply for the loans, and help them grow.

Detroit Future City, the broadly based strategic planning effort, included in its 2012 framework this straightforward assessment: "A crucial step toward equitable job growth will also be the explicit recognition and dismantling of current barriers facing Detroit residents in terms of access to skills development and employment and entrepreneurship opportunities. In fact, those barriers have forced many Detroiters into the informal economy as entrepreneurs, which in turn offers an opportunity to create new pathways to prosperity and job growth for an unknown number of sole proprietors who might someday be employers themselves" (Detroit Future City 2012). More than fifty different support services and funds are available to people starting or managing small businesses, including financing at every stage of the start-up and expansion process, technical assistance and coaching of many kinds, peer mentoring and networking for all types of entrepreneurs, and collaborative workspaces for start-ups. These supports for start-ups operate in an urban environment characterized by clever entrepreneurial improvisation and workarounds, and the assumption of risks that would be uncommon in more orderly, high-functioning municipalities (Cowley 2014). For example, numerous start-ups, mostly run by women of color, are being assisted by FoodLab Detroit and Detroit Kitchen Connect. Many of these enterprises began informally, and are now receiving help with permitting and licensing, shared preparation and storage space, basic business knowledge, and connections to suppliers. As FoodLab describes on its website ,"many of these food businesses continue to operate in an 'informal' or 'underground' economy not by choice, but because policy around the licensing and regulation of food businesses, the long and costly procedure, and the difficulty to access proper information has not yet caught up to the innovation on the ground" (FoodLab Detroit 2015). Detroit Kitchen Connect has helped about a dozen Detroit "foodpreneurs" start and grow their businesses by providing low-cost commercial kitchen space in local churches and community organizations (PolicyLink 2014).

Anchor Institutions as a Vehicle for Equitable Growth and Development

The large institutions such as universities, medical centers, museums, and utility companies that are permanently based in a city play a critically important economic role as major employers, owners of large amounts of property, purchasers of an immense volume of goods and services, and generators of intellectual property and momentum for lead sectors of their regional economies. These anchor institutions' identities are closely linked to their home communities, and they have a substantial stake in the long-term viability of those places. Until relatively recently, most urban anchors did not consciously direct their economic leverage toward the equitable revitalization of their surrounding neighborhoods, and indeed they often used their influence to pursue a unilateral expansion agenda. However, more community-friendly trends have emerged over the past two decades, and many anchors can now be said to be engaged in authentic partnerships with community-based organizations, and hiring, spending, and investing locally with equitable outcomes for residents as a goal.

Cleveland, again, provides leading examples, both from among the individual actions of the large anchors in the University Circle district (The Cleveland Clinic, Case Western Reserve University, and its affiliated University Hospitals System) and their collaborative investments in the neighborhoods and in new, worker-owned enterprises. In total, the Cleveland Clinic Health System employs 43,000 caregivers, and generates over $6 billion in revenue, and its main campus alone creates nearly $4 billion in revenue and procures more than $1.5 billion in goods and services. The system is the largest employer in the northeast part of Ohio and second largest in the state. It has shifted a percentage of its procurement locally and to minority-owned businesses, participating as an anchor partner in a comprehensive neighborhood revitalization effort, implementing childhood wellness programming in local school districts, and positioning itself as a leader in sustainability. The Cleveland Clinic purchases from more than 400 minority vendors, with whom, in 2009, it spent over $150 million. These numbers and those of the other anchors in the district will grow as their administrations commit to higher goals for local purchasing and various steps are taken to build the capacity of suppliers in the central city.

The Cleveland Foundation, one of the country's oldest and largest community trusts, provided the seed funding, convening influence and continuing support to the evolution of the Evergreen Cooperatives, which have launched, so far, three new enterprises owned by their workers, who are residents of the low-income, predominantly African American neighborhoods near the University Circle anchors. The laundry, the solar installation firm, and the urban farm sell their goods and services to the three anchors, whose commitment has allowed the co-ops to grow while providing, at this early stage, dozens of well-paying jobs and the opportunity to build wealth through an ownership stake. The long-term goal is for a network of worker-owned firms with 5,000 employees (Song 2014).

The University of Pennsylvania, in Philadelphia, one of the first anchors to develop and implement a strategy for growing local suppliers, has increased its purchasing from minority-owned, women-owned, and disabled veteran-owned businesses from $2 million to over $100 million over a twenty-year period. The university has put into place a wide range of capacity-building steps for small local firms, redesigned its data base, and structured incentives for its purchasing managers to work with diverse businesses (Schildt and Rubin 2015).

Penn's procurement initiative was part of a much larger set of strategies to revitalize West Philadelphia's housing, education, safety, and commercial environment, and to create a more positive impact on the local economy. Such comprehensive strategies have been undertaken by a number of anchors whose campuses are located in areas of concentrated poverty.

The Johns Hopkins Medical Center is located in one of these distressed neighborhoods in East Baltimore, and the institution, one of the largest employers in the state of Maryland and world-renowned for its care and research, had lived uneasily with its neighbors for decades. More than a decade ago, Hopkins, the city and other institutional partners launched a strategy for transforming the neighborhood which is still underway. Its ultimate outcomes will be an important test of a commitment to economic inclusion, a public-private-philanthropic partnership, and the way in which an anchor institution can grow with its neighboring community.

The East Baltimore Revitalization Initiative involved the expansion of the medical center and the partial demolition and rebuilding of the residential neighborhood. The expansion calls for approximately 1.7 million square feet (originally planned for almost three million) of research and development laboratory and office space, to become a hub for enterprises spun off from Hopkins biotechnological and biomedical research. The new community would include housing at various income levels, plus retail, hotel, and public facilities, including a park and a new public school jointly run by the University's department of education. Original estimates were for approximately 9,000 new jobs on the 88-acre site, as well as several thousand construction jobs during its development (Clinch 2009; Annie E. Casey Foundation 2015).

The plan called for the demolition of many of the existing housing and other buildings, and as a result was intensely controversial. (Gomez 2013; Simmons and Jacobson 2011) Typically, this kind of urban renewal uprooted and dispersed low income, often African American residents with insufficient funds or regard for their future well-being, and the legal minimums did not require much more than that for the 1,667 residents who were displaced. In this case, however, the Annie E. Casey Foundation, based in Baltimore, provided additional resources to substantially augment the amount and nature of housing relocation support, and to establish an organization providing counseling, referrals, and workforce development services for relocated residents (Schachtel 2011). That nonprofit organization, East Baltimore Development Inc., serves more broadly as the embodiment of the partnership of the university, city government, philanthropy, and other entities, and oversees a development agreement with the Forest City property development company and its local business partners.

The initial objectives and strategies for accomplishing the inclusion of local, minority, and women workers and firms owned by these groups, were outlined in a Minority Inclusion Agreement signed in 2002 by the partners, including Johns Hopkins and the city. It included nine objectives pertaining to race and gender diversity and local emphasis in equity ownership in real estate and businesses, hiring, contracting, and business opportunities. It called for training and employment opportunities in the technical workforce, an incubator for local start-ups, a community reinvestment fund, and other vehicles for spreading economic benefits across East Baltimore (EBDI 2002).

After a decade, one of the proposed laboratory buildings and a number of other structures, including the new public school and 18,000 square feet of retail, have been built, making up about 20 percent of the original plan, with roughly 1,000 permanent jobs created. The projected research and laboratory and office space has been scaled back by a third.

There was a steadily improving system of support for potential employees from East Baltimore, although the modest overall numbers of jobs for local residents continued to frustrate some community leaders. Since 2006, 4,700 construction workers have worked on the site, with roughly 30 percent of the work hours completed by residents of Baltimore City and over 12 percent from East Baltimore. A pipeline for job and training referrals, services, and relationships with a wider range of employers was created in 2007 by EBDI. It was continuously improved, and an array of strong workforce organizations has been connected to this effort. Between 2007 and 2013, 357 individuals were placed into jobs through the pipeline, including 67 who were relocated from the project site (Annie E. Casey Foundation 2015).

Improving employment and career opportunities available to East Baltimore residents, and the relocated residents specifically, calls for tailoring workforce development to skill and education levels. Residents with minimal, basic, and advanced levels of education need three different approaches, respectively, and 40 percent of the relocated residents had the minimal level of schooling, while many people in the pipeline, both high school graduates and others, had reading and math proficiency levels below what is needed for good-paying jobs. Many of them had other barriers to employment as well, from a record of incarceration or a drug problem to a family crisis. The workforce system included some exceptional programs and agencies that could work with modest numbers of such clients, but overall, it was not designed, funded, or coordinated to meet the needs of this large constituency.

Among the bright spots is a program that trains local residents for technician positions in biotechnology and medical laboratories with the anchors and with other firms. The entering students of the BioTechnical Institute of Maryland, almost all of whom are African American residents of Baltimore,

have graduated high school but not been to college. Their innovative training makes them competitive for, and gets them hired into, technical associate jobs at the leading labs in the city and region. To date, more than 75 percent
of its 300 graduates have gotten jobs in laboratory settings, and roughly
40 percent of graduates have gone on to pursue advanced degrees (Policy-
Link 2013a). Since the Baltimore region is a national leader in biotechnology
and medical research, with one-third of its new jobs over the recent decade
being in life sciences, this is an important sector for inner-city residents to
gain a foothold (Vey 2012; Roethke 2012).

Maximizing Jobs and Local Employment
Through Public Investment

Contracting by local government for the construction and maintenance of
infrastructure, housing, and myriad other goods and services can be a po-
tent tool for directing employment and business activity to local residents,
firms, and neighborhoods. A growing number of central cities are seeking
to create viable legal and practical frameworks for bringing these opportunities closer to home and, in the process, within reach of more people of color.
Such policies generally aim to accomplish four goals:

- Choose investments that maximize job creation and other community and environmental benefits
- Target investments in communities that have historically been
  underinvested.
- Hire locally for both construction and permanent jobs.
- Create opportunities for local and minority-owned business development along the supply chain.

One of the most ambitious such efforts has been in New Orleans, where
the Regional Transportation Authority (RTA) drastically changed the way it
awards contracts, to make sure that small businesses owned by people of color
and women have a fair chance to compete. The new policy, with its explicit
commitment to equity, has resulted in growth from 11 percent of contract
dollars going to disadvantaged business enterprises from 2001 to 2009 to
31 percent in 2013. This is roughly consistent with African Americans representing 30 percent of business owners in the city, as well as 60 percent of the

population. Setting goals and making traditional "good faith efforts" are not, by themselves, enough to drive tangible change; New Orleans had a 22 percent goal when it was achieving just 11 percent. The progress came only once bidding procedures were restructured, the contracting manual rewritten, practical systems established to guide small firm owners through the often baffling intricacies of attaining public contracts, and the leaders of the agency thoroughly educated and committed to the changes (Policylink 2013c).

In Portland, Oregon, from 2009 to 2011, a pilot program to finance and install energy efficiency upgrades in homes (funded by the U.S. Department of Energy under the Recovery Act), augmented by city funds, included a community workforce agreement requiring that 80 percent of the jobs go to local residents and 30 percent of the trades and technical work hours go to historically underrepresented groups, with wages equal to at least 180 percent of the state median. The results were significant, including

- employment for more than 400 workers, including 48 new hires in the construction trades;
- average wages of nearly $20.34 per hour;
- provision of health insurance by nearly 80 percent of the participating contracting firms;
- 48 percent of the trade and technical hours worked by people of color (22 percent of Portland's residents are people of color; the Community Workforce Agreement [CWA] goal was 30 percent) (City of Portland 2015).

As in New Orleans, attention was paid to the practical steps of bringing the ambitious goals within reach. Beyond that, the Clean Energy Works pilot was consistent with a broader growing intention in Portland to codify these kinds of contracting targets as citywide policy. In 2012, the city passed a model Community Benefits Agreement ordinance for publicly funded projects, with a host of resources for small firms, as well as monitoring, enforcement, and community oversight processes.

In San Francisco, years of grassroots organizing and advocacy led to the adoption of a mandatory local hiring policy on city-funded projects. Passed in 2010, the policy began with a floor of 20 percent local hire, with specific targets to hire apprentices from disadvantaged neighborhoods, and increases up to 50 percent local hire over the next several years. Through strong partnerships with workforce training services, community organizations, and the local unions, the city has so far been able to meet the new goals, with over 300,000 work hours on projects totaling nearly a half billion dollars going to local workers (Brightline Defense Project 2012; San Francisco Office of Economic and Workforce Development 2013). Applying this policy to the city's ten-year capital plan is projected to yield 25,000 jobs for local residents. Additionally, the San Francisco Public Utilities Commission has passed its own community benefits and economic inclusion resolutions, with the goal that local residents receive employment opportunities and neighborhood enhancements from over $8 billion in sewer and water infrastructure upgrades over the next several decades (Ellis 2010; San Francisco Public Utilities Commission 2013).

Across the bay, Oakland is also innovating policies to create opportunities in low-income communities of color. The West Oakland Army Base was closed in the 1990s, eliminating hundreds of good jobs adjacent to a historically African American neighborhood. This was part of a wave of base closings in the region which took a major toll on good-paying, previously secure, skilled blue-collar jobs largely held by people of color. After nearly twenty years of planning, the City of Oakland adopted a plan to turn the former base, which is adjacent to one of the largest ports on the West Coast, into a transportation and logistics center. The first, $500 million phase will include 1,500 construction jobs and another 1,500 permanent positions. Faith leaders, community organizations, and others got the city to pass a good jobs policy for both construction and permanent jobs on the site, including a policy that employers cannot prescreen job applicants for prior criminal records, an important community win, as well as a living wage minimum of $11.70 per hour plus benefits. The project broke ground in late 2013 (PolicyLink 2013d).

Sustainable Development, Good Jobs, and Equity

Local and regional plans to promote more energy-efficient, environmentally sustainable land use and transportation patterns have proliferated, and in the past several years they have more frequently taken up direct focus on employment and economic opportunity. For example, the HUD Office of Sustainable Housing and Communities changed its name in 2013 to the Office of Economic Resilience, and guided its more than 100 grantees toward a stronger emphasis on job creation, and to access to skills and supports for the workforce. This attention to economic growth provides a welcome chance to explore policies that promote equitable development, rather than just a narrower concept of growth management.

In regions such as Minneapolis-St. Paul, Seattle, and Sacramento, the sustainability planning process has been informed and strengthened by regional equity coalitions seeking not only "a seat at the table" but also tangible policy outcomes. The specific issues vary, of course, but there is an underlying interest in seeing that regional visions and plans for transportation, land use, housing, and environmental quality commit to improving the long-term economic prospects of people of color and of low-income communities. This often is expressed as a goal of creating communities of opportunity, to undo the legacy of persistent patterns of racial disparities and to avoid creating new inequities. Creating communities of opportunity does not call for a single solution; sometimes opening up suburban housing markets to families of all incomes and races is a critically important way to provide access to quality education and higher quality jobs. Other times, inner-city neighborhoods need new investments and protections to keep low-income residents and small businesses from being displaced in the wake of transit improvements and the increased market appeal of their communities. Some cities are mainly struggling with how to attract new investment, while others are struggling to manage a flood of it. Whatever the particular growth profile of a region, the new wave of sustainable development planning needs to address access to economic opportunity in a volatile period characterized by rising inequality.

In the San Francisco Bay Area, local initiatives to improve job quality and direct employment to underrepresented groups, while important, are not significant enough on their own to have a noticeable impact on the growing income inequality the region faces; the larger, structural changes to the economy are greater than any one city alone can address. But two regional planning efforts in the past several years have opened an important opportunity to orient the regional economy toward equitable growth.

In 2008, California passed legislation to reduce greenhouse gas emissions through coordinated regional land use, housing, and transportation planning. SB 375 required regional planning agencies to develop Sustainable Community Strategies outlining how they might direct transportation dollars and land use incentives to meet new climate goals. In the Bay Area, local and regional equity advocates saw this as an important opportunity to invest in projects and strategies that would advance equitable and environmentally sustainable regional growth. Several organizations formed the Six

Wins Network in 2010 to create and advance recommendations around six broad community goals: affordable housing; robust and affordable local transit service; development without displacement; healthy communities; economic opportunities; and community power. Over forty organizations were engaged in creating and supporting an Environment, Equity, and Jobs (EEJ) scenario based on these goals. An independent analysis determined that this EEJ scenario was the environmentally superior alternative of all the scenarios developed. The plan adopted by the regional agencies included several key recommendations from the EEJ scenario, including important anti-displacement measures integrated into a new regional housing program (Marcantonio and Karner 2014).

Several of the community groups that formed the Six Wins Network have continued their work to advance equity goals within another regional planning effort currently underway. They are promoting a regional economic development plan that focuses on increasing access to middle-wage jobs for low-income workers. Called "One Bay Area," this $5 million, three-year initiative is supported by the HUD Office of Economic Resilience as part of the Sustainable Communities Initiative. This initiative has three areas of work: housing the regional workforce; expanding economic opportunity; and strengthening equity voices and principles in the planning process. The initiative seeks to understand and address the barriers many workers with less than a four-year college degree face in accessing middle-wage jobs, those that pay between $18 and $30 an hour. The project is conducting worker surveys, doing regional economic analyses of various sectors, and providing grants to local organizations for pilot projects to advance economic opportunity (Metropolitan Transportation Commission 2013). While it is too soon to describe results from this effort, it clearly reflects a new way of defining, and planning for, prosperity in a region with fast-growing technology sectors yet growing inequality and a very high cost of living.

A similar commitment to equity and inclusion in regional economic and workforce development pervades the regional Baltimore Opportunity Collaborative, the current planning process supported by the federal Sustainable Communities Initiative. In June 2014, the Collaborative released a "Study of Barriers to Employment Opportunities in the Baltimore Region" based on extensive survey research, which placed the challenges faced by individuals squarely in the midst of deep structural issues of race and economic change: "There are six barriers to employment opportunities for those living in the Baltimore region, according to the study. Eighty-two percent of those seeking jobs face three or more of those barriers." These barriers include a lack of basic skills; the absence of career pathways for those with limited higher education, skills, and experience; transportation and housing challenges to reaching and holding steady work; a set of problems that are both individual and social, ranging from substance abuse and criminal records to an absence of child care; structural racism, by which is meant "an array of societal dynamics—such as historic wealth disparities, unequal treatment by the justice systems and dissimilar consideration in interviews—that routinely put minority job seekers at a disadvantage relative to their white counterparts"; and limitations in the amount and flexibility of funding for workforce training programs (Opportunity Collaborative 2014).

This assessment—empirically based and linking the economic fortunes of low-income people of color to the broad social trends—provides a strong foundation on which the Collaborative can move forward. Planning for sustainability and equity would be enhanced if more regional efforts incorporated such a forthright account of the barriers which must be faced both by individuals and by advocates for systemic change.

Conclusion

The Great Recession has awakened Americans to a widening inequality of opportunity. In an increasingly global economy, to succeed and prosper, America needs a new growth model—a model of economic growth that is truly inclusive. This chapter points to initiatives that embody an equity-driven growth model. Here, we outline collaborative models: workforce development and training strategies that connect workers to jobs and opportunities; regional economic development strategies that link local workforce, housing, and community development efforts; anchor-based efforts that engage in community partnerships to create positive social and economic impact; and entrepreneurship initiatives that foster and support the creation, innovation, and expansion of local business. Using examples from Detroit, San Francisco, Baltimore, and other postindustrial cities on a path of revitalization, we highlight demonstrated efforts and successes for each of these strategies to illustrate the critical linkages, partnerships, and dynamic relationship that the various components play in achieving a complete vision of equitable growth.

These strategies for equitable and inclusive economic growth are driven by local and regional movements, policy makers, and institutions, which means they will be customized for each situation and responsive to community priorities. Nonetheless, collective partnerships with the private sector, not-for-profits, and all levels of government are necessary to move forward under a guiding set of principles for equitable development. With the creativity, energy, and aspirations of these local leaders to generate equitable urban development, American cities can create change for a modern economy that manifests the potential of its people.

CHAPTER 11

The Fragility of Growth
in a Post-Industrial City

Jeremy Nowak

After decades of decline, there are bright spots for several of America's older industrial cities in the Northeast and Midwest. The 2010 Census and subsequent data from the American Community Survey demonstrate a tapering of population loss, and in a few instances, a slight population recovery for perennial population losers (W. Frey 2013). Recent urban population recovery should be tempered by the fact that cities continue to be major sites of concentrated poverty (Kneebone, Nadeau, and Berube 2011). Moreover, job location and demography continue to favor Southern and Western states, making recovery for many Northeastern and Midwestern cities more difficult.

The past fifty years of urban history demonstrate that there are no quick fixes for our most challenged cities. Local government policy functions in a federalist hierarchy and global economic forces affect success. Many cities work against a backlog of liabilities and constraints: pension fund and healthcare costs, deferred maintenance for critical infrastructure, public management practices resistant to change, a noncompetitive work force, and outmoded cost structures. Moreover, the historical dynamics of regional segregation by race and economic status are strong impediments to change.

In the face of this history and context, local actions and policies still matter. To succeed, older distressed cities must make progress on two simultaneous fronts: one is economic and the other public and civic. In terms of the economy, cities must adopt a cost structure and regulatory environment that is competitive. They must confront historical liabilities that over the long term will make it more difficult to pay for public goods. And they must build on the advantages of place, from cultural institutions to research universities.

From a public and civic perspective, cities must address management practices that have reinforced decline and concentrated poverty, including low-quality public services and a tendency to ignore the implications of declining middle- and modest-income communities. They must offer services in keeping with the expectations of increasingly sophisticated knowledge workers, while focusing attention on those amenities and services that maximize opportunity for lower- and modest-income families.

Cities have to become both more competitive and more equitable. A *competitive* city attracts and retains residents who have options. An *equitable* city improves circumstances for those with more limited choices. The two are not mutually exclusive, although politics often prioritizes one over the other.

There are two approaches to rebuilding cities to promote higher levels of social mobility. One is from *the outside in* where emphasis is given to linking low-income people and places to metropolitan opportunities: suburban housing near better schools, better transportation to employment centers, firm creation along regional growth clusters. A second is to build *from the inside out*, restoring the amenities of place in ways that promote higher levels of urban integration and enable public institutions and private housing markets to maximize opportunity. Both approaches ought to be pursued.

In this chapter I focus on three public and civic practices that enable competitiveness and equity from the *inside out*: 1) the reorganization of urban education, 2) the re-norming of place, and 3) a data-driven approach to city-wide community investment. I use Philadelphia as a case study because the city is at a midpoint between growth and decline, exhibiting dynamic features of the postindustrial American city alongside seemingly intractable communities of poverty. I view its recent demographic growth as demonstrating a demand for urban places while also signaling the dramatic changes that still must occur to succeed over the long term.

Growth Without Middle-Income Families

For the first time in more than half a century Philadelphia's population grew between 2000 and 2010. The growth was slight (about 1.5 percent) but significant given the city's steady population decline during the second half of the twentieth century. Philadelphia's population in 1900 was about 1.3 million persons and reached a high point in 1950 at 2.1 million (Gibson 1998). It then declined steadily back near to its 1900 level at around 1.5 million in 2000. It had its first increase in decades during the first decade of the twenty-first century (Pew Charitable Trusts 2012).

The geography of new residential growth in Philadelphia reflects a recentralization and urban renewal movement that had planning antecedents fifty years ago to salvage the core of the city in the face of suburbanization and white middle-class flight. Since that time, but particularly in the past two decades, population growth has formed around the historical center of the city and near cultural institutions, universities, medical centers, and natural amenities such as riverfronts and parks.

Today Philadelphia's central core contains more than 350 cultural and arts organizations, hundreds of new restaurants, and more than 175,000 residents in what the Center City District[1] terms the extended downtown, which includes the neighborhoods just north and south of the traditional core. Of those 175,000 residents, about 40 percent work in the downtown (Center City District and Central Philadelphia Development Corporation 2013).

The city's downtown has grown by 10 percent over the past decade. Its firms, shops, and institutions account for 38 percent of all wages in the city. And the central core has the most educated population in the city; 76 percent of its twenty-five- to thirty-four-year-olds have college degrees (Center City District and Central Philadelphia Development Corporation 2013).

Just west of the downtown is the city's second growth hub, where the University of Pennsylvania, Drexel University, and a complex of medical centers and research facilities have generated millions of square feet of new commercial real estate over the past decade, thousands of students and new residents, and the retail and cultural amenities associated with the expansion of knowledge industries and higher education. It too has a significantly higher educated population than the city at large,[2] and is among the most important research zones in Pennsylvania. At present, 44 percent of all NIH funding in the state flows through that area (University City District 2014).

These success stories are occurring in an otherwise very poor city. Philadelphia has the highest level of poverty of the ten largest cities in the nation. About 26 percent of Philadelphians live below the poverty line and more than 25 percent of city residents use federal food subsidies (Lubrano and Duchneskie 2013). And despite the fears of gentrification in communities with proximity to the downtown, the overwhelming trend in cities such as Philadelphia is an increase in the number of low-poverty census tracts (Jargowsky 2013).

Unlike New York City, Washington, D.C., or Boston, Philadelphia has not been able to recoup the job losses of the past fifty years (Center City District and Central Philadelphia Development Corporation 2014). New York and Boston also lost manufacturing employment but have done a better job replacing lost manufacturing jobs with postindustrial service employment. The job and firm creation gap is viewed by many as a consequence of the high cost of doing business in the city[3] (tax structure and building costs) (Badenhausen 2013) and the low quality of workforce skills, particularly at middle-range skill requirements (Philadelphia Workforce Investment Board 2009).

Figure 11.1 shows Philadelphia's shifting age demography. From 2000 to 2010 there were population gains for those eighteen to thirty-four. In fact the pace of that growth was more rapid than in all but five other cities with populations over 500,000. There were also population gains among those fifty-five to sixty-four, though at a rate that was slower than most other cities. However Philadelphia continued to lose population for ages 0–17 (particularly 5–17), 35–54, and 65 and older (Minnesota Population Center 2014).

While the city has seen significant growth in residents in the so-called millennial population (in their twenties and early thirties), it has experienced a corresponding loss among school-age children and adults in prime earning age (35–54).

It is instructive to note what the data says about people moving into the city in terms of their educational background and immigrant status. Review of the 2009–2011 American Community Survey data shows that the percentage of new people moving into Philadelphia each year who have at least a college degree is high (52 percent); only six cities with populations above 250,000 had new movers with a higher percentage of college degrees or graduate degrees.[4] But context is important. As a percentage of the overall population the yearly number of college graduates that move into the city is too small (about 1.2 percent of the total city population)[5] to significantly affect the overall workforce quality numbers (Minnesota Population Center 2014).

Among new movers into the city, 23 percent are foreign born and only eight cities with populations of 250,000 or more have a higher percentage of foreign-born newcomers. But once again the share of the city's overall population that are yearly foreign-born movers into Philadelphia, as a percentage of the population (0.53 percent), is small. Philadelphia may be attracting more

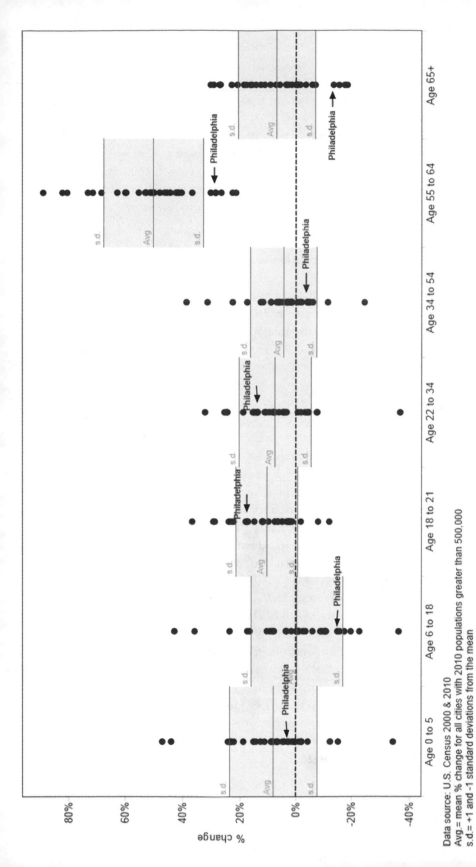

Figure 11.1. Percent change in population by age category, 2000–2010 (cities with 2010 population greater than 500,000). Avg. = mean % change for all cities with 2010 populations greater than 500,000; s.d. = +1 and −1 standard deviations from mean. U.S. Census 2000, 2010.

Data source: U.S. Census 2000 & 2010
Avg.= mean % change for all cities with 2010 populations greater than 500,000
s.d. = +1 and -1 standard deviations from the mean

immigrants than in past years but not at a decisive rate (Minnesota Population Center 2014).

It is difficult to predict whether the growth in the city's population will
continue over the next decade and at what rate. The trend lines appear to be
positive. But the bigger question is: will population growth continue to be a
matter of trading younger households without children for middle-aged headed
households with children? And what are the limits to this growth model?

The Reorganization of Urban Education

The leading driver of people out of Philadelphia is the academic quality of
schools and well-founded fears of the lack of safety in many schools. There
are other factors, but schools are paramount. A recent Pew Charitable Trusts
survey found that 56 percent of Philadelphia millennial aged population
would not recommend the city as a place to raise children (Pew Charitable
Trusts 2014).

Philadelphia cannot grow its population of middle-class families (minority or white) nor do a very good job helping lower-income people attain
middle-class skills without demonstrating vast improvements in education.
This is a matter not only of the public district but the diversity and range of
options in pre-K, K-12, and post-high school.

Accomplishing this requires a civic and public emphasis on quality and
pragmatism. It means using data to track and reward quality. And it means
remaining open to organizational change. Take the case of early childhood
education. There is near universal agreement that early childhood education
pays substantial returns for children (Heckman 2006) but there are caveats
to the research that are important to note. First, the quality of early-childhood
education offered is an important factor, and therefore funding pre-K education without a quality lens diminishes the results substantially (Heckman,
Pinto, and Savelyev 2013). Second, the effects of early-childhood education are
actually more significant for lower-income children (Cascio and Schanzenbach 2013), due to the fact that quality care can compensate for supports not
available at home. And third, the impact fades if students attend poorly
functioning schools. The effects for low-income children will fade more
quickly than for higher-income children, if they are placed in low-achievement
schools, again most likely due to the lack of compensatory influence for lower-
income children (Puma et al. 2012).

If we accept the importance of *quality* early education, the Philadelphia pre-K data is alarming. The best comparative data comes from the State of Pennsylvania's early childhood learning program, which has made strides over the past decade in keeping data, ranking centers, and at least aspiring to build a continuous improvement environment.

The State of Pennsylvania rankings are based on a star system (one star the lowest and four the highest)[6] and the 2013 numbers are worrisome. From a total of 791 centers ranked in Philadelphia, 52 were suspended for noncompliance, 397 were rated as one star, 232 two star, 96 three star, and only 66 were given a four star rating. Only about 20 percent of centers are three- and four-star rated (Pennsylvania Early Learning, n.d.).

The public policy imperative is not just to increase access and funding for early-childhood education, but also to insist on quality and measure the effects. We know the importance of this for lifelong learning, and that is why a good deal of recent education research and public policy has been directed toward making certain that children have literacy competencies by the end of third grade. It is an important predictor of success (Fiester 2013). But third-grade reading levels for district-run schools show that about 56 percent are below proficient, and among charters about 40 percent are below proficient.[7]

The achievement challenges in the overall K-12 systems are just as daunting. During the 2011–2012 school year there were approximately 200,000 students in the city's public district and public charter schools. About half those students performed below the level of proficiency based on statewide tests. Across the state, 28 percent of students were below proficient. In one elite suburban district outside of Philadelphia only 8 percent were below proficient (Pennsylvania Department of Education 2012).

If Philadelphia wants a competitive district it has to dramatically shift the numbers. To get to the state average the Philadelphia schools would need to have 45,000 more of its students reach proficient or above. Getting to a proficient and above level between the state average and an elite district average means raising performance for 70,000 students.

While Philadelphia numbers have recently improved, the improvements have not been fast enough to slow the exit for families with school age children. This has led to a great deal of organizational innovation and political controversy. While some of the controversy has revolved around school funding (particularly in the past two years), two other issues dominate the conversation: teacher quality and charter schools.

There is universal agreement on the impact of high-quality teachers with regard to both the craft of teaching and content knowledge. Teacher quality involves a variety of issues: whom we attract to the profession; how teachers are compensated; how we train teachers; and how we measure performance and incent quality performers.

A 2013 study on the Philadelphia School District conducted by the National Center for Teacher Quality reviewed factors that contribute to a strong teaching culture and found the district's practices lacking significant accountability. Tenure was based on time served (three years) and not performance. It was virtually impossible to remove an underperforming teacher (over a three-year span, only .04 percent of teachers were removed for cause, and it took on average two years to remove the teacher) and there was no data used to recruit or evaluate teachers (student level academic growth data) (National Council on Teacher Quality 2013).

The incentives do not exist to reward teaching excellence or remove low-performing teachers. Principals have limited authority to hire and fire personnel. The labor management atmosphere is *industrial* in that it assumes that each teacher is interchangeable based on time served.

The charter school controversies are part of the larger issue of public school choice. Within most public districts there are select schools that require academic merit or evidence of a particular interest (performance arts, science) to be admitted. In fact, several of Philadelphia's special select schools are among the highest-performing public schools in the state. Those schools draw from a citywide pool and they follow the same rules of the district except admissions criteria. The admissions filter and what it represents (prior performance and preparation) is determinative.

As a reaction to parental dissatisfaction with available school choices, new school options emerged over the past fifteen years, managed differently than conventional district schools. Some are managed through contracts with large institutions (the University of Pennsylvania, the Franklin Institute, for example) that are granted significant autonomy. The larger alternative schools movement has been through charter schools, publicly funded schools with private (overwhelmingly nonprofit) managers.

The concept of charters is based on an agreement that charter operators would get greater autonomy and in return would provide greater performance accountability. The charter school movement took off quickly and today close to one out of three Philadelphia students attend charters (School District of Philadelphia 2013). Charter performance has been uneven but, in general, charters have fared better than comparable nonselect district schools with similar populations.

The most interesting charter experiment in Philadelphia has been the Renaissance schools that combine charter management autonomy with neighborhood catchment areas. These are the closest things we have to a natural experiment, where we keep the same children and change the adults and the management. Several charter management organizations in the city have demonstrated unusually strong results in these turnarounds, according to a recent study put out by the School District of Philadelphia (Wolford, Stratos, and Reitano 2013). Others have lagged behind, showing no improvement or even further decline.

The top charter management organization in the city is the Mastery Charter Schools. They currently manage fifteen schools serving over 9,600 students; all but two are turnaround neighborhood schools. They take over some of the worst schools in the city and in a matter of years have managed to move test scores up while reducing school violence. Two-year turnaround results have demonstrated double digit percent increases in scores; and over a brief period of time, their numbers for some grade levels have reached or exceeded the average state proficiency level (Wolford, Stratos, and Reitano 2013).

Charters are controversial with traditional school advocates and the teacher's union, both of whom view them as nondemocratic privatization mechanisms. Charters are popular with many parents who view them as safe alternatives. The evidence of popularity nationally is based both on increased enrollment numbers and opinion polls (Brushaw and Lopez 2013; National Alliance for Public Charter Schools 2013). The same is true locally. According to a 2010 Pew Philadelphia Research Initiative survey of Philadelphia parents, 72 percent of charter school parents were very satisfied with their child's school while only 40 percent of parents with children in district-run schools were very satisfied. As a result, demand for Philadelphia charter schools exceeds supply, with nearly 30,000 students on charter waiting lists (Pew Charitable Trusts 2010).

The larger charter organizations that manage multiple schools have created their own teacher training programs. The best charters are data-centric in their approach to management, including teacher evaluation. Several charters have made use of teaching techniques that use recent research into the noncognitive aspects of learning. Schools such as KIPP, Mastery, and Young Scholars have pioneered the application of the social-emotional factors that enable better student outcomes. These issues are discussed in Paul Tough's book on the subject (Tough 2012).

The emergence of multiple organizational types within the Philadelphia School District—admission select, contract, citywide charters, and Renaissance charters—is redefining the architecture of the school system. The emerging notion of the district is one where schools or networks of schools move to the center of the system as autonomous managers with stronger or weaker relationships to the central district. The district becomes a multiprovider regulator more than a direct service manager, a service support system more than a full service institution (R. Denhardt and J. Denhardt 2007). They manage relationships with school managers; they maintain standards through a data warehouse that uses information to elevate the closing and opening of schools.

The emergence of a *portfolio management* model (Bulkley, Henig, and Levin 2010) of schools has not come to fruition in the most optimal way but has developed at a piecemeal pace. The optimal portfolio is driven by a commitment to quality in all cases, with a healthy agnosticism regarding the form of management. Using data-based evaluation standards, a smart portfolio approach would be to expand what works, close down what does not, share best practices across sectors (charter, district, and magnate), and seed innovations where possible. But this is hard to accomplish in an environment where closing low-performing schools—district or charter—is politically so difficult and there is significant resistance to a performance culture.

It is true that there are resource constraints for schools in Philadelphia and that high levels of poverty make the job of teaching remarkably difficult. But we know that some schools do much better than others with the same children in terms of academic achievement. The challenge for a city like Philadelphia is to build on what works, which in many instances requires that past practices, from how schools are organized to the choices we give parents to the way we train and evaluate teachers, have to change.

It is interesting to note a similar systems devolution with Philadelphia's Catholic schools. The declining status of urban Catholic schools, driven by shifts in Catholic demography, the decline of the women's religious orders (and the sexual abuse scandals that rocked the church), may have contributed to the popularity of charters. The movement toward charters occurred in many of the city's neighborhoods that were previously well served by the Catholic system.

In 1965, 35 percent of all school-age students in Philadelphia attended Catholic schools; by 2013 the number had declined to about 18 percent and the number continues to move downward. Moreover, in contrast to a time when Catholic schools largely served a Catholic population, today's inner-city Catholic schools are majority non-Catholic (Pennsylvania State Data Center 2013). There has been little written or understood about what the decline of parochial school systems has meant in terms of cost pressures on the public systems.

There are some signs of a Catholic school revival. During the past several years, in response to the continued closing of schools, Catholic business and lay leaders have formed organizations that negotiated management of the schools away from central archdiocese control. One of the networks now manages fifteen inner-city schools and a second manages eighteen high schools in the region. The networks are in many ways similar to charter management groups in that there are common systems and standards driven by the central nonprofit, but strong leadership expected at the school level.

The two networks are engaged in one of the largest urban Catholic school turnaround processes in the nation. They are attempting to change the business model of Catholic education in terms of tuition structure, management authority, and upgrading leadership and teaching. Several of their schools show early signs of repopulation, but it is too early in the turnaround efforts to evaluate impact.

There is historical evidence from many sources that Catholic schools do a better job educating poor and minority children than do the traditional district schools (Chen and Pong 2014; Kim 2011). The question is, can the inner-city Catholic schools be revived and at numbers that move the overall urban picture in the right direction?

As of 2014, Philadelphia's two major school systems are being restructured by school-based managers or subsystem network managers. They are becoming systems of schools and networks rather than centralized districts in the traditional sense. There is some hope that this could pay off in terms of performance numbers and the positioning of the city over the long term. But we are far from knowing whether that can or will happen.

Most important, we do not know what these transformations will mean for the thousands of newcomers to the city who do not yet have school-age children. To create schools that will attract a range of students, and not force families to privatize education costs or to move, is fundamental to changing the trajectory of demography. Will a public choice movement that increases the number of quality schools and a new parochial system generate higher levels of social integration?

The Re-Norming of Place

In too many cities like Philadelphia we have lost the expectation that schools can become integrating public institutions. This is part of a broader construct of decline and segregation where the notion of public becomes synonymous with lower quality and is seen as an amenity reserved for the poorest citizens. This reinforces the sense of economic and racial segregation experienced by residents in their everyday experiences, from who uses public transportation and schools, to the use of public spaces. The metro in Washington and the subway system in New York City work precisely because everyone uses them, across social class and ethnic boundaries. That is not true of the subway system in Philadelphia, which is not regarded as an amenity with middle-class quality.

The most basic attraction and stabilization strategy for cities such as Philadelphia is to increase the volume of high-quality places shared across ethnicity, age, and economic status. The ways in which this has happened historically are tied, in part, to the way we built housing, integrated uses (zoning), and managed public institutions. In earlier periods of urban history, it also reflected the fact that there were fewer residential options. Today we are experimenting with new ways to make cities public once again, at a time when we are still coming to terms with what the abandonment of urban space has meant.

The recent revitalization of cities such as Philadelphia has been a product, in part, of intentional efforts to re-norm places in ways that attract and retain diverse populations. Essential elements of re-norming are often linked to public safety efforts: computer-aided policing around crime hotspots, the so-called "broken window" deployments around nonserious crimes, and community-based policing. Moreover, a significant number of growing urban institutions now employ their own police force and transportation systems to augment public capacity and redefine the value and desirability of their institutions. Temple University in North Philadelphia, for example, currently employs the fourth largest police force in Pennsylvania.

But the restoration of public access and shared spaces has taken many other forms besides public safety concerns: the growth of outdoor cafes; citizen movements around better public transportation and pedestrian rights; new trends in planning and architecture around humanizing small public spaces; the opening up of parks and waterways to increased citizen use; a focus on catalyzing the creative dimensions of place through public art and community festivals; and the repurposing of abandoned industrial buildings for new residential, artisanal, and business uses.

One of the policy initiatives that helped to reshape social integration over the past two decades in Philadelphia were successful applications to the federal government to tear down older public housing high-rises and replace them with lower-density and more economically integrated units (homeownership and rentals). While these policies were not without their critics (public housing advocates decried the reduction in total units and some adjacent communities worried about the use of Section 8 vouchers for relocation), these changes had an enormous real estate value impact on a half dozen neighborhoods not far from the central core. The removal of high crime high-rises opened up areas to higher levels of economic and racial integration.

What all these movements and initiatives have in common is the intentionality of re-use as a way to broaden demand and access. The efforts are often not led by the traditional public sector. If you were to identify one prime mover linked to the revitalization of downtown Philadelphia, for example, it would be a special improvement district (Center City District). Supported by downtown businesses and institutions, this nonprofit organization performs work we associate with government.

The Center City District (CCD) is one of more than a thousand such organizations in the nation (Becker and Grossman 2010).[8] It functions as a parallel government that assesses fees from local businesses (based on an agreement recognized by the city) and uses those fees to provide higher-level services than can be expected from government. Its omnipresent uniformed workers are responsible for cleaning the sidewalks and public spaces; providing information to residents, downtown employees, and tourists; and working with local police to maintain safety.

CCD also functions as a combined planning office, civic organization, and business chamber, publishing information for residents and businesses, advocating for change in public policies, and marketing communities. In some cases CCD raises money to rebuild public spaces and becomes the program manager of those places.

The emergence of nongovernmental managers of place is a tacit admission that cities are not always able to provide the amenities that are required to attract and maintain the highest-quality public use. Whether this is due to issues of public funding or public work force management, or to the breakdown of informal social capital that might have compensated for what the public sector could not do, is not clear. What is clear, is that place-based management requires skills and perspectives that traditional public management is not always able to provide.

The notion of *public* has two common meanings: one related to government and a second linked to the idea of common access and open participation. The two meanings are related in that we assume that a government (especially a democratic one) ensures rights of access and expression as a way of protecting public space and participation. The services of the public sector are, we assume, the precondition to the sustenance of common infrastructure, physical and civic.

But when public goods are degraded to the extent that large numbers of people no longer use them, there are an increasing number of cases where the public management is outsourced to civil society, often with business interests playing a major role.

The example of downtown Philadelphia does not imply that public spaces in other areas of the city are not used and are not safe. Many are vibrant and valuable to their communities. Nor is it possible for all communities (those without a local business base, for example) to create self-funded special service districts. In many communities the informal mechanism of local residents and the activities of conventional public management, often aided by local civic groups, provide access and security. But in too many cases public access is limited by either a lack of security or the lack of ongoing public attention (from cleanups to graffiti removal to repairing old infrastructure).

In neighborhoods with fewer resources than a downtown, the re-norming of place is often done in small-scale, citizen-led ways that are nonetheless significant. Block associations come together to sponsor cleanups and children's events; abandoned lots are turned into gardens and vacant walls are made into murals; a neighborhood business group hangs banners that promote the community; or neighborhood music and art festivals are held. These signs of local social capital are building blocks of public life in the most distressed communities. They are the visible manifestations of informal social contracts about behavior and aspiration.

A primary focus for rebuilding a distressed city must be to support civic efforts—formal and informal—that re-norm everyday expectations about public life. We have important examples of this for downtown public plazas, recreation centers in low income neighborhoods, transportation stops, and parks. The challenge is to accelerate the momentum of reclamation by supporting an ever widening assortment of place-oriented advocates and managers.

Access expands opportunity. Businesses can stay open longer because there is less fear of robbery. Families unable to pay the cost to privatize play and recreation use local parks and playgrounds. Access to employment is eased because travelling at night on public transit becomes a safer option. The need to privatize the cost of education is reduced.

A Data-Driven Approach to Citywide Community Investment

What made cities such as Philadelphia thrive historically was the existence of moderately priced communities, where people chose to live and where there were public amenities that were family friendly, from schools to recreation centers. Many once stable row home neighborhoods went into decline as the economic base of the city changed.

Many of those neighborhoods are still viable. Residents move to them from lower-income areas to establish homeowner equity and find better schools. And in some instances they are places where new immigrants—West Indian, African, Southeast Asian, Dominican, Latin American, and Eastern European—are settling. A major issue for Philadelphia is to figure out how to best reinforce the viability of moderately priced communities of choice, places where newcomers and internal movers are relocating. This is critical to supporting market opportunities that work for moderate-income populations.

At the same time, most community development focuses on subsidized housing investment in lower-income areas, including communities with high levels of residential abandonment. Part of this has to do with public sector income targeting but it also reflects a philosophical perspective around responding to communities with the greatest need. While this is understandable, there are two potential downsides: 1) it ignores market forces that continue to dampen demand in areas where public money is invested, and 2) it can have the effect of reinforcing concentrated poverty.

What can a city like Philadelphia do to manage the dual demands of investing public resources in low-income places while paying attention to areas with more strength that may have greater antipoverty consequences? My understanding of these issues came from working in support of a major public sector initiative.

In 2001 I was asked by Mayor Street of Philadelphia to design a way to use public dollars to manage the seemingly endless expansion of abandoned housing stock. At the time I was the CEO of The Reinvestment Fund, which provides debt financing and policy advisory services for Mid-Atlantic communities. The result of our consultancy with the mayor—what came to be called the Neighborhood Transformation Initiative (NTI)[9]— has been the subject of both praise and critique (McGovern 2006). While the project was popularly viewed as focused on the worst areas of the city (where housing abandonment was the greatest), the major issue that emerged in all of our analysis was the importance of supporting fragile communities that were not the poorest, but could either go into decline or be stabilized; these were the moderately priced communities that were so critical to social mobility.

When I took on the assignment I was struck by the fact that while there was a great deal of work being done in support of regional strategies and neighborhood plans, there was less work being done in understanding the social ecology of cities. The tradition of neighborhood succession and housing filtering analyses had come to an end and in its place was the notion of a region and a neighborhood. In too many instances neighborhood plans lacked context and regional studies left cities on the back burner.

At the same time, advances in data analysis and geographic information systems were creating the opportunity to explore the city with a more refined understanding of the trends effecting change. We went about the analysis of Philadelphia by building extensive geo-coded databases and examining the trends through a statistical cluster analysis. This gave us a vantage point from which to view the city as a whole.

It was important to first measure the extent of decline. Prior to 2001 there was a limited inventory of vacant properties. The NTI initiative had as its first task to catalogue the city's abandoned properties. It turned out that the city had 26,000 abandoned residential units, 31,000 vacant lots, and 2,500 vacant commercial and industrial properties from a real estate parcel map of more than half a million properties. This created the first baseline for analysis after fifty years of steady decline. It was also the first opportunity to set goals for doing everything from cleaning lots to tearing down dangerous buildings.

A second step was to understand the patterns underneath the raw data. The basic arithmetic of decline has very little meaning until you geo-code it, analyze it in terms of other trends and social indicators such as code violations, changing property values, mortgage foreclosures, and so forth. From here you can see the patterns of decline and investment. Spatially displayed patterns have tremendous policy value in that citizens can see how the conditions of their community relate to adjacent and more distant neighborhoods.[10] It gives people a context for public actions.

The most important step was to view the patterns as organizing principles for defining public investment strategies. Spatial analysis of real estate and other data can help identify efficiencies of scale (taking down multiple dangerous buildings in one area at once), areas of greatest leverage (where market activity is emerging and private investment is active), and areas of transitional stability (where small public investments can help maintain neighborhood viability). Public investment products from marketing vacant parcels to foreclosure prevention counseling to scattered site housing rehabilitation can have more or less impact based on their context; and in a city with limited resources and significant real estate and infrastructure issues, the targeting value derived from pattern analysis, was critical.

What I took from this analysis—both the data analytics and many days driving the streets and talking to residents—were four public investment principles: 1) building from strength, 2) stabilizing mid-value communities, 3) emphasizing the importance of people-based strategies for the most depopulated and poorest areas, and 4) identifying places where there is great opportunity for mixed-income communities.

The principle of building from strength refers not only to comparatively better off areas but to the fact that within lower-income and moderately distressed communities, it is imperative to identify nodes of strength that remain: a density of strong blocks, proximity to stable institutions, signs of private investment, access to transportation, and so forth. From these nodes of strength it is more likely that investment into a development and civic strategy will succeed.

A second principle was the importance of concentrating place-based investments in those communities that still have viability but show signs of a downward trajectory because of indicators such as elevated vacancy rates

(one or two on a street), high mortgage foreclosure rates, and visible deterioration of retail quality. These are the mid-value communities that are the
bellwethers for cities such as Philadelphia. They are the places where residents relocate as the next rung up the geographical and social ladder. In
these communities, relatively small investments in housing rehabilitation,
focused code enforcement and streetscape investments, and community
policing efforts are preventive activities that save public resources over the
long term.

The third principle is to emphasize the importance of people-based
investments—from job training to family support—in the poorest communities where there is very little opportunity of real estate markets stabilizing
anytime in the near future. The political symbolism of place has often created a narrative that conflates the rehabilitation of housing with poverty reduction. While the former is certainly an input to the latter, it is very often
not the most important use of public resources if household poverty allevia-
tion is the goal.

Principle four relates to enabling more mixed-income communities. In
those areas of the city where there are multiple market types (some areas rising and others falling) in proximity and where there are large tracts of vacant land, there are opportunities to incent developers and work with civic
groups to build mixed-income communities where market-rate housing will
defray the development cost of the more affordable units. In the absence of
political and civic leadership that helps this come about, there is often a stale-
mate over the use of vacant land, which of course benefits nobody.

When you come to view the complexity of the city as a whole and the importance of building a spatially differentiated public investment strategy,
one of the most important underlying tasks is to manage change at the community level. It is often hard for residents to come to terms with the fact that
the changes of the past several decades mean that their community may never
look the same as it did in the past: retail strips may contract; some vacant
land will become parks; large buildings may never have the same manufacturing use again; streets with 50 or 60 percent vacancy levels are often not
the best streets for revitalization. The civic engagement required to deal with
this kind of change management is intense but necessary.

It is difficult to enact principles such as these, in part because the politics
of constituency services will always seek to spread resources in less strategic
ways. But in cities that have too much land, too many service demands, and
a tier of mid-value communities that are struggling to sustain themselves,

decisions have to be made on the basis of data that supports a theory of change for the overall city.

Conclusion

Cities like Philadelphia have an opportunity to grow for the first time in decades. To do so they need to do the civic and public work of building amenities that attract new residents while also assisting in the social mobility of low-income residents. The three areas discussed in this chapter build on emerging innovations of the past two decades: how to manage public space, how to reorganize schools, and how to best invest in communities with limited public resources.

None of the innovations or perspectives discussed provide simple answers or recipes for success. They are practices that show some promise but also have drawbacks and limits. Perhaps the most controversial perspective revolves around what I view as a gradual transformation of the practical meaning of a public sphere. I see that transformation through the emergence of institutions such as charter schools and special service districts.

As noted in the outset the purpose of this chapter was to propose some of the practices critical to a development and change perspective that works from the city itself rather than regional policies. At the same time, nothing that is discussed here is meant to ignore the metropolitan context. Great urban spaces and neighborhoods become regional assets. And the restoration of value in moderately priced communities (many of which are close to the suburban edge) has significance for inner-ring suburbs, many of which are in a similar position.

CHAPTER 12

Fostering an Inclusive Metropolis:
Equity, Growth, and Community

Chris Benner and Manuel Pastor

Calls for an inclusive metropolis generally appeal to fairness and democracy, conjuring visions of equitable distribution of burdens and benefits and widespread participation in public policy-making processes. In recent years, however, research has suggested that inclusion may not only be good for our moral values or sense of social justice but also for generating long-term economic growth (Benner and Pastor 2015a; Eberts, Erickcek, and Kleinhenz 2006; Pastor and Benner 2008). The statistical work seems to suggest not only that there is a correlation between equity and growth but also that the causal arrow runs from equity to growth (as well as back again); however, in most of the work, the underlying mechanisms for the linkage between equity and growth remain unclear. Explanations for the relationship have varied, some pointing to structural factors (perhaps more equitable distributions of income are consistent with more investment in basic human capital and less investment in financial speculation) and others to what might be termed political economy factors (perhaps more equity leads to less conflict over slices of the pie and more willingness to focus on strategies to grow the pie).

While the structural factors are sometimes examined through statistical analysis, the factors related to political economy are harder to measure or model, and thus need to be analyzed through qualitative case studies. This chapter reports on some of our recent efforts to do just that, reviewing both some suggestive quantitative results and a wide range of cases that are part of an ongoing project to understand real-world causal mechanisms that link social equity and sustained economic growth. Our interest here is to shift the focus from particular policy mechanisms—such as better workforce development systems or more attention to placing transit in low-income neighborhoods—to underlying social, political, and economic processes, not just policies, that may contribute to both social equity and economic growth.

We argue, in particular, that diverse and dynamic regional knowledge networks (or, as described later in more formal terms, "epistemic communities") are an important factor in shaping equity and sustained economic growth. We explored this possibility first in *Just Growth: Inclusion and Prosperity in America's Metropolitan Communities* (Benner and Pastor 2012), suggesting that while collaboration in a region can be incentivized and enforced by jurisdictional authority—such as a central city's power to annex suburbs— it can also be induced through a particularly visionary metropolitan planning agency (such as the Mid-America Regional Council in Kansas City) or effective regional leadership programs (as in Jacksonville, Florida, or Nashville, Tennessee).

As we have refined and tested the concept, we have sought to better differentiate our approach from the simple calls to collaborate that seem to populate some regionalist thinking and writing (Henton, Melville, and Walesh 2003, 1997). Indeed, further research shows that while diverse and dynamic knowledge communities do involve *repeated interactions*, a *sense of place*, and a *commitment to the long run*, they can emerge from struggle as well as consensus. What is critical is how the inevitable conflicts are resolved and whether the parties involved work to create a spirit of shared destiny that is a political and social precondition for a more inclusive policy framework.

In short, a critical factor in generating an inclusive metropolis is what might be termed the deep political economy: the configurations of power and voice that lead multiple interests to be recognized in the policy-making process. It is possible that inclusive regional growth might come about through other processes—structural characteristics of the regional economy, for instance. However, while diverse epistemic communities might not be absolutely necessary for an inclusive metropolis, inclusive processes centered in dynamic knowledge communities create fertile ground in which economic growth and social equity are more likely to go together.

To make this argument, the chapter proceeds as follows. The first section both reviews the recent quantitative work on the equity-growth relationship and introduces an analysis of sustained growth that includes the role of not just income equity but also spatial, social, and political connection.

In particular, we present recent empirical findings from our own work on the relationships among regional government characteristics, various measures of social equity and social connection, and the ability of regions to sustain economic growth; we extend that work slightly here by considering the role of political homogeneity and spatial sorting. We suggest that these findings indeed support the contention that a non-polarized civil society may be useful for economic sustainability.

We then turn to a more specific discussion of diverse and dynamic epistemic communities, based on a series of eleven in-depth regional case studies.[1] Here, we synthesize some of the key findings that emerge across these regions, discussing first how these diverse knowledge networks emerged in particular regions, how they influence regional governance processes, and how this in turn seems to affect processes shaping both economic growth and social equity. We conclude with a discussion of implications for regional leaders and stakeholders who are interested in strengthening and diversifying regional knowledge networks: that is, on building a sense of *place* and a commitment to the long run that ultimately creates a sense of shared destiny across differences.

Equity, Growth, and Community

Equity and Growth: Perspectives and Evidence

While traditional economic theory has generally posited a trade-off between equity and efficiency and thus between income equality and economic growth, recent research from both the international and regionalist literature has challenged this supposition. The first salvos were from studies of the developing world (see Aghion, Caroli, and García-Peñalosa 1999 for an early review), generally with a perspective that targeting poverty and inequality might promote growth because it increases the productive nature of the poor (Birdsall, Ross, and Sabot 1995; Deninger and Squire 1996), because it lowers social tensions and so facilitates more policy certainty (Alesina and Perotti 1996; Rodrik 1999), and because it generates less resentment against the protection of private property (Alesina and Rodrik 1994; Persson and Tabellin 1994).

The questions posed and methods used in this international comparative work have been transplanted into studies of metropolitan regions in the

United States. The first domestic efforts to replicate the findings were at the state level, with more recent work suggesting that inequality does indeed dampen state economies in a way consistent with the international findings (Panizza 2002; Partridge 1997). Meanwhile, a flurry of studies—to which we have contributed—have suggested that income inequality, geographic concentrations of the poor, city-suburb disparities, and residential segregation by race may be negatively associated with economic growth (Pastor 2006; Pastor and Benner 2008; Voith 1998). It is important to note one issue that might immediately come to mind: reverse causality. In fact, the efforts cited have generally relied on multiple regression analysis, sometimes with techniques to control for simultaneity (that is, the impact of growth on equity as well as the impact of equity on growth) and always with the care to consider equity variables at the beginning of a time period, not after.

The results also seem to be robust to alternative testing strategies. Consider, for example, a factor analysis undertaken by economists at the Cleveland Federal Reserve to identify key variables that influence economic growth on the regional level: they found that while variables like a skilled workforce or a diversified economy are important, high levels of racial inclusion and progress on income equality also correlate strongly and positively with economic growth (Eberts et al. 2006).

While these studies have produced findings parallel to those covering developing countries, they have generally been less clear about the mechanisms by which equity can affect growth—is it, as in the developing world context, because of broader investment in human capital and reduced social tension, or other factors? Here we try to uncover a bit of the black box of causation by looking at the role that income equity and social distance may have on *sustaining* growth. Our strategy parallels the pioneering work by IMF economists Berg, Ostry, and Zettelmeyer (2012), which examined sustained periods of growth in GDP in 140 countries (with a "growth spell" defined as continuous growth for at least five years) and found that the variable that was most significant and sizeable in its effect on the length of a growth spell was the Gini coefficient, a measure of income disparity (Berg et al. 2012: 160).

As with the previous international work, this was a methodology just waiting to be applied to metropolitan data—and so we have done just that. We looked at sustained year-over-year quarterly expansion in employment for the period 1990–2011 for the largest 184 metropolitan regions in the United States (that is, all CBSAs or Core Based Statistical Areas that had a population of 250,000 or more as of the 2010 Census) (Benner and Pastor 2015a). We defined a "growth spell" as any period in which such employment growth lasted for three years or more, a characterization that led to identification of 324 such spells (of varying length). The basic idea was to discover which factors lengthen the time before a region slips; these are then considered positive for sustaining growth.[2]

Why is sustaining growth important? In Figure 12.1, we offer a scatterplot of observations for all 184 regions, with the horizontal axis indicating the number of quarters over the twenty-one-year period a region spent in a growth spell and the horizontal axis indicating the total growth in regional employment over the entire time period. Note that there were three regions that had no growth spells at all (in other words, experienced no periods of growth sustained over at least twelve quarters); there were others that experienced the minimum sustained growth to qualify as a spell, twelve quarters, while there were two high-performing regions that experienced growth over seventy quarters.[3] In any case, the pattern is relatively clear (and evidenced by the fitted trend line as well): the more time a region can spend in sustained growth, the more likely it is to experience significant improvement in regional employment over the long haul. Steady (although not necessarily slow) wins the economic race.

So what contributed to sustained growth in our analysis? What we found was striking: as in Berg et al. (2012), the most significant predictor—both in terms of size and consistency over multiple specifications—was the metropolitan Gini coefficient. Even more remarkable: our coefficients were roughly (and eerily) similar to those of Berg et al.—striking considering the very different sorts of datasets being examined. These results are echoed in a different set of specifications by our colleagues Hal Wolman and Ned Hill, who found that regions that were more equal were less likely to wobble into crisis (Hill et al. 2012), although their results also suggest inequality may be associated with higher likelihood of bouncing back from such a crisis.

Other variables made a difference in sustained growth, including measures of economic structure such as the extent of the workforce in manufacturing or construction (higher shares were associated with shorter growth spells, with the first likely because of a reliance on older declining industries and the second because of its association with boom-bust housing cycles), as well as an education measure that captured what share of the population had a mid-range level of schooling (more than a high school degree and less than a college degree). With those other variables in a regression, we find statisti-

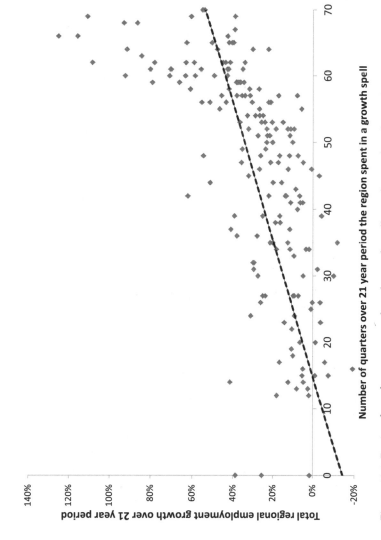

Figure 12.1. Regional employment growth and growth spells: exploring the relationship.

cally significant impacts of metropolitan political fragmentation as well as indicators of social and spatial connection, including residential segregation and differences in the poverty rate between the metro's prime (or central) cities and its suburbs.

Does Social Connection Matter for Sustained Growth?

What broadly seems to matter in whether or not growth was sustained over time was not just the underlying economic structure but also various measures of social distance such as income inequality, metropolitan fragmentation, and residential segregation. Creating community across a region might therefore be a sort of antidote to erratic growth, a sort of elixir to promote resilience and sustained growth. This is exactly what we later argue is a central task of diverse and dynamic epistemic communities: to overcome the tendency to atomistic, self-interested behavior that fails to realize the benefits of collaboration.

But before going there, does disconnection really matter? One way to test the role of shared regional identity is to look at a measure of political polarization, particularly the degree to which voters' ideological leanings are divided by geographic lines that might pose challenges for intraregional collaboration. To get at this, we used voting data from Dave Leip's *Atlas of U.S. Presidential Elections*,[4] with the methods described at more length in our forthcoming book (Benner and Pastor 2015b). To derive a measure of "regional political homogeneity" at the metro level, we began by summing votes for the Democratic and Republican candidates by CBSA. In this case, a bigger regional gap in voter preferences—either really "red" or really "blue"—signals a higher level of ideological similarity. However, because the sort of voter cohesion we were interested in capturing had more to do with differences within a region, we also summarized the data separately for the "core" county and the "outlying" counties in each CBSA and we term this variable "political spatial sorting within region." Our hypothesis was that a larger gap signals more political spatial sorting—that is, geographic polarization—and might be thus associated with less cohesion and perhaps a shorter growth spell.

Unfortunately, the voting data is not available below the county level of geography and this means that we cannot derive this measure of regional voter cohesion for CBSAs consisting of only one county (52 of the 184 CBSAs

Table 12.1. Political Variables and Sustained Growth

	Sample 1 All CBSAs		Sample 2 Multi-county CBSAs	
	Impact	Sig	Impact	Sig
Regional political homogeneity	**positive**	**0.02**	positive	0.80
Political spatial sorting within region	**negative**	**0.03**	**negative**	**0.00**

Bolded Impacts are significant at at least the .20 two-tail level.

we consider). Because of this issue, we present results for two different samples, one that includes all CBSAs and one that includes only multicounty CBSAs. For the sample with all CBSAs, we set the spatial sorting variable equal to zero for single-county CBSAs and also explored other strategies to control for any factors specific to these cases; we should note that the single-county metros tend to be among the smallest; excluding these cases, for example, causes a loss of about one-quarter of the growth spells, a number which would seem to be worrisome until we realize that this represents only about 11 percent of the total metro population in the sample.

What do we find? Table 12.1 presents the results in a relatively simple format: we indicate the direction of the effect (positive or negative) and the degree of statistical significance, bolding all results that meet a certain threshold (below, we occasionally discuss the size of the effect when the differences are quite large). The pattern is, at least to us, quite intriguing: to the extent that there is overall political homogeneity, growth spells are lengthened (although insignificantly so in the case of the multicounty CBSAs) while to the extent that there is political spatial sorting (or geographic polarization) within regions, growth spells are shortened. This is also consistent with our case studies: we find that places that are overwhelming Republican (Salt Lake City) or Democratic (San Antonio) can both find their way to higher levels of collaboration and more steady growth. Note, however, that the effect of overall political homogeneity is not significant when we move to the larger multicounty CBSAs; on the other hand, political spatial sorting rises in both significance and, while not reported here, the size of the effect.

What happens when we test these political variables in the context of a fuller multivariate regression? The results are shown in Table 12.2, which also helps illustrate some of the factors discussed above, including a measure of

Table 12.2. Integrated Model and Sustained Growth

	Sample 1 All CBSAs		Sample 2 Multi-county CBSAs	
	Impact	Sig	Impact	Sig
Metropolitan power diffusion index	**negative**	**0.036**	negative	0.445
Gini coefficient	**negative**	**0.000**	**negative**	**0.000**
Segregation index, Non-Hispanic White	**negative**	**0.078**	**negative**	**0.117**
Ratio, principal city to suburban poverty rates	negative	0.570	positive	0.755
Adult population with HS to AA degree	**positive**	**0.178**	positive	0.639
Percent of population foreign born	**negative**	**0.000**	**negative**	**0.199**
Percent employment in public Madministration	negative	0.557	negative	0.213
Percent employment in manufacturing	**negative**	**0.001**	**negative**	**0.000**
Percent employment in construction	**negative**	**0.047**	**negative**	**0.002**
Percent of workforce covered by a union contract	negative	0.468	negative	0.492
Regional political homogeneity	**positive**	**0.102**	positive	0.873
Political spatial sorting within region	**negative**	**0.014**	**negative**	**0.013**

Bolded Impacts are significant at at least the .20 two-tail level.

jurisdictional fragmentation called the "metropolitan power diffusion index" (Hamilton, Miller, and Paytas 2004; Miller and Lee 2009). Before turning to these results, it is useful to stress something that is obscured by the approach we take here of simply reporting the direction of the effect and whether it is significant: the largest size effect (and, as it turns out, highest level of significance) emerges from our measure of inequality, the Gini coefficient.[5] Residential segregation is also important as are some of the structural variables like percent in manufacturing and construction; percent foreign-born is also negatively associated with sustaining growth.

Note that the results parallel the findings without as many controls (i.e., those in Table 12.1): political spatial sorting has a significant negative impact on sustainable growth while the effect of regional political homogeneity is not significant when we focus on just the multicounty CBSAs that represent 90 percent of the population under consideration. The political variables also have interesting interactions with other variables: for example, the city-suburb poverty ratio is significant if the political variables are not included, suggesting a high correlation with political spatial sorting.[6] Note also that when we move to the multicounty setting, the metropolitan power diffusion index is much less significant: political sorting and jurisdictional fragmentation are likely to go hand in hand in the data as they do in the real world.

Of course, as with the general growth and equity results, one might worry about reverse causality—that it is the lack of growth that generates political and social distance rather than the other way around. While we cannot test this directly in a simultaneous model—the underlying hazard ratio regression strategy used to estimate growth sustainability is not amenable to this— it is useful to stress that we are taking measures of political homogeneity and spatial sorting that are taken *before* the growth periods we consider (specifically, we are using results from elections in 1988 for the growth spells of the 1990s and from 2000 for the growth spells of the 2000s). While there is some possibility that this is picking up the impacts of previous long-run trends in growth, it far more likely that we are not finding a spurious correlation: social disconnection can impact the sustainability of growth.

Indeed, it is of particular interest that while regional political homogeneity and spatial sorting matter, it is the sorting variable that performs more consistently. While this measure of political disconnection is certainly imperfect, the results do point in the direction that having a more like-minded regional polity—and one where that like-mindedness at a metropolitan level does not mask deep divides within the metro—may be more consistent with sustained growth. As we will see, this is exactly what diverse epistemic communities are meant to address—to take disparate groups and help them find new common ground.

Diverse and Dynamic Epistemic Communities

If social and political connections matter for sustained growth, it is useful to know under what circumstances they may be created and sustained. If such connections are simply a structural feature—say, of the racial or political homogeneity of a region—then we are left with an argument that may be satisfying in its explanation but problematic in its prescription. After all, if we want to actually foster an inclusive metropolis, we want to discover not just *where* communities already share a common fate but also *how* leadership can more purposefully craft that sense of common ground.

To understand that process, we have been developing the concept of a diverse and dynamic epistemic community. What is an epistemic community? Our use of the term builds on, but is slightly different than, what has existed heretofore in the literature. Haas (1992) describes an epistemic community as a group of people, usually professionals, who have shared norms, causal beliefs, and validity tests as well as a common policy enterprise—and that such communities are formed through processes of collective knowledge acquisition and understanding of each other's choices, and are then institutionalized via repeated interactions. While the notion of epistemic communities is linked with some kind of common policy enterprise, these enterprises are not limited to formal legislative or policy processes; indeed, as Adler and Haas put it: "the policy ideas of epistemic communities generally evolve independently, rather than under the direct influence of government sources of authority" (Adler and Haas 1992: 374).

Our extension of the concept to the region is a natural: this is an important scale of the economy in which government structures are usually absent and so the formation of consensus is important. We also extend the concept by suggesting that it need not be limited to policy makers and other professionals. Under the guise of regionalism (and often through formal visioning processes or other such mechanisms), key actors develop mechanisms to share facts and communicate concerns, create new ways to share concerns and priorities, and may even generate a new sense of identity.

Of course, members of epistemic communities do not necessarily wind up agreeing on inclusion as a standard element of their policy enterprise. Indeed, as Lester and Reckhow (2013) have convincingly argued, positive outcomes for regional equity may emerge more from skirmishes among competing actors than from pure collaboration. At the same time, diverse and dynamic epistemic communities evolve over time, and in the process of repeated interactions can overcome both the general tendency to atomistic, self-interested behavior that fails to realize the benefits of collaboration *and* the social distance that prevents a sort of solidarity that leads one set of partners to take the interests of another set into account.

We review here research on eleven regions in which we studied the existence of regional integration and social connectedness (Benner and Pastor 2015b). The regions were selected by looking at *both* growth and equity outcomes over a thirty-year period *and* qualitative evidence of regional collaboration. The regions studied include six cases of inclusive metropolises where growth and equity clearly went together (Seattle, Sacramento, Salt Lake City, San Antonio, Grand Rapids, and Raleigh-Durham); two contrasting cases of slow growth and dramatically worsening inequality (Fresno and Greensboro); two cases with strong reputations as collaborative regions but where rapid growth had been (at least recently) associated with slippages in equity measures (Silicon Valley and Charlotte); and one dramatic "turn-around" case, where a stagnant economy and growing inequality in the 1980s and early 1990s was replaced by striking patterns of relatively inclusive growth in the subsequent period (Oklahoma City).

Through these case studies, we sought to understand two things. The first was the extent to which regional performance on growth and equity is linked to collective interpretation and knowledge generation over extended interactions between multiple constituencies. The second was the evolution of those communicative processes, particularly in terms of their capacity to manage conflict. In each region, we interviewed a wide array of actors (from business, government, labor, community, philanthropy), and probed for evidence of both collaboration and conflict. We also reviewed a wide range of secondary material on each region, including academic work, reports, and media coverage.

The driving questions included these. How and why do diverse epistemic communities emerge in certain places, and what hinders their development in others? How does the nature of those epistemic communities shape the processes of regional governance and regional development? And what are the specific mechanisms through which such knowledge communities facilitate or contribute to a more inclusive and economically sustainable metropolis?

Why and How Do Diverse Epistemic Communities Form?

Previous research has identified a number of general conditions that seem to be in place whenever epistemic communities form. The most important seem to be conditions of complexity and uncertainty within a particular domain of subject area interest. This creates the need for interactive processes between people to understand that complexity, and to be able to interpret changes and figure out how best to respond to unexpected dynamics. There is also a need for some level of expertise or specialized knowledge to effectively interpret the complex information and related processes generated in the community. Typically in epistemic communities there is some set of processes for institutionalizing both the interaction itself and for acting upon the ideas and beliefs that emerge from the knowledge generated in those communities.

At first glance, the conditions identified above might appear to describe any region. After all, regional development is always characterized by complex and uncertain change driven by a large array of actors and processes. But uncertainty does not necessarily lead actors to search outside their established operating procedures or existing networks, and in the most fragmented regions, different constituencies and geographies may not see their future as closely or even not so closely linked with other constituencies in the region—in these cases, the interactions are generally less collaborative and the results can reflect that. We are interested in circumstances and cases where mechanisms are developed such that there is a *diverse and dynamic* epistemic community with a common domain of knowledge interest in the *region's* development.

So what contributes to the development of an epistemic community focused on regional development, and what contributes to it being more or less diverse and dynamic in its membership, focus, and long-term viability? In our case studies, we found three broad factors that seemed to contribute to diverse constituencies coming together in regional knowledge sharing networks. The first factor—really more of a catalyst—is economic shocks. Widespread threats to economic security, especially those that add uncertainty to the future, can be the catalyst for regional leaders to come together to fully understand causes of economic decline and to collaborate to turn things around. While these shocks are typically negative, we also found cases of positive economic shocks, where rapid growth threatens quality of life or contributes to growing air pollution, loss of farmland and green space on the urban periphery. Regardless of whether the economic shock is negative or positive, it seems that it is a sense of urgency and rapid change that helps stimulate diverse constituencies to come together to try to understand and address what is going on in the region.

The second factor for developing and strengthening diverse epistemic communities may come from internal regional characteristics and leadership strategies pursued in the region. Frequently some form of regional government—whether in the form of city-county mergers (e.g., Nashville or Jacksonville) or aggressive annexation policies of central cities (e.g., Oklahoma

City)—more or less enforces a sense of common fate. But beyond the structural conditions, there is also a role here for deliberate collaborative efforts, often driven by particular individuals or groups of individuals. A drive for inclusion from regional elites may be driven more by moral values and a broad culture of inclusion, rather than a sense of crisis—or it may emerge from visionary leaders who see the potential value of broadly collaborative approaches to shaping regional development. The risk with elite-driven processes is that they can be paternalistic but, despite this, the results still can be the creation of "tables" that facilitate the emergence and maintenance of regional strategies.

The third factor that can contribute to diverse regional knowledge networks emerges from the other side of the social balance: the actions and motivations of social movements and others concerned with social equity. Here, the demands made to regional leadership for inclusion of marginalized populations can play an important role in catalyzing processes that result in the institutionalization of knowledge sharing processes. From our research, it seems that this happens most effectively when social movements are less focused on or faced with a zero-sum situation. This might help explain, for example, why union demands in Detroit that focused most dominantly on bargaining within the auto sector were less effective in stimulating regional dialogue, while union demands in Milwaukee that focused on training and industrial upgrading helped stimulate a number of institutional supports for cross-sector dialogue and action (Pastor and Benner 2008). For social movement activism to stimulate the development of diverse epistemic communities probably also requires some level of governance opportunity or regional champion to help translate between the worldviews of activists and elite leadership.

Economic shocks, effective regional leadership, and social movements obviously don't always lead to diverse and dynamic epistemic communities. In some places—Detroit and Fresno come to mind—deep racial and regional conflicts that underpin economic and institutional divides may hinder diverse constituencies from coming together. In other places—Silicon Valley and Charlotte in our research—paternalistic regional leadership may have obtained a measure of consensus in decades past, but are increasingly less effective at broadening knowledge networks in the face of rapid demographic change and increasingly entrenched economic divides. But in those places where diverse epistemic communities have formed, it seems to be some combination of economic shock, enlightened regional leadership, and aspirational social movements that have been essential in building and sustaining their existence.

How Do Epistemic Communities Impact Regional Outcomes?

Once the process of building diverse regional epistemic communities is underway, how does the information sharing and knowledge development in these communities actually change governance processes in the region? One important qualifier is essential: structural forces, such as deindustrialization, can overwhelm almost any intentional effort to adjust. However, as Sean Safford (2009) convincingly argues, the local response can matter even in the face of huge structural pressures. So while we acknowledge the limits of intentional action—perhaps it is just nibbling at the edge of structural impediments—we have identified five specific mechanisms by which knowledge or epistemic communities can impact outcomes.

First, in regions with diverse epistemic communities, regional priorities are more likely to reflect a diverse set of interests, rather than those of dominant elites in the region, and these priorities are more likely to have been determined through interactive communication that helps them be broadly understood. In Salt Lake City, for example, the small nonprofit organization Envision Utah led a broad collaborative visioning process in which regional priorities emerged from a broad consultative, knowledge generation process that included more than 2,000 people in fifty public workshops and more than 17,000 responses over the internet and newspaper surveys. This process helped ensure that priorities for development in the region were not limited to those developed in the narrow halls of power, but were rooted in the lived experience and values of diverse communities and were broadly shared by leaders throughout the region.

Similarly, in Oklahoma City, the original Metropolitan Area Projects (MAPS) investment in 1993 included nine diverse projects developed by a mayor-appointed Metro Area Projects Task Force consisting of a diversity of public officials; project ideas were also developed by various other committees consisting of city council members and civic leaders. The mayor also created a city council committee to review the task force's work, and appointed as head of this committee the council member he thought would be the strongest *opponent* of the whole initiative. In arguing for voters to pass new taxes to pay for these projects, Mayor Norick emphasized the multiple beneficia- ries of the projects and the importance of focusing on the city as a whole, telling arts patrons, for example: "Are you willing to defeat your symphony because you don't like baseball?" (Lackmeyer and Money 2006: 127). By con- sciously bringing opponents and supporters together, and directly connect- ing the interests of different constituencies, the process in Oklahoma City ensured a diversity of priorities were represented in the MAPS projects.

Second, diverse epistemic communities can also help issues in the region be framed not in terms of zero-sum or us-versus-them terms, but rather around a respect for difference and a sense of a common future together. Again in Salt Lake City, multiple stakeholders told us that the long-term perspective of the Envision Utah approach helped them overcome short-term, zero-sum conflicts and recognize common interests that facilitated medium- term creative solutions. One oft-cited example involved a controversial new freeway project. Negotiations in Salt Lake City county resulted in a substan- tial redesign of the project including more green landscaping, expanded frontage roads with bike lanes and trails, and signalized intersections includ- ing a new radar-activated bike turn signal to facilitate both bike and car traffic in the corridor—a result that emerged from a perspective that it was possible to meet multiple interests in development and design of the project. And back to Oklahoma City, the mayor lobbying for MAPS attracted senior voters by appealing to intergenerational solidarity: "You may not like it. You may not even be around for it. But aren't your grandkids?" (Lackmeyer and Money 2006: 127).

Third, with diverse and dynamic epistemic communities, leadership within the region develops capacities for interacting with diverse constitu- encies. In San Antonio, for example, initially high levels of conflict between equity advocates and city elites were overcome when both sides of the divide shifted their perspectives and strategies to embrace the contributions of the other side. Henry Cisneros was a particularly visible and important public sector leader in this process. With roots in poor west side communities, but reaching the highest levels of political influence in the city, he was able to gar- ner trust and support from both sides of this divide and help strengthen a culture of collaboration that was later institutionalized even after he left the mayor's office. Ernie Cortes, the dynamic community organizer responsible for the founding of COPS (Communities Organized for Public Service), was also important in his ability to move from a typical Saul Alinsky-ist confron- tational style to the more collaborative approach required to build Project

Quest, an award-winning and influential workforce development initiative in the region (Racemacher, Bear, and Conway 2001). Banking executive Tom Frost, once the object of COPS protests (which led him to distribute copies of Saul Alinsky's *Rules for Radicals* to his banking colleagues so they would be better prepared to fight their adversaries), eventually came to appreciate COPS and became chairman of the board of Project Quest.

Fourth, with the ability to build ties across diverse institutions and constituencies, diverse epistemic communities influence regional governing processes through their ability to help coordinate actions among different institutions in the region. This was perhaps most evident in our research in Grand Rapids, where there was widespread agreement about the value of the "four-legged stool" in shaping economic development trajectories in the region. Consisting of Grand Action, the Chamber of Commerce, The Right Place, and Experience Grand Rapids, this mix of public, private, and nonprofit entities maintained an informal division of labor encompassing regional research, place marketing, downtown redevelopment, policy advocacy, economic development, tourism and convention development, and regional leadership training. The four organizations complemented each other, regularly sharing information and knowledge that ensured they were moving in coordinated directions in their programmatic work. Similar cross organizational and cross sector dynamics were evident in Sacramento, Salt Lake City, Raleigh-Durham, and Oklahoma City.

Finally, of course, as has been shown in research on epistemic communities in other contexts, the existence of such strong, collaborative knowledge networks contributes to a greater likelihood that regional policies will actually be developed and passed, rather than be constrained by unproductive conflicts and knowledge differences. In cases where these epistemic communities are particularly diverse, we believe that the policies passed are also likely to be more inclusive.

As these cases suggest, these various processes of shared regional priority setting, inclusive issue framing, collaborative leadership development, coordinating action, and passing policies all contribute to a more fundamental transformation in people's sense of place, identity, and belonging. Key regional actors come to see themselves as being part of the region as a whole, and see their regional destiny as being tied up with a diverse range of other constituencies and actors, not just their own immediate constituencies or networks.

We are not suggesting that the creation of regional identity papers over conflicts or happens without tension. Different priorities, values, or interests persist. Moreover, no degree of collaboration can fully overcome structural factors like the collapse of the auto industry or a housing crash that devastates assets and attitudes. What we are suggesting here is more modest: diverse epistemic communities help constituencies recognize a common future together. In such settings, conflicts are played out in a context of long-term and repeated interactions in an interdependent world, rather than winner-take-all battles in an unrealistic vision where opponents are vanquished and made irrelevant—and that can allow for a more successful approach to structural challenges.

Epistemic Communities and the Inclusive Metropolis

Epistemic communities may be good things in and of themselves—they connect people across boundaries, they develop a shared sense of destiny, and surely they appeal to a sense of identity and purpose. All of this may matter for psychic well-being—and we have suggested that it might allow regional actors to better coordinate when faced with a sudden external or internal shock. This is particularly true given the competitive relationship between suburbs and central cities that have generally characterized our major metros. But why would we expect a high level of social connection to actually impact longer-term economic and social outcomes?

Before answering that question, a key caveat is in order: we are not trying to suggest that diverse epistemic communities *necessarily* result in greater growth and equity. Nor are we suggesting that inclusive growth can only happen when diverse and dynamic epistemic communities are present. Our case studies (and the quantitative work we reviewed earlier) simply suggest that an inclusive knowledge community *may* contribute to a higher *likelihood* of producing an inclusive metropolis—that is, they create a more fertile environment in which policies such as better transportation systems or job training programs that can contribute to economic growth and social equity are more likely to take place.

Why might that be possible? In an intriguing new article in the *Journal of Economic Perspectives*, Dani Rodrik, one of the earlier researchers looking at the equity-efficiency relationship in the developing world, tries to explain why policies that might actually benefit multiple actors fail to get enacted (Rodrik 2014). He argues that often the set of political possibilities—and so the range of policy choices—lies well within the range of economic possibilities (or more formally, there is a bounded political possibilities frontier that is within the production possibilities frontier). He suggests that ideas can lead actors to see and then realize new forms of mutual gain—with one of his examples being the negotiated end to apartheid, a process that included repeated interactions, the call to a sense of place, and a commitment to a long-term future that led white elites to realize that their interests could be secured even as the black masses gained a rightful place in South Africa.

Certainly, America's regions are less extreme in their divides but there are gains to be made by incorporating those so often left behind. After all, in the process of adjusting to changed economic circumstances, regional growth is shaped by the extent to which important economic actors are able to work together to capitalize on innovations and new markets (Benner 2003; Saxenian 1994). This includes everything from firms and their suppliers coordinating activities, to links with community college curriculum and nonprofit workforce development and training programs, to individual career aspirations and motivations (Maskell and Malmberg 1999; Storper 1997). This, in turn, is shaped by diverse sources of information on labor market opportunities that may come from a variety of sources, ranging from public school teachers, peer networks, mentors, and broad news sources. In short, it takes a village to make a regional economy thrive (Storper 2013)—and when economic winds are shifting, the more the village can work together in recognizing and then capitalizing on positive new directions of change, the better the economy is likely to perform.

Diverse and dynamic epistemic communities can contribute to fostering greater social equity within regions as well. In a way, this linkage is more straightforward: the very appearance of the word "diversity" suggests greater inclusion. But we are not referring to a mechanical process in which the deals that get struck between multiple partners necessarily include multiple interests. Rather, we are talking about the transformation of underlying social processes, structural conditions, and actor identities.

One of the clearest recent examples is the way the San Antonio Chamber of Commerce joined up in 2012 with political leaders and social equity actors to champion an increased sales tax to fund pre-K education for the most disadvantaged children in the city. Their rationale was that this was key to workforce development in the long run—reflecting exactly that rooted perspective we have stressed—but there is also little doubt that continued interactions among all the parties essentially shifted the self-identity and self-conception of key chamber leaders to see why this was in their own interest as well.

It is also the case that collaboration in one realm may spill over to another. We have highlighted the role of Envision Utah in creating a new approach to regional planning, one that has led to agreements about light rail and environmental protection (Scheer 2012). While not the only reason, we think that the history of problem solving based on shared knowledge is not disconnected to the emergence of the Utah Compact, a remarkable agreement between civic, business, faith, and immigrant leaders to have a civil discussion about immigration (Jameson 2012). And it is not just talk: Utah has extended driving privileges and in-state tuition, and undertaken other pro-immigrant policies one would not usually associate with such a politically conservative area.

Another recent example seems apparent in Seattle's success in becoming the first city in the country with a plan to raise the city minimum wage to $15 an hour. Elsewhere, increases in the minimum wage have been achieved through typical political processes involving the need to get a simple majority of either voters or legislators to pass it. In Seattle, however, Mayor Ed Murray appointed an Income Inequality Advisory Committee with twenty-four members representing a wide range of stakeholders, and charged them with coming up with a proposal that would be acceptable to all, and in the end only two members opposed the final recommendations (one because the recommendations did not go far enough and the other because they went too far). But in creating this committee, Mayor Murray built on at least three decades of a deep culture of diverse dialogue, deliberation, and participation that has characterized city and regional decision making, and has come to be known in regional leadership circles as "the Seattle process," which then becomes institutionalized in a variety of forums, from local conflicts over day-labor sites to regional wage policies.

Ultimately, the inclusive metropolis involves these sorts of conversations and transformations. The policies to get there are important but so is the development of the underlying political economy: a shared sense of destiny between diverse constituencies that evolve from repeated interactions, a commitment to place, and repeated interactions that help to build a commitment to principled struggle as well as facilitated consensus. While more research is certainly needed on the econometric connections and policy linkages between equity and growth, so too is it needed on the leadership skills, styles, and challenges needed to foster and forge the inclusive metropolis.

NOTES

Chapter 1. Socioeconomic Mobility in the United States:
New Evidence and Policy Lessons

This chapter is adapted from "Improving Opportunities for Economic Mobility in the United States," written testimony for the U.S. Senate Budget Committee hearing on "Opportunity, Mobility, and Inequality in Today's Economy" on April 1, 2014. It presents a nontechnical summary of research findings originally published in Chetty et al. (2014a, b).

1. Other measures of mobility—such as the probability of reaching the middle class or the correlation between parent and child income—exhibit similar patterns. I focus on the probability of moving from the bottom to the top fifth for simplicity.

2. In interpreting such international comparisons, it is important to keep in mind that the income distribution in Denmark and Canada is more compressed than in the United States, which may make it easier to move up in the income distribution in those countries than in the United States in percentile terms. Hence, such comparisons, while useful for illustrative purposes, are more difficult to interpret than the within-U.S. comparisons I focus on below.

3. The fraction of teenagers fourteen to sixteen who work is also strongly correlated with higher absolute upward mobility, which is consistent with a general pattern that the strongest correlates of absolute upward mobility often tend to affect children before they enter the labor force.

Chapter 2. Neighborhoods and Segregation

Parts of this chapter summarize results and discussions presented in earlier work, particularly concentration of poverty figures from Jargowsky (2013) and segregation results from Jargowsky (2014a), although the figures presented herein have been updated to include ACS 2008–2012 data.

1. This analysis is based on American Community Survey (ACS) data collected over sixty months spanning 2008–2012; calculations by the author. See Jargowsky (2013) for a discussion of issues related to measuring the concentration of poverty.

2. The official categories are "White," "Black or African American," "American Indian and Alaska Native," "Asian," "Native Hawaiian and Other Pacific Islander," or "Some Other Race."

3. It should be noted that Asians consist of a number of heterogeneous groups, reflecting different countries of origin, cultures, and periods and circumstances of immigration to the United States. The trends in segregation for Asians represent an amalgamation of these differing populations. Separate analyses for the subgroups are highly desirable but beyond the scope of this chapter.

4. Jargowsky's measure was the neighborhood sorting index, which reflects the variance in income between neighborhoods as a proportion of the total variance. Reardon and Bischoff's measure was the rank order information theory index.

5. This analysis uses 2005–2009 ACS data and was previously reported in Jargowsky (2014a).

Chapter 3. The Changing Geography of Disadvantage

1. The figures on the national poverty rate and poor population come from the U.S. Census Bureau Current Population Survey. They are based on the official federal poverty thresholds and calculated based on gross, pre-tax income. Among other limitations, these figures do not take into account differences in the cost of living across places or tax-based or in-kind government benefits.

2. These estimates come from Brookings State of Metropolitan America Indicator Map: www.brookings.edu/research/interactives/state-of-metropolitan-america-indicator-map.

3. These numbers exclude census tracts with small populations (fewer than 500 people), or where college and graduate students make up more than 50 percent of residents. Contemporaneous census tract boundaries were used in each year.

4. This analysis uses official metropolitan statistical area definitions from 2009 and identifies the 100 largest metro areas based on population data from the 2010 Census. These regions range in size from Modesto, California (514,453), to the New York-Northern New Jersey-Long Island, NY-NJ-PA metro area (18,897,109), and together they represent two-thirds of the nation's population.

5. The impact of Hurricane Katrina meant that, even with poverty increases in the latter half of the decade, the region remained below pre-storm poverty levels by 2008–2012.

6. Madison, Wisconsin, did not contain a high-poverty neighborhood in 2000 or in 2008–2012, so its concentrated poverty rate remains zero.

7. Pittsburgh was the exception, as its concentrated poverty rate held statistically steady at roughly 6 percent.

8. Within the nation's largest metro areas, "cities" are defined as the first city that appears in the official metropolitan statistical area (MSA) name and any other city in

the MSA's title that had a population of 100,000 or more as of the 2010 Census. "Suburbs" are the remainder of the MSA outside the primary city (or cities). Small metro areas include all metropolitan statistical areas, based on 2009 definitions, outside the 100 largest MSAs. Nonmetro (or "rural") areas include all counties that are not a part of an official MSA.

9. For example, see Sharkey (2013) for a discussion.

Chapter 4. U.S. Workers' Diverging Locations: Causes and Inequality Consequences

1. Throughout this chapter I use "city" and "metropolitan area" synonymously. All analysis and discussion refers to metropolitan areas, which bundles together central cities with their surrounding suburbs, even though I refer to them as cities.

2. Estimates refer to workers employed at least thirty-five hours per week and fifty weeks per year, ages twenty-five to fifty-five. Controls include race, Hispanic origin, sex, and experience. Data are from 1980 and 2000 U.S. Censuses, and the 2011 American Community Survey.

3. Wages are controlled for housing cost. "High-skill city" is used as a short form for cities with a high share of high-skilled workers as defined above.

4. There are interesting life cycle dynamics related to which types of amenities are valued at different points of the life cycle and how these interact with which neighborhoods households choose to live in (e.g., city versus suburb.) This chapter focuses on choice of metropolitan area and abstracts away from neighborhood choice within the city. An interesting point of future research would be to explore how life-cycle dynamics interact with neighborhood choices and influence the provision of local amenities.

5. The impact of land use regulation on housing prices has also been studied by Glaeser, Gyourko, and Saks (2006). They show that land-use regulation creates a regulatory "tax" on land where the cost of complying with regulation constraints is reflected in land prices. The cost of buying and developing unused land is usually less than that of buying similar already developed land. This price "discount" to undeveloped land reflects the many hidden costs of complying with regulation.

6. See Quigley and Raphael (2004) for a discussion of the determinants of housing affordability and Linneman and Wachter (1989) for a discussion of the concept.

7. These data come from Zillow.com.

Chapter 5. Building Shared Prosperity Through Place-Conscious Strategies That Reweave the Goals of Fair Housing and Community Development

1. Most researchers use the poverty rate of a census tract as the primary proxy for neighborhood distress, with tract-level poverty rates above 30 or 40 percent serving as

indicators of severe distress (see Jargowsky 1997 for the seminal research on concentrated neighborhood poverty). However, not every neighborhood with a high rate of poverty suffers from the same degree of social and economic distress.

2. Some economists have argued that place-focused investments of this type are inherently inefficient because they merely relocate key assets (or problems) from one place to another, but others suggest that place-focused investments can yield important spillover benefits that increase welfare overall. For a thoughtful discussion of this debate, see Kline and Moretti (2013).

3. See Tach, Pendall, and Derian (2014) for a much more extensive discussion of the evidence regarding income mixing at differing geographic scales.

4. A demonstration of this approach, called the Bridges to Work Initiative, found no evidence of higher employment or earnings among participants than for a control group (Palubinsky and Watson 1997).

5. See for example, Pendall and Turner (2014), which presents analysis that groups metros into clusters based on regional economic, demographic, and equity indicators.

6. The administration has committed to partnering with up to 20 "Promise Zones" (not to be confused with Promise Neighborhoods), the first five of which were announced in 2014, providing access to technical assistance resources and expertise each zone needs to achieve its goals. Other recent initiatives of note include the Clinton administration's Empowerment Zones program, which focused primarily on job creation in inner-city locations. Empowerment Zones achieved spotty success and have not received much attention or follow-up. Clinton's Community Development Financial Institutions (CDFIs), however, have proven more durable and play a useful role providing credit and technical sophistication to fuel investment in underserved communities.

7. Section 3608 of the 1968 Fair Housing Act.

8. HUD, "Affirmatively Furthering Fair Housing Proposed Rule," May 14, 2015; see http://www.huduser.org/portal/affht_pt.html.

9. The new rule also encourages localities to work together to develop regional fair housing assessments, even when regions cross state boundaries. And it creates explicit opportunities for public review and input.

Chapter 7. Expanding Educational Opportunity in Urban School Districts

1. "[E]valuation of students who had applied to one or more of the 123 new small high schools of choice that opened . . . between September 2002 and September 2006 . . . [considered] more than 21,000 students, 93 percent of whom were black or Latino. Of that group, 83 percent came from low-income families, and more than two-thirds entered ninth grade reading below grade level" (G. Duncan and Murnane 2014).

Chapter 8. Preparing Today's Youth for Tomorrow's Jobs

1. Economists disagree as to whether labor shortages exist at all (Sumption 2011; Barnow, Trutko, and Piatak 2013; Salzman 2013). This is primarily because economic theory teaches us that wages move to restore equilibrium in labor markets. If particular skills are scarce, employers will raise wages and more workers will come forward or seek training to join the occupation. In practice, however, the lag between the signal of higher wages and the response of increased supply often results in short-term capacity scarcities. In some circumstances, periods of tight labor supply are short-lived, disappearing once supply adjusts to the temporarily increased demand. In other circumstances, however, shortages persist because demand rises at a faster pace than supply's ability to catch up, or the job might be inherently unappealing, or wage rigidities might halt wage increase necessary to precipitate the increased supply. Regardless, techniques for measuring the level of skills shortage in the labor force are complex and often controversial.

2. Preliminary estimates for the shortage extended to 2025 are very similar to the 2020 estimates due to the depth of the 2007 recession.

3. Not all credentials, however, are created equal. And in today's tight labor market, what you take, where you take it, and whether or not you work in field after taking it, all matter in determining post-college economic success (Carnevale, Rose, and Cheah 2011, Hoxby and Avery 2013). In this analysis, we consider only those credentials with labor market value, or credentials that are able to generate earnings of at least $35,000 per year.

4. Underqualification is not synonymous with undercredentialed. It is clear that many people hired in positions for which the average education level is higher than they currently possess, may have other desirable characteristics that they bring to bear on the job—such as experience or work ethic. Underqualification therefore is a purely relative term that compares one's current attainment level to that which is average for the occupation in question.

5. CRF (2015) define a bachelor's job as an occupational category for which a significant percentage of the workers have a bachelor's degree and/ or wages for bachelor's degree holders in this occupational category must be at or above the median wages for bachelor's degrees overall, with a reasonable premium over high school diplomas. This composite definition of a bachelor's degree job incorporates information on the preponderance of degree types as well as the median wages to determine whether a worker's education level is adequate for the job. In so doing, CRF take into account demand considerations also met—in addition to the education distribution—as determinants of the occupation's categorization.

6. The relatively lower wages paid to undercredentialed workers—on average— make the prima facie case for upskilling. In a market economy, where wages are the marginal product of labor, the fact that less credentialed workers systematically

make less implies they are relatively less productive than more credentialed workers in the same occupation.

7. In general, the regulation applies to most for-profit institutions and some non-profit and public institutions that provide certificate programs. But the greatest likely impact will be on for-profit colleges and universities.

Chapter 9. Labor-Demand-Side Economic Development Incentives and Urban Opportunity

1. Increasing local employment rates has some potential opportunity costs of reducing "leisure." But the stigma costs of involuntary unemployment are sufficient that the net benefits of reducing unemployment are probably at least equal to the earnings increase (Bartik 2015).

2. More formally, if we do everything in terms of logarithms, the following equations exactly hold:

$$\begin{aligned} \mathrm{d}\ln E &= \mathrm{d}\ln(E/P) + \mathrm{d}\ln P = \mathrm{d}\ln(E/L) + \mathrm{d}\ln(L/P) + \mathrm{d}\ln P \\ &= \mathrm{d}\ln(1 - U) + \mathrm{d}\ln(LFPR) + \mathrm{d}\ln P, \text{ and if } U \text{ is close to zero,} \\ &\approx -\mathrm{d}U + \mathrm{d}\ln(LFPR) + \mathrm{d}\ln P, \end{aligned}$$

where d indicates a change in a variable over some time period, E is employment, P is population, L is the labor force, U is the unemployment rate, and $LFPR$ is the labor force participation rate.

3. These equations simplify the analysis by ignoring that costs and benefits vary over time, so these equations should be interpreted as average annual figures.

4. Annual costs in forgone revenue from lower business taxes is equal to average state and local business tax revenue per job, divided by the negative of the elasticity of business activity with respect to state and local business taxes (Bartik and Hollenbeck 2012). The cost of an incentive per job created, ignoring fiscal effects of the job increase, is $\mathrm{d}B^*J/\mathrm{d}J$, where J is private jobs, $\mathrm{d}J$ is the induced private jobs, B is state and local business tax revenue per job, and $\mathrm{d}B$ is the change in that variable. The elasticity of business activity with respect to state and local business taxes is $E = (\mathrm{d}J/J)/(\mathrm{d}B/B)$. With some substitution, $\mathrm{d}B^*J/\mathrm{d}J = B/(-E)$. State and local business tax revenue per private sector job is \$6,053, based on the findings of Phillips et al. (2013). At an elasticity of -0.2, the cost of inducing jobs is \$6,053/0.2 = \$30,000.

5. The \$1,300 annual costs of typical state and local business tax incentives comes from Peters and Fisher (2002), updated to 2013 dollars. The assumption is that new business location decisions have a similar sensitivity to the long-run business tax elasticity. This will occur, for example, if business death rates are fixed, and new business location decisions drive long-run responsiveness of business activity with respect to

local costs. The available evidence indicates that elasticities of new business locations are similar to long-run business tax elasticities (Wasylenko 1997; Bartik 1991).

6. Under special circumstances, incentives might allow efficiency gains. Suppose we finance the incentives by an efficient tax. If the incentives are modeled as reducing the marginal tax burden on investment and job creation, then the incentives can be viewed as allowing an efficient expansion of business activity. However, national effects of marginal cost reductions will be far lower than local effects, as local effects include job relocations. National job creation effects might be 10 to 20 percent of local effects (Bartik 2011). Furthermore, discretionary incentives may not affect all firms at the margin, which reduces the efficiency gain. In addition, subsidizing export-base businesses produces an efficiency loss from distorting business activity across industries.

7. The −0.2 business elasticity, if firms use a 12 percent discount rate (L. Summers and Poterba 1994), implies present value costs from the firm's perspective of $282, 000 to create one job. Suppose some business service increases productivity by k times its one-time cost, and that this cost reduction then depreciates at rate d. The present value of this cost reduction per dollar of public one-time cost is $k(1+r)/(r+d)$, where r is the firm's discount rate. $282,000 divided by this amount then gives the one-time public sector cost of creating the equivalent of one full-time permanent job. The annual equivalent cost is equal to s times this one-time payment, where s is the social discount rate.

8. These are annual costs to create the equivalent of a permanent job. They are calculated by multiplying the one-time cost per job created by 3 percent plus 25 percent, which accounts for both social discounting and job depreciation.

9. Tax incentives could also be provided up front, but then this requires recovering the cash if the firm leaves via clawback contracts (Weber 2007). This is less of an issue for customized services because the firm will lose trained workers and services if it leaves.

10. This calculation takes the $600 million in Social Services Block Grants and allocates these equally to each year from 1994 to 2003. It also assumes that $55 million in tax credits for hiring occur each year from 1994 to 2003. I adjust these numbers to 2013 dollars, and discount the present value to the year 2000, the year in which Busso et al. (2013) observe the employment effects.

11. This multiplies the $22,000 by 28 percent to get the annual cost for the equivalent of one permanent job.

Chapter 11. The Fragility of Growth in a Post-Industrial City

The author wishes to thank his colleague Ken Gross, Ph.D for his assistance with census research and bibliographic citations.

1. The Center City District is a private-sector sponsored organization with a mission "to enhance the vitality of Center City Philadelphia as a thriving 24-hour downtown and a great place to live, work or have fun," http://www.centercityphila.org/.

2. 54 percent of University City residents twenty-five or older have a bachelor's or advanced degree (University City District 2014).

3. In Forbes 2013 "Cost of Business Rank" Philadelphia ranked 173rd of 200 cities (Badenhausen 2013).

4. Cities with percentage of movers into the city with a BA degree or higher greater than Philadelphia's rate: Atlanta, Seattle, San Francisco, Boston, Washington, Chicago.

5. For Austin, Denver, Atlanta, Seattle, San Francisco, Boston, and Washington new movers each year with a college degree or higher represent greater than 2.5 percent of each city's total population.

6. The standards address staff qualifications and professional development, the early-learning program, partnerships with family and community, and leadership and management. More information on the PA Keystone Stars early childhood facility assessment can be found at http://www.pakeys.org/.

7. Calculations were made by aggregating school level PSSA results provided by the Pennsylvania Department of Education, http://www.portal.state.pa.us/portal/server.pt /community/school_assessments/7442.

8. These organizations are referred to by different names, which include business improvement districts, business improvement areas, business revitalization zones, community improvement districts, special service areas, and special improvement districts.

9. For more detail on the city's NTI plan see http://www.phila.gov/ohcd/conplan31 /strategy.pdf.

10. For the NTI project the Reinvestment Fund created the Market Value Analysis methodology to classify neighborhoods by housing market type and the spatial representation of these classifications. More information on the method can be found at http://www.trfund.com/policy/public-policy/market-value-analysis/.

Chapter 12. Fostering an Inclusive Metropolis: Equity, Growth, and Community

1. These are discussed more fully in a forthcoming book (Benner and Pastor 2015b).

2. The actual specification of our hazard model was a Cox regression, a statistical strategy that examines the likelihood an event will occur at time t, with the event being a fall from (sustained employment growth) grace. Methodological details are available in Benner and Pastor (2015a), but suffice it to say that we were careful to control for a variety of important technical issues that would affect the analysis, including issues of data censoring (when the spell might have begun before the first year available in the data or continue beyond the end of the available data) as well as the proper timing of the initial variables (so that their values are taken before the growth spell and not during the growth spell to clarify issues of causality).

3. Note that the actual range of possible quarters of growth over the twenty-one-year period is actually 80 since the measure of growth is year over year and so the first year is lost to the count; as a result, 70 quarters of growth spells is impressive indeed.

4. Dave Leip, *Atlas of U.S. Presidential Elections* website, http://uselectionatlas.org/.

5. For a series of technical reasons explained in Benner and Pastor (2015a), the Gini used in the multivariate specifications is actually detrended from its high correlation with the education measure; in fact, this is a reasonable approach as it gets us to consider the level of inequality more associated with political or social factors than economic structural factors.

6. To investigate that, we dropped the spatial sorting variable and the city-suburb poverty ratio did indeed return to significance.

REFERENCES

Abel, Jaison R., Richard Deitz, and Yaqin Su. 2014. "Are Recent College Graduates Finding Good Jobs?" *Current Issues in Economics and Finance* (Federal Reserve Bank of New York) 20 (1).

Abramson, Alan J., and Mitchell S. Tobin. 1994. *The Changing Geography of Metropolitan Opportunity: The Segregation of the Poor in U.S. Metropolitan Areas, 1970 to 1990.* Washington, D.C.: Fannie Mae Office of Housing Policy Research.

Abramson, Alan J., Mitchell S. Tobin, and Matthew R. VanderGoot. 1995. "The Changing Geography of Metropolitan Opportunity: The Segregation of the Poor in U.S. Metropolitan Areas, 1970 to 1990." *Housing Policy Debate* 6 (1): 45–72.

Acemoglu, Daron. 2002. "Directed Technical Change." *Review of Economic Studies* 69 (4): 781–809.

———. 2003. "Patterns of Skill Premia." *Review of Economic Studies* 70 (243): 199–230.

Adler, Emanual, and Peter Haas. 1992. "Epistemic Communities, World Order and the Creation of a Reflective Research Program." *International Organization* 46 (1): 367–90.

Aghion, Philippe, Eve Caroli, and Cecilia García-Peñalosa. 1999. "Inequality and Economic Growth: The Perspective of the New Growth Theories." *Journal of Economic Literature* 37, 4: 1615–60.

Alba, Richard D. 1985. *Italian Americans: Into the Twilight of Ethnicity.* Englewood Cliffs, N.J.: Prentice Hall.

———. 1992. *Ethnic Identity: The Transformation of White America.* New Haven, Conn.: Yale University Press.

Alesina, Alberto, and Roberto Perotti. 1996. "Income Distribution, Political Instability, and Investment." *European Economic Review* 40: 1203–28.

Alesina, Alberto, and Dani Rodrik. 1994. "Distributive Politics and Economic Growth." *Quarterly Journal of Economics* 109, 2: 465–90.

Allard, Scott W., and Benjamin Roth. 2010. "Strained Suburbs: The Social Service Challenges of Rising Suburban Poverty." Metropolitan Opportunity Series 7. Washington, D.C.: Brookings Institution.

Amezcua, Alejandro S., Matthew G. Grimes, Steven W. Bradley, and Johan Wiklund. 2013. "Organizational Sponsorship and Founding Environments: A Contingency View on the Survival of Business-Incubated Firms, 1994–2007." *Academy of Management Journal* 56 (6): 1628–54.

Anderson, Judith, Debra Hollinger, and Joseph Conaty. 1992. "Poverty and Achieve-
ment: Re-Examining the Relationship Between School Poverty and Student
Achievement: An Examination of Eighth Grade Student Achievement Using the
National Education Longitudinal Study of 1988." Paper presented at the Annual
Meeting of the American Educational Research Association, San Francisco,
April 20–24, 1992. http://eric.ed.gov/?id=ED346207.

Anderson, Michael L. 2008. "Multiple Inference and Gender Differences in the Effects of
Early Intervention: A Reevaluation of the Abecedarian, Perry Preschool, and Early
Training Projects." *Journal of the American Statistical Association* 103 (484): 1481–95.

Andrews, Rodney, Stephen L. DesJardins, and Vimal Ranchhod. 2010. "The Effects of
the Kalamazoo Promise on Student College Choice." *Economics of Education Review* 29 (5): 722–37.

Angrist, Joshua D., Susan M. Dynarski, Thomas J. Kane, Parag A. Pathak, and Christopher R. Walters. 2010a. "Who Benefits from KIPP?" NBER Working Paper 15740.
Cambridge, Mass.: National Bureau of Economic Research.

———. 2010b. "Inputs and Impacts in Charter Schools: KIPP Lynn." *American Economic Review* 100 (2): 239–43.

Annie E. Casey Foundation. 2015. "Expanding Economic Opportunity: Lessons from
the East Baltimore Revitalization Initiative." Report. Baltimore: Annie E. Casey
Foundation.

Arab American Institute Foundation. Michigan. 2011. Data on Arab American Population.

Aretha, David. 2001. *With All Deliberate Speed: Court-Ordered Busing and American
Schools.* Greensboro, N.C.: Morgan Reynolds.

Autor, David H. 2014. "Skills, Education, and the Rise of Earnings Inequality Among
the 'Other 99 Percent.'" *Science* 344 (6186): 843–51.

Autor, David H., and David Dorn. 2013. "The Growth of Low-Skill Service Jobs and the
Polarization of the US Labor Market." *American Economic Review* 103 (5): 1553–97.

Autor, David H., David Dorn, and Gordon H. Hanson. 2013. "The China Syndrome:
Local Labor Market Effects of Import Competition in the United States." *American
Economic Review* 103 (6): 2121–68.

Autor, David H., Lawrence F. Katz, and Alan B. Krueger. 1998. "Computing Inequality:
Have Computers Changed the Labor Market?" *Quarterly Journal of Economics*
113 (4): 1169–1213.

Badenhausen, Kurt, ed. 2013. "Best Places for Business and Careers." *Forbes.com*, Au-
gust 7. Retrieved March 27, 2014. http://www.forbes.com/best-places-for-business
/list/#page:1_sort:2_direction:asc_search:_filter:All%20states.

Bailey, Martin J., and Susan M. Dynarski. 2011. "Gains and Gaps: Changing Inequality in U.S. College Entry and Completion." NBER Working Paper 17633, December. Cambridge, Mass.: National Bureau of Economic Research.

Balfanz, Robert, and Nettie Legters. 2004. "Locating the Dropout Crisis: Which High
Schools Produce the Nation's Dropouts? Where Are They Located? Who Attends

Them? Report 70." Center for Research on the Education of Students Placed at Risk CRESPAR. http://files.eric.ed.gov/fulltext/ED484525.pdf.

Baltimore Neighborhood Indicators Alliance. 2012. "Percent of Properties That Are Vacant and Abandoned by Community Statistical Area, 2012." http://bniajfi.org/wp-content/uploads/2014/04/Vacants-2012.jpg, retrieved May 31, 2014.

Barnett, W. Steven, Megan E. Carolan, James H. Squires, and Kirsty Clarke Brown. 2013. *The State of Preschool 2013: State Preschool Yearbook.* New Brunswick, N.J.: National Institute for Early Education Research.

Barnow, Burt S., John Trutko, and Jaclyn Schede Piatak. 2013. "How Do We Know Occupational Labor Shortages Exist?" *Employment Research Newsletter* (W. E. Upjohn Institute for Employment Research) 20 (2).

Barrington, Wendy E., Mai Stafford, Mark Hamer, Shirley A. A. Beresford, Thomas Koepsell, and Andrew Steptoe. 2014. "Neighborhood Socioeconomic Deprivation, Perceived Neighborhood Factors, and Cortisol Responses to Induced Stress Among Healthy Adults." *Health & Place* 27: 120–26.

Bartik, Timothy J. 1991. *Who Benefits from State and Local Economic Development Policies?* Kalamazoo, Mich.: W. E. Upjohn Institute for Employment Research.

———. 1993. "Economic Development and Black Economic Success." Upjohn Institute Technical Report 93-001. Kalamazoo, Mich.: W. E. Upjohn Institute for Employment Research.

———. 2001. *Jobs for the Poor: Can Labor Demand Policies Help?* Kalamazoo, Mich.: W. E. Upjohn Institute for Employment Research.

———. 2005. "Solving the Problems of Economic Development Incentives." *Growth and Change* 36 (2): 139–66.

———. 2010. "Bringing Jobs to People: How Federal Policy Can Target Job Creation for Economically Distressed Areas." Hamilton Project Discussion Paper. Washington, D.C.: Brookings Institution.

———. 2011. *Investing in Kids: Early Childhood Programs and Local Economic Development.* Kalamazoo, Mich.: Upjohn Institute.

———. 2013. "Effects of the Pre-K Program of Kalamazoo County Ready 4s on Kindergarten Entry Test Scores: Estimates Based on Data from the Fall of 2011 and the Fall of 2012." Upjohn Institute Working Paper 13-198. Kalamazoo, Mich.: Upjohn Institute.

———. 2015. "How Effects of Local Labor Demand Shocks Vary with the Initial Local Unemployment Rate." *Growth and Change* (forthcoming).

Bartik, Timothy J., and John H. Bishop. 2009. "The Job Creation Tax Credit: Dismal Projects for Employment Call for a Quick, Efficient, and Effective Response." Brief Paper 248. Washington, D.C.: Economic Policy Institute.

Bartik, Timothy J., Randall Eberts, and Wei-Jang Huang. 2010. "The Kalamazoo Promise, and Enrollment and Achievement Trends in Kalamazoo Public Schools." Paper presented at PromiseNet 2010 Conference, Kalamazoo, Mich., June 16–18.

Bartik, Timothy J., and George Erickcek. 2014. "Simulating the Effects of the Tax Credit Program of the Michigan Economic Growth Authority on Job Creation and Fiscal Benefits." *Economic Development Quarterly* 28 (4): 314–27.

Bartik, Timothy J., William T. Gormley, Jr., and Shirley Adelstein. 2012. "Earnings Benefits of Tulsa's Pre-K Program for Different Income Groups." *Economics of Education Review* 31 (6): 1143–61.

Bartik, Timothy J., and Kevin Hollenbeck. 2012. "An Analysis of the Employment Effects of the Washington High Technology Business and Occupation (B&O) Tax Credit: Technical Report." Upjohn Institute Working Paper 12-187. Kalamazoo, Mich.: Upjohn Institute.

Bartik, Timothy J., and Marta Lachowska. 2013. "The Short-Term Effects of the Kalamazoo Promise Scholarship on Student Outcomes." *Research in Labor Economics* 38: 37–76.

Bates, Timothy. 2009. "Utilizing Affirmative Action in Public Sector Procurement as a Local Economic Development Strategy." *Economic Development Quarterly* 23 (3): 180–92.

Batt, Rosemary, and Paul Osterman. 1993. "Workplace Training Policy: Case Studies of State and Local Experiments." Working Paper 106. Washington, D.C.: Economic Policy Institute.

Beaudry, Paul, Mark Doms, and Ethan Lewis. 2010. "Should the Personal Computer Be Considered a Technological Revolution? Evidence from U.S. Metropolitan Areas." *Journal of Political Economy* 118 (5): 988–1036.

Becker, Carol, and Seth Grossman. 2010. *Census of United States BIDs*. Washington, D.C.: International Downtown Association.

Benner, C. 2003. "Learning Communities in a Learning Region: The Soft Infrastructure of Cross-Firm Learning Networks in Silicon Valley." *Environment and Planning A* 35 (10): 1809–30.

Benner, C., and M. Pastor. 2012. *Just Growth: Inclusion and Prosperity in America's Metropolitan Regions*. New York: Routledge.

———. 2015a. "Brother, Can You Spare Some Time? Sustaining Prosperity and Social Inclusion in America's Metropolitan Regions." *Urban Studies* 52 (7): 1339–56.

———. 2015b. *Equity, Growth and Community: What the Nation Can Learn from America's Metro Areas*. Berkeley: University of California Press.

Benus, Jacob M., Michelle L. Wood, and Neelima Grover. 1994. "A Comparative Analysis of the Washington and Massachusetts UI Self-Employment Demonstrations." Report to U.S. Department of Labor, Employment and Training Administration. Unemployment Insurance Service. Cambridge, Mass.: Abt Associates.

Berg, A., J. D. Ostry, and J. Zettelmeyer. 2012. "What Makes Growth Sustained?" *Journal of Development Economics* 98 (2): 149–66.

Berry, Christopher R., and Edward L. Glaeser. 2005. "The Divergence of Human Capital Levels Across Cities." *Papers in Regional Science* 84 (3): 407–44.

Berube, Alan, and Elizabeth Kneebone. 2006. "Two Steps Back: City and Suburban Poverty Trends 1999–2005." Washington, D.C.: Brookings Institution.

Birdsall, N., D. Ross, and R. Sabot. 1995. "Inequality and Growth Reconsidered: Lessons from East Asia." *World Bank Economic Review* 9(3): 477.

Bischoff, Kendra, and Sean F. Reardon. 2013. "Residential Segregation by Income, 1970–2009." Providence, R.I.: Spatial Structures in the Social Sciences, Brown University. http://www.s4.brown.edu/us2010/Data/Report/report10162013.pdf

Bishop, John II. 1993. "Improving Job Matches in the U.S. Labor Market." *Brookings Papers on Economic Activity: Microeconomics*, 335–400.

Blank, Rebecca M., Marilyn Dabady, and Constance F. Citro, eds. 2004. *Measuring Racial Discrimination*. Washington, D.C.: National Academy Press.

Blau, Francine, and Lawrence Kahn. 2007. "The Gender Pay Gap: Have Women Gone as Far as They Can?" *Academy of Management Perspectives*, 7–23.

Bloom, Howard S., and Rebecca Unterman. 2013. "Sustained Progress: New Findings About the Effectiveness and Operation of Small Public High Schools of Choice in New York City." MDRC.

Bluestone, Barry, and Bennett Harrison. 1982. *The Deindustrialization of America: Plant Closings, Community Abandonment, and the Dismantling of Basic Industry*. New York: Basic.

Bobo, Lawrence D. 1989. "Keeping the Linchpin in Place: Testing the Multiple Sources of Opposition to Residential Integration." *International Review of Social Psychology* 2: 305–23.

Borjas, George J. 1998. "To Ghetto or Not to Ghetto: Ethnicity and Residential Segregation." *Journal of Urban Economics* 44: 228–53.

Boserup, Simon, Wojciech Kopczuk, and Claus Kreiner. 2013. "Intergenerational Wealth Mobility: Evidence from Danish Wealth Records of Three Generations." University of Copenhagen mimeo.

Briggs, Xavier de Souza, Susan J. Popkin, and John Goering. 2010. *Moving to Opportunity: The Story of an American Experiment to Fight Ghetto Poverty*. New York: Oxford University Press.

Brightline Defense Project. 2012. "Putting Local Hire to Work." Brightline Report. San Francisco: Brightline Defense Project.

Brooks-Gunn, Jeanne, Greg J. Duncan, and J. Lawrence Aber, eds. 1997. *Neighborhood Poverty*. Vol. 2, *Policy Implications in Studying Neighborhoods*. New York: Russell Sage.

Brooks-Gunn, Jeanne, Greg J. Duncan, Pamela Kato Klebanov, and Naomi Sealand. 1993. "Do Neighborhoods Influence Child and Adolescent Development?" *American Journal of Sociology* 99 (2): 353–95.

Brushaw, W. J., and S. J. Lopez. 2013. "The 45th Annual PDK/Gallup Poll of the Public's Attitudes Toward the Public Schools." Phi Delta Kappa International, September. http://pdkintl.org/noindex/2013_PDKGallup.pdf, retrieved April 1, 2014.

Bulkley, K., J. R. Henig, and H. M. Levin. 2010. *Between Public and Private Politics, Governance and the New Portfolio Models for Urban School Reform.* Cambridge, Mass.: Harvard Education Press.

Burdick-Will, Julia, Jens Ludwig, Stephen W. Raudenbusch, Robert J. Sampson, Lisa Sanbonmatsu, and Patrick Sharkey. 2011. "Converging Evidence for Neighborhood Effects on Children's Test Scores: An Experimental, Quasi-Experimental, and Observational Comparison." In *Whither Opportunity? Rising Inequality, Schools, and Children's Life Chances,* ed. Greg J. Duncan and Richard J. Murnane, 255–76. New York: Russell Sage.

Bureau of Labor Statistics. 2004. "Unemployed New Entrants and Reentrants to the Labor Force." LAUS Research Report.

Burtless, Gary. 1985. "Are Targeted Wage Subsidies Harmful? Evidence from a Wage Voucher Experiment." *Industrial and Labor Relations Review* 39 (1): 105–14.

Bush-Baskette, Stephanie R., Kelly Robinson, and Peter Simmons. 2011. "Residential and Social Outcomes for Residents Living in Housing Certified by the New Jersey Council on Affordable Housing." *Rutgers Law Review* 63 (3): 879–904.

Busso, Matias, Jesse Gregory, and Patrick Kline. 2013. "Assessing the Incidence and Efficiency of a Prominent Place Based Policy." *American Economic Review* 103 (2): 897–947.

Campbell, Frances A., Craig T. Ramey, Elizabeth Pungello, Joseph Sparling, and Shari Miller-Johnson. 2002. "Early Childhood Education: Young Adult Outcomes from the Abecedarian Project." *Applied Developmental Science* 6 (1): 42–57.

Card, David and John E. DiNardo. 2002. "Skill-Biased Technological Change and Rising Wage Inequality: Some Problems and Puzzles." *Journal of Labor Economics* 20 (4): 733–83.

Cárdenas, Vanessa, and Sarah Treuhaft, eds. 2013. "All-In Nation: An America That Works for All." PolicyLink and Center for American Progress.

Carey, N. 2013. "Detroit Blight Battle to Take Down Abandoned Buildings Could Be Key to Bankrupt City's Survival." Huffpost Detroit, July 25.

Carnevale, Anthony P., Tamara Jayasundera, and Ban Cheah. 2012. "The College Advantage: Weathering the Economic Storm." Washington, D.C.: Georgetown University Center on Education and the Workforce.

Carnevale, Anthony P., Stephen J. Rose, and Ban Cheah. 2011. "The College Payoff: Education, Occupations, Lifetime Earnings." Washington, D.C.: Georgetown University Center on Education and the Workforce.

Carnevale, Anthony P., Stephen J. Rose, and Megan Fasules. 2015. *Mismatch: Defining and Explaining Over and Underqualified Workers.* Washington, D.C.: Georgetown University Center on Education and the Workforce.

Carnevale, Anthony P., Stephen J. Rose, and Jeff Strohl. 2014. "Achieving Racial and Economic Diversity with Race-Blind Admissions Policy." In *The Future of Affirmative Action: New Paths to Higher Education Diversity After Fisher v. University of Texas,* ed. Richard Kahlenberg. Washington D.C.: Century Foundation Press.

Carnevale, Anthony P., Nicole Smith, and Jeff Strohl. 2010. "Help Wanted: Projections of Jobs and Education Requirements Through 2018." Washington, D.C.: Georgetown University Center on Education and the Workforce.

———. 2013. "Recovery: Job Growth and Education Requirements Through 2020." Washington, D.C.: Georgetown University Center on Education and the Workforce.

Carnevale, Anthony P., and Jeff Strohl. 2013. "Separate and Unequal: How Higher Education Reinforces the Intergenerational Reproduction of White Racial Privilege." Washington, D.C.: Georgetown University Center on Education and the Workforce.

Carnevale, Anthony P., Jeff Strohl, and Michelle Melton. 2011. "What's It Worth: The Economic Value of College Majors." Washington, D.C.: Georgetown University Center on Education and the Workforce.

Carr, James H., and Nandinee K. Kutty. 2008. *Segregation: The Rising Costs for America*. New York: Routledge.

Carrillo-Tudela, Carlos, Bart Hobijn, and Ludo Visschers. 2014. "Career Changes Decline During Recessions." *FRBSF Economic Letter* 2014–9, Federal Reserve Bank of San Francisco.

Cascio, Elizabeth U., and Diane Whitmore Schanzenbach. 2013. "The Impacts of Expanding Access to High-Quality Preschool Education." NBER Working Paper 19735. Cambridge, Mass.: National Bureau of Economic Research.

Cashin, Sheryll. 2014. *Place, Not Race: A New Vision of Opportunity in America*. Boston: Beacon.

Center City District and Central Philadelphia Development Corporation. 2013. "State of Center City Philadelphia 2013."

———. 2014. "Center City Reports: Pathways to Job Growth," January. https://www.centercityphila.org/docs/CCR14_employment.pdf.

Chen, V., and S. L. Pong. 2014. "Within-District Effects of Catholic Schooling on 12th Grade Math Achievement." *Journal of School Choice* 8: 1–19.

Chetty, Raj, John N. Friedman, Nathaniel Hilger, Emmanuel Saez, Diane Whitmore Schanzenbach, and Danny Yagan. 2011. "How Does Your Kindergarten Classroom Affect Your Earnings? Evidence from Project STAR." *Quarterly Journal of Economics* 126 (4): 1593–1660.

Chetty, Raj, John N. Friedman, and Jonah E. Rockoff. 2014. "Measuring the Impacts of Teachers II: Teacher Value-Added and Student Outcomes in Adulthood." *American Economic Review* 104 (9): 2633–79.

Chetty, Raj, Nathaniel Hendren, and Lawrence Katz. 2015. "The Effects of Exposure to Better Neighborhoods on Children: New Evidence from the Moving to Opportunity Experiment." Harvard University unpublished manuscript.

Chetty, Raj, Nathaniel Hendren, Patrick Kline, and Emmanuel Saez. 2014. "Where Is the Land of Opportunity? The Geography of Intergenerational Mobility in the United States." NBER Working Paper 19843. Boston: National Bureau of Economic Research.

Chetty, Raj, Nathaniel Hendren, Patrick Kline, Emmanuel Saez, and Nicholas Turner. 2014a. "Is the United States Still a Land of Opportunity? Recent Trends in Intergenerational Mobility." *American Economic Review Papers and Proceedings*, May.

———. 2014b. "Where Is the Land of Opportunity? The Geography of Intergenerational Mobility in the United States." *Quarterly Journal of Economics* 129 (4): 1553–1623.

Chrisman, James J. 2002. "Economic Impact of Small Business Development Center Counseling Activities in the United States: 2000–2001." Report for Association of Small Business Development Center.

Chrisman, James J., Ed McMullan, and Jeremy Hall. 2005. "The Influence of Guided Preparation on the Long-Term Performance of New Ventures." *Journal of Business Venturing* 20: 769–91.

Christensen, C. M., M. B. Horn, and C. W. Johnson. 2008. *Disrupting Class: How Disruptive Innovation Will Change the Way the World Learns.* New York: McGraw-Hill.

City of Philadelphia. 2002. "The Mayor's Operating Budget in Brief for Fiscal Year 2003," May. http://www.phila.gov/pdfs/Budget_in_Brief.pdf.

———. 2012. "The Mayor's Operating Budget in Brief for Fiscal Year 2013," March. http://www.phila.gov/pdfs/Mayors_Operating_Budget_In_Brief_FY2013.pdf.

City of Portland, Oregon. Bureau of Planning and Sustainability. Date? "Clean Energy Works Portland." https://www.portlandoregon.gov/bps/article/431322, accessed April 2015.

Clampet-Lundquist, Susan, and Douglas S. Massey. 2008. "Neighborhood Effects on Economic Self-Sufficiency: A Reconsideration of the Moving to Opportunity Experiment." *American Journal of Sociology* 114 (1): 107–43.

Clark, Gregory. 2014. "Your Ancestors, Your Fate." *New York Times*, February 21.

Clark, William A. V., and Jun L. Onaka. 1983. "Life Cycle and Housing Adjustment as Explanations of Residential Mobility." *Urban Studies* 20 (1): 47–57.

Clinch, Richard P. 2009. The Workforce Supply and Demand Characteristics of the East Baltimore Development Inc. Redevelopment Effort. Report. Jacob France Institute.

Cochrane, Steven, Sophia Koropeckyj, Aaron Smith, and Sean Ellis. 2014. "Central Cities and Metropolitan Areas: Manufacturing and Nonmanufacturing Employment as Drivers of Growth." In *Revitalizing American Cities*, ed. Susan M. Wachter and Kimberly A. Zeuli, 65–80. Philadelphia: University of Pennsylvania Press.

Coleman, James S., Ernest Q. Campbell, Carol J. Hobson, James McPartland, Alexander M. Mood, Frederic D. Weinfeld, and Robert York. 1966. "Equality of Educational Opportunity." Washington, D.C., 1066–5684.

Congressional Budget Office. 2014. "The Slow Recovery of the Labor Market."

Corak, Miles. 2013. "Income Inequality, Equality of Opportunity, and Intergenerational Mobility." *Journal of Economic Perspectives* 27 (3): 79–102.

Corak, Miles, and Andrew Heisz. 1999. "The Intergenerational Earnings and Income Mobility of Canadian Men: Evidence from Longitudinal Income Tax Data." *Journal of Human Resources* 34 (3): 504–33.

Coulton, Claudia J., Brett Theodos, and Margery Austin Turner. 2009. "Family Mobility and Neighborhood Change: New Evidence and Implications for Community Initiatives." Washington, D.C.: Urban Institute.

Covington, Kenya, Lance Freeman, and Michael Stoll. 2011. "The Suburbanization of Housing Choice Voucher Recipients." Washington, D.C.: Brookings Institution.

Cowley, Stacy. 2014. "Hanging a Shingle in Detroit." *New York Times*, April 17.

Cronin, J. M. 2011. *Reforming Boston Schools, 1930 to the Present: Overcoming Corruption and Racial Segregation*. New York: Palgrave Studies in Urban Education, Palgrave Macmillan.

Currie, Janet. 2011. "Health and Life Chances." In *Neighborhood and Life Chances: How Place Matters in Modern America*, ed. Harriet B. Newburger, Eugenie L. Birch, and Susan M. Wachter, 3–17. Philadelphia: University of Pennsylvania Press.

Currie, Janet, and Duncan Thomas. 1995. "Does Head Start Make a Difference?" *American Economic Review* 85 (3): 341–64.

Cutler, David M., and Edward L. Glaeser. 1997. "Are Ghettos Good or Bad?" *Quarterly Journal of Economics* 112 (3): 827–72.

Cutler, David M., Edward L. Glaeser, and Jacob L. Vigdor. 1999. "The Rise and Decline of the American Ghetto." *Journal of Political Economy* 107 (3): 455–506.

Dale, Stacy Berg, and Alan B. Krueger. 2002. "Estimating the Payoff to Attending a More Selective College: An Application of Selection Based on Observables and Unobservables." *Quarterly Journal of Economics* 117 (4) (November): 1491–1527.

Darling-Hammond, Linda. 2009. "President Obama and Education: The Possibility for Dramatic Improvements in Teaching and Learning." *Harvard Educational Review* 79 (2): 210–23.

Darrah, Jennifer, and Stefanie DeLuca. 2014. "Living Here Has Changed My Whole Perspective: How Escaping Inner-City Poverty Shapes Neighborhood and Housing Choice." *Journal of Policy Analysis and Management* 33 (2): 350–84.

Davidson, Chandler, and Bernard Grofman. 1994. *Quiet Revolution in the South: The Impact of the Voting Rights Act 1965–1990*. Princeton, N.J.: Princeton University Press.

De Sousa, Christopher A. 2013. "Publicly Subsidized Brownfields Redevelopment." In *Financing Economic Development in the 21st Century*, 2nd ed., ed. Sammis B. White and Zenia Z. Kotval, 150–67. New York: M.E. Sharpe.

DeGenova, Alexandra, Brendan Goodwin, Shannon Moriarty, and Jeremy Robitaille. 2009. "On the Ground: 40B Developments Before and After." Medford, Mass.: Tufts University Department of Urban and Environmental Policy and Planning.. http://community-wealth.org/sites/clone.community-wealth.org/files/downloads/report-de_genova-et-al.pdf, accessed June 27, 2014.

DeLuca, Stefanie, and Peter Rosenblatt. 2011. "Increasing Access to High Performing Schools in an Assisted Housing Voucher Program." In *Finding Common Ground: Coordinating Housing and Education Policy to Promote Integration*, ed. Philip Tegeler, 35–42. Washington, D.C.: Poverty and Race Research Action Council.

DeNavas-Walt, Carmen, Bernadette Proctor, and Jessica Smith. 2013. "Income, Poverty, and Health Insurance Coverage in the United States: 2012." Current Population Reports. Washington, D.C.: U.S. Census Bureau.

Denhardt, R. B., and J. V. Denhardt. 2007. *The New Public Service: Serving Rather Than Steering.* New York: M. E. Sharpe.

Deninger, K., and L. Squire. 1996. "Measuring Income Inequality: A New Database." *World Bank Economic Review* 10 (3): 565–91.

Department of Health and Human Services. 2014. "Annual Update of the HHS Poverty Guidelines." *Federal Register* 9 (14): 3593–94.

Desforges, Charles, and Alberto Abouchaar. 2003. *The Impact of Parental Involvement, Parental Support and Family Education on Pupil Achievement and Adjustment: A Review of Literature.* London: DfES Publications.

Detroit Future City. 2012. "Detroit Strategic Framework Plan." Report. Detroit Future City.

Diamond, Rebecca. 2013. "The Determinants and Welfare Implications of US Workers' Diverging Location Choices by Skill: 1980–2000." Stanford University, mimeograph. http://web.stanford.edu/~diamondr/jmp_final_all_files.pdf.

Dickens, William T. 2011. "Has the Recession Increased the NAIRU?" Northeastern University and Brookings Institution. Working Paper.

DiNardo, J., N. Fortin, and T. Lemieux. 1996. "Labor Market Institutions and the Distribution of Wages, 1973–1992: A Semiparametric Approach." *Econometrica* 64 (95): 1001–44.

Dobbie, Will, and Roland G. Fryer, Jr. 2009. "Are High Quality Schools Enough to Close the Achievement Gap? Evidence from a Social Experiment in Harlem." NBER Working Paper 15473. Cambridge, Mass.: National Bureau of Economic Research.

———. 2011. "Are High-Quality Schools Enough to Increase Achievement Among the Poor? Evidence from the Harlem Children's Zone." *American Economic Journal: Applied Economics* 3 (3): 158–87.

Duncan, Cynthia. 1999. *Worlds Apart: Why Poverty Persists in Rural America.* New Haven, Conn.: Yale University Press.

Duncan, Greg J., and Richard J. Murnane, eds. 2011. *Whither Opportunity? Rising Inequality, Schools, and Children's Life Chances.* New York: Russell Sage.

———. 2014. *Restoring Opportunity: The Crisis of Inequality and the Challenge for American Education.* Cambridge, Mass.: Harvard Education Press.

Duncan, Otis Dudley. 1969. "Inheritance of Poverty or Inheritance of Race?" In *On Understanding Poverty*, ed. Daniel P. Moynihan, 85–110. New York: Basic.

Duncan, Otis Dudley, and Beverly Duncan. 1955. "A Methodological Analysis of Segregation Indexes." *American Sociological Review* 20 (2): 210–17.

Dye, Richard, and David Merriman. 2003. "The Effect of Tax Increment Financing on Land Use." In *The Property Tax, Land Use and Land Use Regulation*, ed. Richard Netzer, 37–61. Northampton, Mass.: Elgar.

Dynarski, Susan, Joshua Hyman, and Diane Schanzenbach. 2013. "Experimental Evidence on the Effect of Childhood Investments on Postsecondary Attainment and Degree Completion." *Journal of Policy Analysis and Management* 32 (4): 692–717.

East Baltimore Development Inc. (EBDI). 2002. "Minority Inclusion Agreement for the East Baltimore Development Initiative." Report. East Baltimore Development, Inc.

Eberts, R., G. Erickcek, and J. Kleinhenz. 2006. "Dashboard Indicators for the Northeast Ohio Economy: Prepared for the Fund for Our Economic Future." Working Paper 06-05. Cleveland, Ohio: Federal Reserve Bank of Cleveland.

Economist. 2013. "Reshoring Manufacturing: Coming Home. Special Report: Outsourcing and Offshoring." print edition, January 19.

Ehlen, Mark. 2001. "The Economic Impact of Manufacturing Extension Centers." *Economic Development Quarterly* 15 (1): 36–44.

Ellen, Ingrid Gould, Keren Mertens Horn, and Katherine M. O'Regan. 2013. "Why Do Higher-Income Households Choose Low-Income Neighbourhoods? Pioneering or Thrift?" *Urban Studies* 50 (12): 2478–95.

Ellen, Ingrid Gould, Tod Mijanovich, and Keri-Nicole Dillman. 2001. "Neighborhood Effects on Health: Exploring the Links and Assessing the Evidence." *Journal of Urban Affairs* 23 (3–4): 391–408.

Ellen, Ingrid Gould, and Margery Austin Turner. 1997. "Does Neighborhood Matter? Assessing Recent Evidence." *Housing Policy Debate* 8 (4): 833–66.

Ellis, Juliet. 2010. "The San Francisco PUC: Working for the Community." *Race, Poverty, and the Environment* 17, 2 (Fall).

Elvery, Joel A. 2009. "The Impact of Enterprise Zones on Resident Employment: An Evaluation of the Enterprise Zone Programs of California and Florida." *Economic Development Quarterly* 23 (1): 44–59.

EuQuant. 2007. "Increasing the Capacity of the Nation's Small Disadvantaged Businesses (SDBs)." Report Commissioned by Congressional Black Caucus Foundation.

Farley, Reynolds, and William H. Frey. 1994. "Changes in the Segregation of Whites from Blacks During the 1980s: Small Steps Toward a More Integrated Society." *American Sociological Review* 59 (1): 23–45.

Farley, Reynolds, Sheldon Danziger, and Harry J. Holzer. 2002. *Detroit Divided.* New: Russell Sage.

Federal Reserve System. Division of Consumer and Community Affairs Offices, and Brookings Institution. 2008. *The Enduring Challenge of Concentrated Poverty in America: Case Studies from Communities Across the U.S.* Richmond, Va.: Federal Reserve Bank of Richmond.

Fiester, L. 2013. "Early Warning Confirmed: A Research Update on Third-Grade Reading." Baltimore: Annie E. Casey Foundation.

Finn, Jeremy D., and Charles M. Achilles. 1999. "Tennessee's Class Size Study: Findings, Implications, Misconceptions." *Educational Evaluation and Policy Analysis* 21 (2): 97–109.

Finn, Jeremy D., Susan B. Gerber, and Jayne Boyd-Zaharias. 2005. "Small Classes in the Early Grades, Academic Achievement, and Graduating from High School." *Journal of Educational Psychology* 97 (2): 214–23.

Fischel, W. A. 2004. "An Economic History of Zoning and a Cure for Its Exclusionary Effects." *Urban Studies* 41 (2): 317–40.

Fitchen, Janet. 1981. *Poverty in Rural America: A Case Study.* Boulder, Colorado: Westview Press.

Fogg, Neeta P. and Paul E. Harrington. 2011. "Rising Mal-Employment and the Great Recession: The Growing Disconnection Between Recent College Graduates and the College Labor Market." *Continuing Higher Education Review* 75: 51–65.

FoodLab Detroit. 2015. "Operation Above Ground." Website accessed April 2015. https://foodlabdetroit.com/what-we-do/programs/operation-above-ground, accessed April 2015.

Fredriksson, Peter, Björn Öckert, and Hessel Oosterbeek. 2013. "Long-Term Effects of Class Size." *Quarterly Journal of Economics* 128 (1): 249–285.

Freedman, Matthew. 2013. "Targeted Business Incentives and Local Labor Markets." *Journal of Human Resources* 48 (2): 311–44.

Frey, Richard, and Paul Taylor. 2012. "The Rise of Residential Segregation by Income." Washington, D.C.: Pew Research Center.

Frey, William H. 2011. "Melting Pot Cities and Suburbs: Racial and Ethnic Change in Metro America in the 2000s." Washington, D.C.: Brookings Institution.

——. 2013. "A Big City Growth Revival?" Brookings, May 28.

——. 2014. "A Population Slowdown for Small Town America." Washington, D.C.: Brookings Institution.

Fujita, Shigeru. 2014. "On the Causes of Declines in the Labor Force Participation Rate." Special Report. Research Rap. Federal Reserve Bank of Philadelphia.

Galster, George. 2012. *Driving Detroit: The Quest for Respect in the Motor City.* Philadelphia: University of Pennsylvania Press.

Ganong, Peter, and Daniel Shoag. 2013. "Why Has Regional Income Convergence in the U.S. Stopped?" Harvard Kennedy School Working Paper RWP12-028. Harvard University.

Ghayad, Rand. 2013. "A Decomposition of Shifts of the Beveridge Curve." Public Policy Briefs 13 (1). Federal Reserve Bank of Boston.

Ghayad, Rand, and William Dickens. 2012. "What Can We Learn by Disaggregating the Unemployment-Vacancy Relationship?" Public Policy Briefs 12 (3). Federal Reserve Bank of Boston.

Gibson, C. 1998. "Population of the 100 Largest Cities and Other Urban Places in the United States: 1790 to 1990." June. U.S. Bureau of the Census. Population Division Working Paper 27.

Gillen, K. 2012. "Testimony of Kevin Gillen," June 20. http://www.jerichohousing.org/enewsletters/theskinny_june2012/images/Testimony_City_Council_Vacant_Land_June20_2012.pdf, retrieved May 30, 2014.

Gillette, Howard, Jr. 2011. *Camden After the Fall: Decline and Renewal in a Post-Industrial City.* Philadelphia: University of Pennsylvania Press.

Glaeser, Edward L., and Joshua D. Gottlieb. 2009. "The Wealth of Cities: Agglomeration Economies and Spatial Equilibrium in the United States." *Journal of Economic Literature* 47 (4): 983–1028.

Glaeser, Edward L., Joseph Gyourko, and Raven E. Saks. 2006. "Urban Growth and Housing Supply." *Journal of Economic Geography* 6 (1): 71–89.

Glaeser, Edward L., Jed Kolko, and Albert Saiz. 2001. "Consumer City." *Journal of Economic Geography* 1 (1): 27–50.

Glaeser, Edward L., and Jacob L. Vigdor. 2012. "The End of the Segregated Century: Racial Separation in America's Neighborhoods, 1890–2010." Manhattan Institute for Policy Research, Civic Report 66.

Goldin, Claudia. 2014. "A Grand Gender Convergence: Its Last Chapter." *American Economic Review* 104 (4): 1–30.

Goldin, Claudia, and Lawrence Katz. 2008. *The Race Between Education and Technology.* Cambridge, Mass.: Belknap Press of Harvard University Press.

Gomez, Marisela B. 2013. *Race, Class, Power, and Organizing in East Baltimore: Rebuilding Abandoned Communities in America.* Lanham, Md.: Lexington Books.

Gordon, Robert. 2013. "The Phillips Curve is Alive and Well: Inflation and the NAIRU During the Slow Recovery." NBER Working Paper 19390. Cambridge, Mass.: National Bureau of Economic Research.

Grady, Sue, and Joe Darden. 2012. "Spatial Methods to Study Local Racial Residential Segregation and Infant Health in Detroit, Michigan." *Annals of the Association of American Geographers* 102 (5): 922–31.

Graham, Bryan, and Patrick Sharkey. 2013. "Mobility and the Metropolis: How Communities Factor into Economic Mobility." Pew Charitable Trusts.

Green, Francis, and Steven McIntosh. 2007. "Is There a Genuine Under-Utilization of Skills Amongst the Overqualified?" *Applied Economics* 39: 427–39.

Greenbaum, Robert T., and Jim Landers. 2009. "Why Are State Policy Makers Still Proponents of Enterprise Zones? What Explains Their Action in the Face of a Preponderance of the Research?" *International Regional Science Review* 32 (4): 466–79.

Greene, Jay, Tom Loveless, W. Bentley MacLeod, Thomas Nechyba, Paul Peterson, Meredith Rosenthal, and Grover Whitehurst. 2010. "Expanding Choice in Elementary and Secondary Education: A Report on Rethinking the Federal Role in Education." Washington, D.C: Brookings Institution.

Greenstone, Michael, Richard Hornbeck, and Enrico Moretti. 2010. "Identifying Agglomeration Spillovers: Evidence from Winners and Losers of Large Plant Openings." *Journal of Political Economy* 118 (3): 536–98.

Haas, P. M. 1992. "Introduction: Epistemic Communities and International Policy Coordination." *International Organization* 46 (1): 1–35. doi:10.1017/S0020818300001442.

Hall, Matthew, and Jonathan Stringfield. 2014. "Undocumented Migration and the Residential Segregation of Mexicans in New Destinations." *Social Science Research* 47 (1): 61–78.

Ham, John C., Charles Swenson, Ayse Imrohoroglu, and Heonjae Song. 2011. "Government Programs Can Improve Local Labor Markets: Evidence from State Enterprise Zones, Federal Empowerment Zones and Federal Enterprise Community." *Journal of Public Economics* 95: 779–97.

Hamersma, Sarah. 2003. "The Work Opportunity and Welfare-to-Work Tax Credits: Participation Rates Among Eligible Workers." *National Tax Journal* 56: 725–38.

———. 2008. "The Effects of an Employer Subsidy on Employment Outcomes: A Study of the Work Opportunity and Welfare-to-Work Tax Credits." *Journal of Policy Analysis and Management* 27 (3): 498–520.

Hamilton, D. K., D. Y. Miller, and J. Paytas. 2004. "Exploring the Horizontal and Vertical Dimensions of the Governing of Metropolitan Regions. *Urban Affairs Review* 40 (2), 147–182.

Handbury, Jessie. 2013. "Are Poor Cities Cheap for Everyone? Non-Homotheticity and the Cost of Living Across US Cities." Job Market Paper.

Harrington, Michael. 1962. *The Other America: Poverty in the United States.* New York: Macmillan.

Hanson, Danielle. 2013. "Assessing the Harlem Children's Zone." Heritage Foundation Center for Policy Innovation Discussion Paper 8, March 6. http://report.heritage .org/cpi_dp08.

Hanushek, Eric A., John F. Kain, Jacob M. Markman, and Steven G. Rivkin. 2003. "Does Peer Ability Affect Student Achievement?" *Journal of Applied Econometrics* 18 (5): 527–44.

Heckman, James J. 2006. "Skill Formation and the Economics of Investing in Disadvantaged Children." *Science* 312 (5782): 1900–1902.

Heckman, James J., Seong Hyeok Moon, Rodrigo Pinto, Peter Savelyev, and Adam Yavitz. 2010a. "Analyzing Social Experiments as Implemented: A Reexamination of the Evidence from the HighScope Perry Preschool Program." *Quantitative Economics* 1 (1): 1–46.

———. 2010b. "The Rate of Return to the HighScope Perry Preschool Program." *Journal of Public Economics* 94 (1–2): 114–28.

Heckman, James J., and Brook S. Payner. 1989. "Determining the Impact of Federal Antidiscrimination Policy on the Economic Status of Blacks: A Study of South Carolina." *American Economic Review* 79 (1): 138–77.

Heckman, James J., Rodrigo Pinto, and Peter Savelyev. 2013. "Understanding the Mechanisms Through Which an Influential Early Childhood Program Boosted Adult Outcomes." *American Economic Review* 103 (6): 2052–86.

Helper, Rose. 1969. *Racial Policies and Practices of Real Estate Brokers.* Minneapolis: University of Minnesota Press.

Henton, D., J. Melville, and K. A. Walesh. 1997. *Grassroots Leaders for a New Economy: How Civic Entrepreneurs Are Building Prosperous Communities.* San Francisco: Jossey-Bass.

———. 2003. *Civic Revolutionaries: Igniting the Passion for Change in America's Communities.* New York: Wiley.

Hershberg, Theodore, Alan N. Burstein, Eugene P. Ericksen, Stephanie W. Greenberg, and William L. Yancey. 1981. "A Tale of Three Cities: Blacks, Immigrants, and Opportunity in Philadelphia, 1850–1880, 1930, 1970." In *Philadelphia: Work, Space, Family, and Group Experience in the 19th Century,* ed. Theodore Hershberg, 461–91. New York: Oxford University Press.

Hertz, Thomas. 2007. "Trends in the Intergenerational Elasticity of Family Income in the United States." *Industrial Relations: A Journal of Economy and Society* 46 (1): 22–50.

Heymann, S. Jody, and Alison Earle. 2000. "Low-Income Parents: How Do Working Conditions Affect Their Opportunity to Help School-Age Children at Risk?" *American Educational Research Journal* 37 (4): 833–48.

Hickey, Robert. 2014. "'Inclusionary Upzoning' is Gaining Ground. Here's Why." *Rooflines: The Shelterforce* (blog), October 10.

Hill, E., T. St. Clair, H. Wial, H. Wolman, P. Atkins, P. Blumenthal, S. Ficenec, and A. Friedhoff. 2012. "Economic Shocks and Regional Economic Resilience." In *Urban and Regional Policy and Its Effects: Building Resilient Regions*, ed. N. Pindus, H. Wial, H. Wolman, and M. Weir, 24–59. Washington, D.C.: Brookings Institution Press.

Hirsch, Arnold R. 1983. *Making the Second Ghetto: Race and Housing in Chicago, 1940–1960.* Cambridge: Cambridge University Press.

Holifield, Johnathan, Adam Kamins, and Teresa Lynch. 2012. "Inclusive Clusters." *Economic Development Journal* 11 (4).

Hollenbeck, Kevin. 2008. "Is There a Role for Public Support of Incumbent Worker On-the-Job Training?" Upjohn Institute Working Paper 08-138. Kalamazoo, Mich.: W. E. Upjohn Institute for Employment Research.

Holzer, Harry J., Richard N. Block, Marcus Cheatham, and Jack H. Knott. 1993. "Are Training Subsidies for Firms Effective? The Michigan Experience." *Industrial and Labor Relations Review* 46 (4): 625–36.

Horn, Keren M., and Katherine M. O'Regan. 2011. "The Low Income Housing Tax Credit and Racial Segregation." *Housing Policy Debate* 21 (3): 443–73.

Hoxby, Caroline, and Christopher Avery. 2013. "The Missing 'One-Offs': The Hidden Supply of High-Achieving, Low-Income Students." *Brookings Papers on Economic Activity*, Spring.

Jackson, Kenneth T. 1985. *Crabgrass Frontier: The Suburbanization of the United States.* New York: Oxford University Press.

Jacobs, J. 1961. *The Death and Life of Great American Cities.* New York: Random House.

Jameson, K. 2012. "A Successful Experience of Immigrant Integration: Evidence from Utah." *Journal of Community Positive Practices*, (4), 601–15.

Jargowsky, Paul A. 1996. "Take the Money and Run: Economic Segregation in US Metropolitan Areas." *American Sociological Review* 61(6): 984–98.

———. 1997. *Poverty and Place: Ghettos, Barrios, and the American City.* New York: Russell Sage.

———. 2002. "Sprawl, Concentration of Poverty, and Urban Inequality." In *Urban Sprawl: Causes, Consequences, and Policy Responses*, ed. Gregory Squires, 39–72. Washington, D.C.: Urban Institute Press.

———. 2003. "Stunning Progress, Hidden Problems: The Dramatic Decline of Concentrated Poverty in the 1990s." Living Cities Census Series. Washington, D.C.: Brookings Center on Urban and Metropolitan Policy.

———. 2013. "Concentration of Poverty in the New Millennium: Changes in the Prevalence, Composition, and Location of High-Poverty Neighborhoods." Report of the Century Foundation and the Rutgers Center for Urban Research and Education. New York: Century Foundation.

———. 2014a. "Segregation, Neighborhoods, and Schools." In *Choosing Homes, Choosing Schools*, ed. Annette Lareau and Kimberly Goyette, 97–136. New York: Russell Sage Foundation.

———. 2014b. "Concentration of Poverty: An Update." *Century Foundation. Blog of the Century.*

Jargowsky, Paul A., and Mary Jo Bane. 1991. "Ghetto Poverty in the United States: 1970 to 1980." In *The Urban Underclass*, ed. Christopher Jencks and Paul E. Peterson, 235–73. Washington, D.C.: Brookings Institution.

Jargowsky, Paul A., and Mohamed El Komi. 2011. "Before or After the Bell? School Context and Neighborhood Effects on Student Achievement." In *Neighborhood and Life Chances: How Place Matters in Modern America*, ed. Harriet B. Newburger, Eugenie L. Birch, and Susan M. Wachter, 50–72. Philadelphia: University of Pennsylvania Press.

Jarmin, Ron. 1998. "Manufacturing Extension and Productivity Dynamics." Discussion Paper 98-8. Center for Economic Studies. Washington, D.C.: U.S. Census Bureau.

———. 1999. "Evaluating the Impact of Manufacturing Extension on Productivity Growth." *Journal of Policy Analysis and Management* 18 (1): 99–119.

Jencks, Christopher, and Susan E. Mayer. 1990. "The Social Consequences of Growing Up in a Poor Neighborhood." In *Inner-City Poverty in the United States*, ed. Laurence E. Lynn, Jr., and Michael G. H. McGeary, 111–86. Washington, D.C.: National Academies Press.

Johnson, Gordon. 1982. "Racial Segregation in the Professions: Recent National Industry-Specific Trends: 1968–1980." CDE Working Paper 82-20. Madison: Center for Demography and Ecology, University of Wisconsin at Madison.

Kahlenberg, Richard D. 2001. *All Together Now: Creating Middle-Class Schools Through Public School Choice.* Washington, D.C.: Brookings Institution Press.

Kain, John F. 1968. "Housing Segregation, Negro Employment, and Metropolitan Decentralization." *Quarterly Journal of Economics* 82 (2): 175–97.

Kasarda, John D. 1993. "Inner-City Concentrated Poverty and Neighborhood Distress,
1970 to 1990." *Housing Policy Debate* 4: 253–302.

Kehoe, Timothy J., Kim J. Ruhl, and Joseph B. Steinberg. 2013. "Global Imbalances and
Structural Change in the United States." NBER Working Paper 19339. Cambridge,
Mass.: National Bureau of Economic Research.

Kennedy, Mary M. 1986. "Poverty, Achievement and the Distribution of Compensatory Education Services. An Interim Report from the National Assessment of
Chapter 1." http://files.eric.ed.gov/fulltext/ED271546.pdf.

Kim, Young-Jiu. 2011. "Catholic Schools or School Quality? The Effects of Catholic
Schools on Labor Market Outcomes." *Economics of Education Review* 30: 546–58

Kimelberg, Shelley McDonough. 2014. "Beyond Test Scores: Middle-Class Mothers,
Cultural Capital, and the Evaluation of Urban Public Schools." *Sociological Perspectives*, April.

Kingsley, G. Thomas, and Kathryn L. S. Pettit. 2003. "Concentrated Poverty: A Change
in Course." Neighborhood Change in Urban America Brief 2. Washington, D.C.:
Urban Institute.

Kirp, David L., John P. Dwyer, and Larry A. Rosenthal. 1995. *Our Town: Race,
Housing, and the Soul of Suburbia*. New Brunswick, N.J.: Rutgers University
Press.

Kline, Patrick, and Enrico Moretti. 2013. "People, Places and Public Policy: Some Simple Welfare Economics of Local Economic Development Programs." NBER Working Paper 19659. Cambridge, Mass.: National Bureau of Economic Research.

———. 2014. "Local Economic Development, Agglomeration Economies, and the Big
Push: 100 Years of Evidence from the Tennessee Valley Authority." *Quarterly Journal of Economics* 129 (1): 275–331.

Kneebone, Elizabeth. 2013. "Job Sprawl Stalls: The Great Recession and Metropolitan
Employment Location." Washington, D.C.: Brookings Institution.

Kneebone, Elizabeth, and Alan Berube. 2013. *Confronting Suburban Poverty in America*. Washington, D.C.: Brookings Institution Press.

Kneebone, Elizabeth, C. Nadeau, and Alan Berube. 2011. "The Re-Emergence of Concentrated Poverty: Metropolitan Trends in the 2000s." Brookings Institution.

Knotek, Edward S. 2007. "How Useful Is Okun's Law?" *Economic Review* (4th Quar-
ter): 73–103.

Knudsen, Eric I., James J. Heckman, Judy L. Cameron, and Jack P. Shonkoff. 2006.
"Economic, Neurobiological, and Behavioral Perspectives on Building America's
Future Workforce." *Proceedings of the National Academy of Sciences* 103 (27):
10155–62.

Krueger, Alan B. 2012. "The Rise and Consequences of Inequality in the United States."
Speech at the Center for American Progress, Washington, D.C., January 12.

Krueger, Alan B., Judd Cramer, and David Cho. 2014. "Are the Long-Term Unemployed on the Margins of the Labor Market?" Brookings Panel on Economic Activity. Economic Studies at Brookings. Conference Proceedings. Brookings Institution.

Kubisch, Anne C., Patricia Auspos, Prudence Brown, and Tom Dewar. 2010. "Community Change Initiatives from 1990–2010: Accomplishments and Implications for Future Work." *Community Investments* 22 (1): 8–12.

Lackmeyer, S., and J. Money. 2006. *OKC Second Time Around: A Renaissance Story.* Oklahoma City: Full Circle Press.

Lacy, Karyn. 2007. *Blue-Chip Black: Race, Class, and Status in the New Black Middle Class.* Berkeley: University of California Press.

Ladd, Helen F. 2012. "Education and Poverty: Confronting the Evidence." *Journal of Policy Analysis and Management* 31 (2): 203–27.

Ladd, Helen F., Clara G. Muschkin, and Kenneth A. Dodge. 2014. "From Birth to School: Early Childhood Initiatives and Third-Grade Outcomes in North Carolina." *Journal of Policy Analysis and Management* 33 (1): 162–87.

Lee, Chul-In, and Gary Solon. 2009. "Trends in Intergenerational Income Mobility." *Review of Economics and Statistics* 91 (4): 766–72.

Lester, T. W., and S. Reckhow. 2013. "Network Governance and Regional Equity: Shared Agendas or Problematic Partners?" *Planning Theory* 12 (2): 115–38.

Leventhal, Tama, and Jeanne Brooks-Gunn. 2000. "The Neighborhoods They Live In: The Effects of Neighborhood Residence on Child and Adolescent Outcomes." *Psychological Bulletin* 126, 2: 309–37.

Licht, W. 2011. "Rise and Fall of City's Manufacturing Sector." Philly.com., October 16. http://articles.philly.com/2011-10-16.

Lieberson, Stanley. 1963. *Ethnic Patterns in American Cities.* New York: Free Press.

———. 1980. *A Piece of the Pie: Blacks and White Immigrants Since 1880.* Berkeley: University of California Press.

Linneman, Peter and Susan Wachter. 1989. "The Impacts of Borrowing Constraints on Homeownership." *Real Estate Economics* 17 (4): 389–402.

Lippman, Laura, Shelley Burns, and Edith McArthur. 1996. *Urban Schools: The Challenge of Location and Poverty.* Diane Publishing. http://nces.ed.gov/pubs/96184all.pdf.

Logan, John R., and Brian J. Stults. 2010. "Racial and Ethnic Separation in the Neighborhoods: Progress at a Standstill." Census Brief prepared for US2010. http://www.s4.brown.edu/us2010/Data/Report/report1.pdf.

Lubrano, A., and J. Duchneskie. 2013. "Poverty Dips in City, But Need for Food Stamps Rises." *Philadelphia Inquirer,* September 20.

Ludwig, Jens, Greg J. Duncan, Lisa A. Gennetian, Lawrence F. Katz, Ronald C. Kessler, Jeffrey R. Kling, and Lisa Sanbonmatsu. 2013. "Long-Term Neighborhood Effects on Low-Income Families: Evidence from Moving to Opportunity." *American Economic Review Papers and Proceedings* 103 (3): 226–31.

Ludwig, Jens, Lisa Sanbonmatsu, Lisa Gennetian, Emma Adam, Greg J. Duncan, Lawrence F. Katz, Ronald C. Kessler, et al. 2011. "Neighborhoods, Obesity, and Diabetes—A Randomized Social Experiment." *New England Journal of Medicine* 365 (16): 1509–19.

Marcantonio, Richard A., and Alex Karner. 2014. "Disadvantaged Communities Teach Regional Planners a Lesson in Equitable and Sustainable Development." *Poverty & Race* 23 (1) (January/February).

Martelle, Scott. 2012. *Detroit: A Biography*. Chicago: Chicago Review Press.

Maskell, P., and A. Malmberg. 1999. "The Competitiveness of Firms and Regions: 'Ubiquitification' and the Importance of Localized Learning." *European Urban and Regional Studies* 6 (1): 9–25. doi:10.1177/096977649900600102.

Massey, Douglas S. 1990. "American Apartheid: Segregation and the Making of the Underclass." *American Journal of Sociology* 96 (2): 329–57.

———. 2004. "Segregation and Stratification: A Biosocial Perspective." *DuBois Review: Social Science Research on Race* 1: 1–19.

———. 2007. *Categorically Unequal: The American Stratification System*. New York: Russell Sage.

———. 2011. "The Past and Future of American Civil Rights." *Daedalus* 140 (2): 37–54.

Massey, Douglas S., Len Albright, Rebecca Casciano, Elizabeth Derickson, and David Kinsey. 2013. *Climbing Mount Laurel: The Struggle for Affordable Housing and Social Mobility in an American Suburb*. Princeton, N.J.: Princeton University Press.

Massey, Douglas S., and Rebecca M. Blank. 2006. "Assessing Racial Discrimination: Methods and Measures." In *Fairness in the Housing Market*, ed. John Goering, 61–80. Lanham, Md.: Rowman and Littlefield.

Massey, Douglas S., and Stefanie Brodmann. 2014. *Spheres of Influence: The Social Ecology of Race-Class Inequality*. New York: Russell Sage.

Massey, Douglas S., and Nancy A. Denton. 1988a. "The Dimensions of Racial Segregation." *Social Forces* 67 (2): 281–315.

———. 1988b. "Suburbanization and Segregation in U.S. Metropolitan Areas." *American Journal of Sociology* 94 (3): 592–626.

———. 1989. "Hypersegregation in U.S. Metropolitan Areas: Black and Hispanic Segregation Along Five Dimensions." *Demography* 26 (3): 373–93.

———. 1993. *American Apartheid: Segregation and the Making of the Underclass*. Cambridge, Mass.: Harvard University Press.

Massey, Douglas S., and Mitchell L. Eggers. 1990. "The Ecology of Inequality: Minorities and the Concentration of Poverty, 1970–1980." *American Journal of Sociology* 95 (5): 1153–88.

Massey, Douglas S., and Mary J. Fischer. 2000. "How Segregation Concentrates Poverty." *Ethnic and Racial Studies* 23 (4): 670–91. doi:10.1080/01419870050033676.

———. 2003. "The Geography of Inequality in the United States, 1950–2000." In *Brookings-Wharton Papers on Urban Affairs*, ed. William G. Gale and Janet Rothenberg Pack, 1–40. Washington, D.C.: Brookings Institution.

Mazzucato, Mariana. 2013. *The Entrepreneurial State: Debunking Public vs. Private Sector Myths*. London: Anthem Press.

McGee, Glenn W. 2004. "Closing the Achievement Gap: Lessons from Illinois' Golden Spike High-Poverty High-Performing Schools." *Journal of Education for Students Placed at Risk (JESPAR)* 9 (2): 97–125.

McGovern, Steven J. 2006. "Philadelphia's Neighborhood Transformation Initiative: A Case Study of Mayoral Leadership, Bold Planning and Conflict." *Housing Policy Debate* 17 (3): 529–70.

Metcalf, Gabriel. 2013. "The San Francisco Exodus." *Atlantic Cities*, October 14.

Metropolitan Transportation Commission. 2013. "Bay Area Regional Prosperity Plan Economic Opportunity Sub-Grants 2014–2015 Call for Projects." September 30.

Mieskowski, Peter, and Edwin S. Mills. 1993. "The Causes of Metropolitan Suburbanization." *Journal of Economic Literature* 7: 135–47.

Miller, D. Y., and J. H. Lee. 2009. "Making Sense of Metropolitan Regions: A Dimensional Approach to Regional Governance." *Publius: The Journal of Federalism* 41(1), 126–45.

Minnesota Population Center. 2014. "National Historical Geographic Information System: Version 2.0." Minneapolis: University of Minnesota. https://www.nhgis.org/, retrieved January 14.

Mirel, Jeffrey. 1999. *The Rise and Fall of an Urban School System: Detroit, 1907–81*. Ann Arbor: University of Michigan Press.

Molina, Frieda. 1998. *Making Connections: A Study of Employment Linkage Programs*. Washington, D.C.: Center for Community Change.

Molloy, Raven, Christopher L. Smith, and Abigail Wozniak. 2014. "Declining Migration Within the US: The Role of the Labor Market." NBER Working Paper 20065. Cambridge, Mass.: National Bureau of Economic Research.

Molnar, Lawrence, Donald Grimes, Jack Edelstein, Rocc DePietro, Hugh Sherman, Dinah Adkins, and Lou Tomatzky. 1997. *Impact of Business Incubator Investments*. Athens, Ohio: National Business Incubation Association and University of Michigan.

Moore, Mark A., Anthony E. Boardman, Aidan R. Vining, David L. Weimar, and David H. Greenberg. 2004. "Just Give Me a Number! Practical Values for the Social Discount Rate." *Journal of Policy Analysis and Management* 23 (4): 789–812.

Moretti, Enrico. 2004. "Estimating the Social Return to Higher Education: Evidence from Longitudinal and Repeated Cross-Sectional Data." *Journal of Econometrics* 121 (1): 175–212.

———. 2010. "Local Multipliers." *American Economic Review* 100, 2: 373–77.

———. 2011. "Local Labor Markets." In *Handbook of Labor Economics*. Vol. 4, 1237–1313. Amsterdam: Elsevier.

———. 2013. "Real Wage Inequality." *American Economic Journal: Applied Economics* 5 (1): 65–103.

Moretti, Enrico, and Daniel J. Wilson. 2014. "State Incentives for Innovation, Star Scientists and Jobs: Evidence from Biotech." *Journal of Urban Economics* 79: 20–38.

National Alliance for Public Charter Schools. 2013. "National Charter School Wait-list Numbers Approach One Million," June 27. http://www.publiccharters.org/press/national-charter-school-waitlist-numbers-approach-million/, retrieved April 1, 2014.

National Center for Education Statistics. 2013. "The Condition of Education 2013." Washington, D.C.: U.S. Department of Education.

National Commission on Fair Housing and Equal Opportunity. 2008. "The Future of Fair Housing: Report of the National Commission on Fair Housing and Equal Opportunity." Washington, D.C.: Leadership Conference for Civil Rights.

National Council on Teacher Quality. 2013. "Teacher Quality Roadmap: Improving Policies and Practices in the School District of Philadelphia," May. http://www.nctq.org/dmsView/Teacher_Quality_Roadmap_Improving_Policies_and_Practices_in_Philadelphia_NCTQ_Report, retrieved March 26, 2014.

Neumark, David, and Jed Kolko. 2010. "Do Enterprise Zones Create Jobs? Evidence from California's Enterprise Zone Program." *Journal of Urban Economics* 68: 1–19.

NorTech. 2012. "Inclusive Competitiveness in Northeast Ohio." Report. NorTech. Opportunity Collaborative. http://www.opportunitycollaborative.org/.

Office of Management and Budget (OMB). 2010. "2010 Standards for Delineating Metropolitan and Micropolitan Statistical Areas." *Federal Register* 75, 123: 37246–52.

Olds, David L. 2006. "The Nurse-Family Partnership: An Evidence-Based Preventive Intervention." *Infant Mental Health Journal* 27 (1): 5–25.

Opportunity Collaborative. 2014. "Barriers to Employment Opportunities in the Baltimore Region." Report. Baltimore Metropolitan Council.

Osterman, Paul and Andrew Weaver. 2014. "Why Claims of Skills Shortages in Manufacturing Are Overblown." Issue Brief 376. Economic Policy Institute.

Otterman, Sharon. 2010. "Lauded Harlem Schools Have Their Own Problems." *New York Times*, October 12, A20.

Pack, Janet. 1998. "Poverty and Urban Public Expenditures." *Urban Studies* 35: 1995–2019.

Palubinsky, Beth Z., and Bernardine H. Watson. 1997. "Getting from Here to There: The Bridges to Work Demonstration First Report to the Field." Philadelphia: Public/Private Ventures.

Panizza, U. 2002. "Income Inequality and Economic Growth: Evidence from American Data." *Journal of Economic Growth* 7 (1), 25–41. doi:10.1023/A:1013414509803.

Park, Julie, and John Iceland. 2011. "Residential Segregation in Metropolitan Established Immigrant Gateways and New Destinations, 1990–2000." *Social Science Research* 40 (3): 811–81.

Park, Robert E. 1926. "The Urban Community as a Spatial Pattern and a Moral Order." *Urban Community*: 3–18. Chicago: University of Chicago Press.

Partridge, M. D. 1997. "Is Inequality Harmful for Growth? Comment." *American Economic Review* 87 (5): 1019–32.

Pastor, Manuel 2006. "Cohesion and Competitiveness: Business Leadership for Regional Growth and Social Equity." In *OECD Territorial Reviews: Competitive Cities in the Global Economy*, 393–406. OECD Publishing.

Pastor, Manuel, and Chris Benner. 2008. "Been Down So Long: Weak Market Cities and Regional Equity." In *Retooling for Growth: Building a 21st Century Economy in America's Older Industrial Areas*, ed. R. M. McGahey and J. S. Vey. Washington, D.C: Brookings Institution Press.

Pattillo-McCoy, Mary. 2000. *Black Picket Fences: Privilege and Peril Among the Black Middle Class*. Chicago: University of Chicago Press.

Pendall, Rolf. 2000. "Local Land-Use Regulation and the Chain of Exclusion." *Journal of the American Planning Association* 66: 125–42.

Pendall, Rolf, Christopher Hayes, Arthur (Taz) George, Zach McDade, Casey Dawkins, Jae Sik Jeon, Eli Knaap, et al. 2014. "Driving to Opportunity: Understanding the Links Among Transportation Access, Residential Outcomes, and Economic Opportunity for Housing Voucher Recipients." Washington, D.C.: Urban Institute.

Pendall, Rolf, and Margery Austin Turner. 2014. "Expanding Access to Opportunity in Fast-Growth Metropolitan Areas." Washington, D.C.: Urban Institute.

Pennsylvania Department of Education. 2012. "2011–2012 PSSA and AYP Results." http://www.portal.state.pa.us/portal/server.pt/community/school_assessments, retrieved March 30, 2014.

Pennsylvania Early Learning. n.d. "Early Childhood Programs." http://www.pakeys.org /pages/stars_centers.aspx, retrieved March 31, 2014.

Pennsylvania State Data Center. 2013. "Pennsylvania Abstract: A Statistical Fact Book." Harrisburg: Pennsylvania State Data Center.

Persky, Joseph, Daniyel Felzenshtain, and Virginia Carlson. 2004. *Does "Trickle Down" Work? Economic Development Strategies and Job Chains in Local Labor Markets*. Kalamazoo, Mich.: W. E. Upjohn Institute for Employment Research.

Persson, T., and G. Tabellin. 1994. "Is Inequality Harmful for Growth?" *American Economic Review* 84(3): 600–621.

Peters, Alan H., and Peter S. Fisher. 2002. *State Enterprise Zone Programs: Have They Worked?* Kalamazoo, Mich.: W. E. Upjohn Institute for Employment Research.

Pettigrew, Thomas. 1979. "Racial Change and Social Policy." *Annals of the American Academy of Political and Social Science* 441: 114–31.

Pew Charitable Trusts. 2010. "Philadelphia's Changing Schools and What Parents Want from Them." Philadelphia Research Initiative. Philadelphia: Pew Charitable Trusts.

———. 2012. "Philadelphia: The State of the City, 2012 Update," March 31. Philadelphia Research Initiative. Philadelphia: Pew Charitable Trusts.

———. 2014. "Millennials in Philadelphia: A Promising But Fragile Boom." Philadelphia Research Initiative. Philadelphia: Pew Charitable Trusts.

Phelps, Edmund. 1972. *Inflation Policy and Unemployment Theory*. New York: Norton.

Philadelphia Workforce Investment Board. 2009. "Help Wanted: Knowledge Workers Needed." Philadelphia: Philadelphia Workforce Investment Board.

Phillips, Andrew, Robert Cline, Caroline Sallee, Michelle Klassen, and Daniel Sufranski. 2013. "Total State and Local Business Taxes: State-by-State Estimates for Fiscal

Year 2012." Washington, D.C.: Ernst & Young, LLP Quantitative Economics and Statistics (QUEST) Practice and the Council on State Taxation (COST).

Piketty, Thomas. 2014. *Capital in the 21st Century*. Cambridge, Mass.: Belknap Press of Harvard University Press.

Piketty, Thomas, and Emmanuel Saez. 2003. "Income Inequality in the United States, 1913–1998." *Quarterly Journal of Economics* 118 (1): 1–41.

PolicyLink. 2013a. "Breaking into Biotech in Baltimore." *America's Tomorrow Newsletter*, May 9.

———. 2013b. "Changing the Face of Silicon Valley Start-Ups." *America's Tomorrow Newsletter*, May 23.

———. 2013c. "New Orleans Fast-Tracks Equitable Transit Investment." *America's Tomorrow Newsletter*, June 6.

———. 2013d. "Port of Opportunity: Landmark Jobs Deal in Oakland, California." *America's Tomorrow Newsletter*, December 18.

———. 2013e. "Small Business on a Big Mission: Twin Cities Model Comes to Detroit." *America's Tomorrow Newsletter*, November 7.

———. 2014. "Incubating Good-Food Businesses in Detroit." *America's Tomorrow Newsletter*, June 12.

Polikoff, Alexander. 2006. *Waiting for Gautreaux: A Story of Segregation, Housing, and the Black Ghetto*. Evanston, Ill.: Northwestern University Press.

Porter, Eduardo. 2014. "A Smart Way to Skip College in Pursuit of a Job." *New York Times*, June 17.

Puma, M., S. Bell, R. Cook, C. Heid, P. Broene, F. Jenkins, Andrew Mashburn, et al. 2012. "Third Grade Follow-Up to the Head Start Impact Study." Washington D.C.: U.S. Department of Health and Human Services.

Putnam, Robert D. 1995. "Bowling Alone: America's Declining Social Capital." *Journal of Democracy* 6 (1): 65–78.

Quigley, John M. and Steven Raphael. 2004. "Is Housing Unaffordable? Why Isn't It More Affordable?" *Journal of Economic Perspectives* 18 (1): 191–214.

Quillian, Lincoln. 2012. "Segregation and Poverty Concentration: The Role of Three Segregations." *American Sociological Review* 77 (3): 354–79.

Racemacher, I., M. Bear, and M. Conway. 2001. *Project QUEST: A Case Study of a Sectoral Employment Development Approach*. Washington D.C.: Aspen Institute.

Raphael, Steven and Michael Stoll. 2010. "Job Sprawl and the Suburbanization of Poverty." Metropolitan Opportunity Series 4. Washington DC: Brookings Institution.

Ravitch, Diane. 2010. "The Myth of Charter Schools." *New York Review of Books*, November 11.

Reardon, Sean F. 2011. "The Widening Academic Achievement Gap Between the Rich and the Poor: New Evidence and Possible Explanations." In *Whither Opportunity? Rising Inequality, Schools, and Children's Life Chances*, ed. Greg J. Duncan and Richard J. Murnane, 91–115. New York: Russell Sage.

Reardon, Sean F., and Kendra Bischoff. 2011a. "Growth in the Residential Segregation of Families by Income, 1970–2009." Providence, R.I.: US2010 Census Project. http://www.s4.brown.edu/us2010/Data/Report/report111111.pdf, accessed June 27, 2014.

———. 2011b. "Income Inequality and Income Segregation." *American Journal of Sociology* 116 (4): 1092–1153.

Reynolds, Arthur J., Judy A. Temple, Suh-Ruu Ou, Irma A. Arteaga, and Barry A. B. White. 2011. "School-Based Early Childhood Education and Age-28 Well-Being: Effects by Timing, Dosage, and Subgroups." *Science* 333 (6040): 360–64.

Rode, Peter. 1988. "MEED Means More Business: Job Growth Through Minnesota's Wage Subsidy Program." Minneapolis: Jobs Now Coalition.

Roder, Anne, and Mark Elliott. 2013. "Stimulating Opportunity: An Evaluation of ARRA-Funded Subsidized Employment Programs." New York: Economic Mobility Corporation.

Rodrik, D. 1999. "Where Did All the Growth Go? External Shocks, Social Conflict, and Growth Collapses." *Journal of Economic Growth*, 4(4): 385–412.

———. 2014. When Ideas Trump Interests: Preferences, Worldviews, and Policy Innovations. *Journal of Economic Perspectives*, 28(1): 189–208.

Roethke, Andrea. 2012. "Investing in Baltimore's Workforce: Leveraging Opportunity and Moving to Scale." Report. Job Opportunities Task Force and Baltimore Integration Partnership.

Ross, Stephen L., and John Yinger. 2002. *The Color of Credit: Mortgage Discrimination, Research Methodology, and Fair-Lending Enforcement*. Cambridge, Mass.: MIT Press.

Rossi, Peter H. 1955. *Why Families Move: A Study in the Social Psychology of Urban Residential Mobility*. Glencoe, Ill.: Free Press.

Rothstein, Jesse. 2012. "The Labor Market Four Years into the Crisis: Assessing Structural Explanations." NBER Working Paper 17966. Cambridge, Mass.: National Bureau of Economic Research.

Rothwell, Jonathan T., and Douglas S. Massey. 2009. "The Effect of Density Zoning on Racial Segregation in U.S. Urban Areas." *Urban Affairs Review* 44: 799–806.

———. 2010. "Density Zoning and Class Segregation in U.S. Metropolitan Areas." *Social Science Quarterly* 91: 1123–43.

Rubinowitz, Leonard S., and James E. Rosenbaum. 2000. *Crossing the Class and Color Lines: From Public Housing to White Suburbia*. Chicago: University of Chicago Press.

Rugh, Jacob S., and Douglas S. Massey. 2014. "Segregation in Post-Civil Rights America: Stalled Integration or End of the Segregated Century?" *DuBois Review: Social Science Research on Race*. doi:10.10170S1742058X13000180.

Rusk, David. 2011. "Housing Policy Is School Policy: A Commentary." In *Finding Common Ground: Coordinating Housing and Education Policy to Promote Integration*, ed. Philip Tegeler, 21–30. Washington, D.C.: Poverty and Race Research Action Council.

Saez, Emmanuel. 2013. "Striking It Richer: The Evolution of Top Incomes in the United States (Updated with 2012 Preliminary Estimates)." University of California, Berkeley.

Safford, S. 2009. *Why the Garden Club Couldn't Save Youngstown: The Transformation of the Rust Belt*. Cambridge, Mass.: Harvard University Press.

Salzman, Hal. 2013. "What Shortages? The Real Evidence About the STEM Workforce. The Online Challenge to Higher Education." *Issues in Science and Technology*, Spring.

Salzman, Hal, Daniel Kuehn, and B. Lindsay Lowell. 2013. "Guestworkers in the High-Skill U.S. Labor Market: An Analysis of Supply, Employment, and Wage Trends." Economic Policy Institute.

Sampson, Robert J. 2012a. *Great American City: Chicago and the Enduring Neighborhood Effect*. Chicago: University of Chicago Press.

———. 2012b. "Moving and the Neighborhood Glass Ceiling." *Science* 337 (6101): 1464–65.

Sampson, Robert J. and Patrick Sharkey. 2008. "Neighborhood Selection and the Social Reproduction of Concentrated Racial Inequality." *Demography* 45 (1): 1–29.

San Francisco Mayor's Office. 2009. Report of the San Francisco Mayor's Task Force on African-American Out-Migration. Report. San Francisco.

San Francisco Office of Economic and Workforce Development. 2013. "San Francisco Local Hiring Policy for Construction: 2012–2013 Annual Report." Report. San Francisco.

San Francisco Public Utilities Commission. 2013. "Community Benefits Program: Creating Sustainable and Equitable Communities." Report.

Sanbonmatsu, Lisa, Jeffrey R. Kling, Greg J. Duncan, and Jeanne Brooks-Gunn. 2006. "Neighborhoods and Academic Achievement Results from the Moving to Opportunity Experiment." *Journal of Human Resources* 41 (4): 649–91.

Sanbonmatsu, Lisa, Jens Ludwig, Lawrence F. Katz, Lisa A. Gennetian, Greg J. Duncan, Ronald C. Kessler, Emma Adam, et al. 2011. "Impacts of the Moving to Opportunity for Fair Housing Demonstration Program After 10 to 15 Years." Washington, D.C.: U.S. Department of Housing and Urban Development. Office of Policy Development and Research.

Sanchez, Juan M., and Costanza Liborio. 2012. "The Relationships Among Changes in GDP, Employment, and Unemployment: This Time, It's Different." *Economic Synopses* (Federal Reserve Bank of St. Louis) 13.

Santiago, Catherine DeCarlo, Martha E. Wadsworth, and Jessica Stump. 2011. "Socioeconomic Status, Neighborhood Disadvantage, and Poverty-Related Stress: Prospective Effects on Psychological Syndromes Among Diverse Low-Income Families." *Journal of Economic Psychology* 32 (2): 218–30.

Saxenian, A. 1994. *Regional Advantage: Culture and Competition in Silicon Valley and Route 128*. Cambridge, Mass.: Harvard University Press.

Schachtel, Marsha. 2011. "The East Baltimore Revitalization Initiative: A Commitment to Economic Inclusion." Report. Baltimore: Annie E. Casey Foundation.

Schauben, Laura. 2013. "Neighborhood Development Center: Outcomes Evaluation." Report. Saint Paul, Minn.: Wilder Research.

Scheer, B. 2012. "The Utah Model: Lessons for Regional Planning." Las Vegas: Brookings Mountain West. University of Nevada, Las Vegas. http://www.unlv.edu/sites /default/files/TheUtahModel_0.pdf.

Schildt, Chris, Naomi Cytron, Elizabeth Kneebone, and Carolina Reed. 2013. "The Subprime Crisis in Suburbia: Exploring the Links Between Foreclosures and Suburban Poverty." Community Development Working Paper 2013-02. San Francisco: Federal Reserve Bank of San Francisco.

School District of Philadelphia. 2013. "The School District of Philadelphia," December. http://www.phila.k12.pa.us.

Schwartz, Heather L. 2010. "Housing Policy Is School Policy: Economically Integrative Housing Promotes Academic Success in Montgomery County, Maryland." New York: Century Foundation.

———. 2011. "Integrating Schools Is a Matter of Housing Policy." In *Finding Common Ground: Coordinating Housing and Education Policy to Promote Integration*, ed. Philip Tegeler, 15–20. Washington, D.C.: Poverty and Race Research Action Council.

Schwartz, Heather L., Liisa Ecola, Kristin J. Leuschner, and Aaron Kofner. 2012. "Is Inclusionary Zoning Inclusionary? A Guide for Practitioners." Santa Monica, Calif.: RAND.

Schweinhart, Lawrence J., J. Montie, Z. Xiang, W. S. Barnett, C. R. Belfield, and M. Nores. 2005. "Lifetime Effects: The High/Scope Perry Preschool Study Through Age 40." http://works.bepress.com/william_barnett/3, retrieved July 9, 2014.

Scorsone, Eric, and David Zin. 2010. "The Michigan Economy and State Review: A 10-Year History (1999–2009)." Issue Brief. Lansing, Mich.: Senate Fiscal Agency.

Scott, Molly M., Mary Cunningham, Jennifer Biess, Jennifer Lee O'Neil, Philip Tegeler, Ebony Gayles, and Barbara Sard. 2013. "Expanding Choice: Building a Successful Housing Mobility Program." Washington, D.C.: Urban Institute and Poverty and Race Research Action Council.

Seo, Joo Hwan, Vanessa G. Perry, David Tomczyk, and George T. Solomon. 2012. "Who Benefits Most? The Effects of Managerial Assistance on High- Versus Low-Performing Small Businesses." *Journal of Business Research* 67 (1): 2845–52.

Sharkey, Patrick. 2009. Neighborhoods and the Black-White Mobility Gap." Pew Charitable Trusts Economic Mobility Project.

———. 2013. *Stuck in Place: Urban Neighborhoods and the End of Progress Toward Racial Equality*. Chicago: University of Chicago Press.

Shierholz, Heidi. 2013. "Is There Really a Shortage of Skilled Workers?" In *Restoring Shared Prosperity: A Policy Agenda from Leading Keynesian Economists*, ed. Thomas I. Palley and Gustav A. Horn.

Simmons, Melody, and Joan Jacobson. 2011. "A Dream Derailed." *Maryland Daily Record*, January 31.

Singer, Audrey. 2013. "Contemporary Immigrant Gateways in Historical Perspective." *Daedalus, the Journal of the American Academy of Arts and Sciences* 142: 76–91.

Sinnaeve, Adinda. 2007. "How the EU Manages Subsidy Competition." In *Reining in the Competition for Capital*, ed. Ann Markusen, 87–101. Kalamazoo, Mich:. Upjohn Institute for Employment Research.

Skrentny, John D. 1996. *The Ironies of Affirmative Action: Politics, Culture, and Justice in America*. Chicago: University of Chicago Press.

Song, Lily. 2014. "Evergreen Cooperative Initiative: Anchor-Based Strategy for Inner City Regeneration." *Urban Solutions* 4 (February): 50–56.

Squires, Gregory D., and Jan Chadwick. 2006. "Linguistic Profiling: A Continuing Tradition of Discrimination in the Home Insurance Industry." *Urban Affairs Review* 41: 400–415.

Storper, M. 1997. *The Regional World: Territorial Development in a Global Economy*. New York: Guilford.

———. 2013. *Keys to the City: How Economics, Institutions, Social Interactions, and Politics Shape the Development*. Princeton, N.J.: Princeton University Press.

Story, Louise. 2012. "As Companies Seek Tax Deals, Governments Pay High Price." *New York Times*, December 1.

Sugrue, Thomas. 2005. *Origins of the Urban Crisis: Race and Inequality in Postwar Detroit*. Princeton, N.J.: Princeton University Press.

———. 2011. "A Dream Still Deferred." *New York Times*, March 26.

Summers, Anita A., and Barbara L. Wolfe. 1977. "Do Schools Make a Difference?" *American Economic Review* 67, 4: 639–52.

Summers, Lawrence, and James Poterba. 1994. "Time Horizons of American Firms: New Evidence from a Survey of CEOs." In *Capital Choices: Changing the Way America Invests in Industry*, ed. Michael Porter. Boston: Harvard Business School Press.

Sumption, Madeleine. 2011. "Filling Labor Shortages Through Immigration: An Overview of Shortage Lists and Their Implications." Migration Policy Institute.

Suro, Roberto, Jill H. Wilson, and Audrey Singer. 2011. "Immigration and Poverty in America's Suburbs." Washington, D.C.: Brookings Institution.

Swanson, Christopher B. 2009. "Closing the Graduation Gap." America's Promise Alliance and the Bill and Melinda Gates Foundation.

Tach, Laura, Rolf Pendall, and Alexandra Derian. 2014. "Income Mixing Across Scales: Rationale, Trends, Policies, Practice, and Research for More Inclusive Neighborhoods and Metropolitan Areas." Washington, D.C.: Urban Institute.

Terplan, Egon, and Imron Bhatti. 2013. "Seeking Prosperity: Middle-Wage Job Opportunities in the Bay Area." *SPUR: Action and Ideas for a Better City* (blog), November 5.

Thomas, June M. 2013. *Redevelopment and Race: Planning a Finer City in Postwar Detroit*. Detroit: Wayne State University Press.

Thomas, Kenneth P. 2010. *Investment Incentives and the Global Competition for Capital*. New York: Palgrave Macmillan.

————. 2012. "NYT: $80 Billion in State and Local Subsidies Annually (Updated)." *Middle Class Political Economist* (blog), December 2.

Tomer, Adie, Elizabeth Kneebone, Robert Puentes, and Alan Berube. 2011. "Missed Opportunity: Transit and Jobs in Metropolitan America." Washington, D.C.: Brookings Institution.

Tough, Paul. 2008. *Whatever It Takes: Geoffrey Canada's Quest to Change Harlem and America.* New York: Houghton Mifflin.

————. 2012. *How Children Succeed: Grit, Curiosity, and the Hidden Power of Character.* New York: Houghton Mifflin.

Treuhaft, Sarah, and Victor Rubin. 2013. "Economic Inclusion: Advancing an Equity-Driven Growth Model." Big Ideas for Jobs. University of California. Berkeley Institute for Research on Labor and Employment, and Institute of Urban and Regional Development.

Turner, Margery Austin, Austin Nichols, and Jennifer Comey. 2012. "Expanding Choice in Elementary and Secondary Education: A Report on Rethinking the Federal Role in Education." Washington, D.C.: Urban Institute.

Turner, Margery Austin, and Lynette A. Rawlings. 2009. "Promoting Neighborhood Diversity: Benefits, Barriers, and Strategies." Washington, D.C.: Urban Institute.

U.S. Census Bureau. 1998. "Population of the 100 Largest Urban Places: 1870." http://www.census.gov/population/www/documentation/twps0027/tab10.txt.

————. 2013. "City and Town Totals: Vintage 2012," May. http://www.census.gov/popest/data/cities/totals/2012/index.html.

————. 2014. "Asians Fastest-Growing Race or Ethnic Group in 2012, Census Bureau Reports." Washington, D.C.: U.S. Census Bureau.

U.S. Department of Education. 2013. "Promise Neighborhoods." https://www2.ed.gov/programs/promiseneighborhoods/index.html?exp=0.

University City District. 2014. "The State of University City 2013/2014." Retrieved March 28, 2014. http://universitycity.org/sites/default/files/State-of-UC-2013-web.pdf.

Vedder, Richard, Christopher Denhart, and Johnathan Robe. 2013. "Why Are Recent College Graduates Unemployed? University Enrollments and Labor-Market Realities." Washington, D.C.: Center for College Affordability and Productivity.

Vey, Jennifer S. 2012. "Building from Strength: Creating Opportunity in Greater Baltimore's Next Economy." Report. Brookings Institution. Metropolitan Policy Program.

Vigdor, Jacob L. 2013. "Weighing and Measuring the Decline in Residential Segregation." *City & Community* 12 (2): 169–77.

Voith, R. 1998. "Do Suburbs Need Cities?" *Journal of Regional Science*, 38(3), 445–64. doi:10.1111/0022-4146.00102.

Wasylenko, Michael. 1997. "Taxation and Economic Development: The State of the Economic Literature." *New England Economic Review* (March/April): 37–52.

Weber, Rachel. 2007. "Negotiating the Ideal Deal: Which Local Governments Have the Most Bargaining Leverage?" In *Reining in the Competition for Capital*, ed. Ann

Markusen, 141–60. Kalamazoo, Mich.: W. E. Upjohn Institute for Employment Research.

———. 2013. "Tax Increment Financing in Theory and Practice." In *Financing Economic Development in the 21st Century*, 2nd ed., ed. Sammis B. White and Zenia Z. Kotval, 283–301. New York: M.E. Sharpe.

Weiland, Christina, and Hirokazu Yoshikawa. 2013. "Impacts of a Prekindergarten Program on Children's Mathematics, Language, Literacy, Executive Function, and Emotional Skills." *Child Development* 84 (6): 2112–30.

Weir, Margaret, Jane Rongerude, and Christopher K. Ansell. 2011. "Collaboration is Not Enough: Virtuous Cycles of Reform in Transportation Policy." *Urban Affairs Review* 44 (4): 455–89.

White, Michael J. 1987. *American Neighborhoods and Residential Differentiation*. New York: Russell Sage Foundation.

Whitehurst, Grover J., and Michelle Croft. 2010. "American Neighborhoods and Residential Differentiation. The Harlem Children's Zone, Promise Neighborhoods, and the Broader, Bolder Approach to Education." Washington, D.C.: Brown Center on Education Policy, Brookings Institution.

Wilkes, Rima, and John Iceland. 2004. "Hypersegregation in the Twenty-First Century: An Update and Analysis." *Demography* 41 (1): 23–36.

Williams, Jane, and Alan Berube. 2014. "The Metropolitan Geography of Low-Wage Work." *The Avenue: Rethinking Metropolitan America* (blog), February 10. Metropolitan Policy Program. Brookings Institution. www.brookings.edu/blogs/the-avenue/posts/2014/02/10-metropolitan-geography-low-wage-work-williams-berube.

Wilson, William Julius. 1987. *The Truly Disadvantaged: The Inner City, the Underclass and Public Policy*. Chicago: University of Chicago Press.

———. 1996. *When Work Disappears: The World of the New Urban Poor*. New York: Knopf.

Winerip, Michael. 2011. "For Detroit Schools, Mixed Picture on Reforms." *New York Times*, March 13.

Wolford, Tonya, Katherine Stratos, and Adrienne Reitano. 2013. "The School District of Philadelphia. Renaissance Schools Initiative: Progress Report." Philadelphia: School District of Philadelphia.

Zandi, Mark. 2011. "Manufacturing in the USA: Why We Need a National Manufacturing Strategy." Testimony of Mark Zandi, Chief Economist, Moody's Analytics. Before Joint Economic Committee. U.S. Senate and House of Representatives.

Zimmer, Ron W., and Eugenia F. Toma. 2000. "Peer Effects in Private and Public Schools across Countries." *Journal of Policy Analysis and Management* 19 (1): 75–92.

CONTRIBUTORS

J. Cameron Anglum is a doctoral student in education policy and a dean's scholar at the Graduate School of Education at the University of Pennsylvania. Formerly of the Penn Institute for Urban Research (PennIUR), he is interested in research centered on domestic urban educational reform in the context of myriad interdependent urban concerns including fiscal policy, spatial analysis, and public-private partnerships, subjects often siloed in public dialogue.

Timothy J. Bartik is a senior economist at the W. E. Upjohn Institute for Employment Research, an independent nonprofit and nonpartisan research organization. His research focuses on state and local economic development and local labor markets. Prior to joining Upjohn in 1989, he was an assistant professor of economics at Vanderbilt University. His book *Who Benefits from State and Local Economic Development Policies?* is widely cited as an important review of the evidence on how local policies affect economic development. Bartik's other books include *Jobs for the Poor: Can Labor Demand Policies Help?* and *Investing in Kids: Early Childhood Programs and Local Economic Development.* He is coeditor of *Economic Development Quarterly*, which focuses on local economic development in the United States. He has a Ph.D. and MS in economics from the University of Wisconsin-Madison and a BA from Yale University in political philosophy.

Chris Benner is Dorothy E. Everett Chair in Global Information and Social Entrepreneurship, Director of the Everett Program for Digital Tools for Social Innovation, and Professor of Environmental Studies and Sociology at the University of California, Santa Cruz. His research deals with the relationships between technological change, regional development, and the structure of economic opportunity, focusing on regional labor markets and the transformation of work and employment patterns. His applied policy work centers on workforce development policy, the structure, dynamics and evaluation of workforce intermediaries, and strategies for promoting regional equity. Significant authored or co-authored book publications include *Equity, Growth and Community: What the nation can learn from America's metro regions* (with Manuel Pastor); *Just Growth: Inclusion and Prosperity in America's Metropolitan Regions* (with Manuel Pastor); *This Could Be the Start of Something Big: How Social Movements for Regional Equity Are Reshaping Metropolitan America* (with Manuel Pastor and Martha Matsuoka); and *Work in the New Economy: Flexible Labor Markets in Silicon Valley*. He received his Ph.D. in city and regional planning from the University of California-Berkeley.

Angela Glover Blackwell is founder and CEO of PolicyLink. Prior to creating PolicyLink, she was senior vice president at the Rockefeller Foundation, where she oversaw the domestic and cultural divisions. She gained national recognition as founder of the Oakland, California Urban Strategies Council, where she pioneered new approaches to neighborhood revitalization. She is coauthor of *Uncommon Common Ground: Race and America's Future* and has contributed to several other books. She has previously served on the President's Advisory Council on Faith-Based and Neighborhood Partnerships and was co-chair of the task force on poverty for the Center for American Progress. She now serves on numerous boards as well as on the President's Advisory Commission on Educational Excellence for African Americans. She has a law degree from the University of California-Berkeley and a bachelor's degree from Howard University.

Anthony P. Carnevale is director and research professor at the Georgetown University Center on Education and the Workforce, and an internationally renowned authority and scholar on education, training, and employment. Earlier in his career, he founded and became president of the Institute for Workplace Learning, where he remained for ten years. He also was director of human resource and employment studies at the Committee for Economic Development, where he was appointed by President Clinton to chair the National Commission on Employment Policy. He coauthored the principal affidavit in *Rodriguez v. San Antonio*, a national Supreme Court action to reform unequal tax burdens and education benefits. This historic case resulted in significant fiscal reforms in a wide variety of important states, and remains prevalent to this day.

Raj Chetty is Bloomberg Professor of Economics at Harvard University. His research combines empirical evidence and economic theory to help design more effective government policies. His work on tax policy, unemployment insurance, and education has been widely cited in media outlets and congressional testimony. He was recently awarded a MacArthur "Genius" fellowship and the John Bates Clark medal, given by the American Economic Association to the best American economist under age forty. He has a Ph.D. from Harvard University, which he received at twenty-three, and he is one of the youngest tenured professors in the university's history.

Rebecca Diamond teaches economics at the Stanford Graduate School of Business. She is an applied microeconomist studying local labor and housing markets. Her recent research focuses on the causes and consequences of diverging economic growth across U.S. cities and its effects on inequality. Previously, she was a postdoctoral fellow at the Stanford Institute for Economic Policy Research. She has a Ph.D. in economics from Harvard University.

Lei Ding is a community development economic advisor in the Community Development Studies and Education Department at the Federal Reserve Bank of Philadelphia. His research interests include housing and mortgage finance, community and economic development, and housing policy. Prior to joining the Philadelphia Fed in 2013, he was on the faculty of the Department of Urban Studies and Planning at Wayne State University. Previously he was a senior research associate at the University of North Carolina at Chapel Hill. He holds a BS and an MS from Tsinghua University and a Ph.D. in public policy from George Mason University.

Paul A. Jargowsky is professor of public policy and director of the Center for Urban Research and Urban Education at Rutgers University-Camden. His principal research interests are inequality, the geographic concentration of poverty, and residential segregation by race and class. His book, *Poverty and Place: Ghettos, Barrios, and the American City*, is a comprehensive examination of poverty at the neighborhood level in U.S. metropolitan areas between 1970 and 1990. In December 2013, the Century Foundation published his report "Concentration of Poverty in the New Millennium," the first published comparison of 2000 Census data with the 2007–2011 American Community Survey. In 1993, he was a visiting scholar at the U.S. Department of Health and Human Services, and in 1986, he was project director for the New York State Task Force on Poverty and Welfare Reform. He teaches courses on economics, sociology, social policy, and empirical methods.

David N. Karp is a researcher at the Perelman School of Medicine in Philadelphia, where he works with a team of population health researchers in the Center for Clinical Epidemiology and Biostatistics. His current work employs geographic and spatial statistical analysis to explore variability in community health outcomes. Previously, he worked as senior research coordinator for the Wharton Geospatial Initiative at the Wharton School and as a program coordinator for the Penn Institute for Urban Research (PennIUR). His research interests are in topics of urban geography, community and economic development, and broadly around issues of spatial and social inequality. He holds a master's degree in Urban Spatial Analytics and a BA in Urban Studies, both from the University of Pennsylvania.

Elizabeth Kneebone is a fellow at the Metropolitan Policy Program at the Brookings Institution and coauthor of the book *Confronting Suburban Poverty in America.* Her work primarily focuses on urban and suburban poverty, metropolitan demographics, and tax policies that support low-income workers and communities. Prior to joining Brookings, Kneebone was a research project manager for IFF (formerly the Illinois Facilities Fund), where her work assessed the geographic distribution of need for services and programs targeted to low-income people and places. She has a master's degree in public policy from the University of Chicago's Harris School of Public Policy and a BA in history from Indiana University.

Douglas S. Massey is Henry G. Bryant Professor of Sociology and Public Affairs at Princeton University. He has served on the faculties of the University of Chicago and the University of Pennsylvania. His research focuses on international migration, race and housing, discrimination, education, urban poverty, and Latin America, especially Mexico. He is author, most recently, of *Climbing Mount Laurel: The Struggle for Affordable Housing and Social Mobility in an American Suburb* and *Brokered Boundaries: Creating Immigrant Identity in Anti-Immigrant Times.* He is a member of the National Academy of Sciences, the American Academy of Arts and Sciences, and the American Philosophical Society. He is currently president of the American Academy of Political and Social Sciences and past president of the American Sociological Association and the Population Association of America. He has a Ph.D. from Princeton University.

Jeremy Nowak owns J Nowak Associates, LLC, a small consulting firm that provides advisory services for private and civic sector clients, including the Kauffman Foundation, the Knight Foundation, Acelero Learning, Living Cities, ArtPlace America, the Lenfest Foundation, and the Berwind family trust. He was the chair of the board of directors of the Federal Reserve Bank of Philadelphia in 2012 and 2013, the former president of the William Penn Foundation, and the founding CEO of the Reinvestment Fund. Nowak was also founding chair of Mastery Charter Schools, a network of fifteen inner-city schools that are success stories. He is now a nonresident senior fellow at the Brookings Institution, a PennIUR Scholar at the Penn Institute for Urban Research, and has published on a variety of issues, including housing policy, creativity, cities, and development finance.

Manuel Pastor is professor of sociology and American studies and ethnicity at the University of Southern California (USC). As founding director of the Center for Justice, Tolerance, and Community at the University of California-Santa Cruz, he also directs the Program for Environmental and Regional Equity at USC and codirects the USC Center for the Study of Immigrant Integration. He has written several books and speaks frequently on a variety of topics including demographic change, economic inequality, and community empowerment. In 2012, he received the Liberty Hill Foundation's Wally Marks Changemaker of the Year Award for social justice research partnerships. He has a Ph.D. in economics from the University of Massachusetts-Amherst and has received fellowships from the Danforth, Guggenheim, and Kellogg foundations and grants from the Irvine Foundation, the Rockefeller Foundation, the Ford Foundation, the National Science Foundation, the Hewlett Foundation, the MacArthur Foundation, and many others.

Victor Rubin is vice president for research at PolicyLink. He has been an urban planning researcher, teacher, and consultant for more than thirty years. Recently, he led a number of PolicyLink's engagement strategies for equitable economic growth and inclusion in Detroit, Baltimore, San Diego, and Oakland. He also coauthored, with Sarah Treuhaft, "Economic Inclusion: Advancing an Equity-Driven Growth Model," a report for the Big Ideas for Job Creation project for the Institute for Research on Labor and Employment at the University of California-Berkeley. Before joining PolicyLink, he had been Director of the HUD Office of University Partnerships and director of the University Oakland Metropolitan Forum. He is a member of the California Planning Roundtable and was an adjunct associate professor in the department of city and regional planning at the University of California-Berkeley, the department where he earned his Ph.D. and MCP.

Chris Schildt, senior associate at PolicyLink, conducts research on equitable economic growth strategies, including best practices for advancing equity in job creation, entrepreneurship, job quality, and workforce development. Prior to joining PolicyLink, she researched job creation strategies at the University of California-Berkeley Labor Center and has worked on community engagement and local hiring campaigns related to transportation and land-use planning in the Bay Area. She holds a BA and an MCP from the University of California-Berkeley.

Nicole Smith is a research professor and senior economist at the Georgetown University Center on Education and the Workforce, where she leads the center's econometric and methodological work. She has developed a framework for restructuring long-term occupational and educational projections and is part of a team of economists working on a project to map, forecast, and monitor human capital development and career pathways. Her current research investigates the role of education and socioeconomic factors in intergenerational mobility. Prior to joining the center, Smith was a faculty member in economics at Gettysburg College and the University of the West Indies (UWI)-St. Augustine. She has a Ph.D. in economics from American University and graduated with honors in economics and mathematics from UWI-St. Augustine campus. She was the recipient of the Sir Arthur Lewis Memorial Prize for outstanding research at the master's level at UWI.

Margery Austin Turner is senior vice president for program planning and management at the Urban Institute, where she leads efforts to frame and conduct policy research. A nationally recognized expert on urban policy and neighborhood issues, Turner has analyzed issues concerning residential location, racial and ethnic discrimination and its contribution to neighborhood segregation and inequality, and the role of housing policies in promoting residential mobility and location choice. Turner was deputy assistant secretary for research at the Department of Housing and Urban Development (HUD) from 1993 to 1996. During that time, she focused HUD's research agenda on the problems of racial discrimination, poverty, and economic opportunity in America's metropolitan areas. In her tenure, HUD's research office launched three major social science demonstration projects to test different strategies for helping families from distressed inner-city neighborhoods access opportunities through residential mobility, employment, and education.

Susan M. Wachter is Albert Sussman Professor of Real Estate at the Wharton School of the University of Pennsylvania and codirector of the Penn Institute for Urban Research (PennIUR). She is a former assistant secretary for policy development and research at the U.S. Department of Housing and Urban Development and chairperson of Wharton's real estate department. She is cofounder and current codirector of PennIUR and author of more than 200 scholarly publications, including fifteen books. She frequently comments on national media and testifies to the U.S. Congress on housing policy.

Zachary D. Wood is currently a Ph.D. candidate in public affairs and community development at Rutgers University-Camden. His primary research focus is around issues of urban poverty and social change through civic engagement and political advocacy. His recent research explores the role of nonprofits as advocates for social and policy change. Previously, he held numerous leadership roles in the nonprofit world, most recently as the director of development and the director of advocacy and public policy for Covenant House Pennsylvania, a shelter and service provider for homeless and marginalized youth in the Philadelphia area. He has also served as executive director of Habitat for Humanity on the Crow Creek Lakota Reservation in South Dakota.

INDEX

Note: Figures and tables are represented by italicized page numbers followed by the letter *f* or *t*.

housing affordability (continued)
desirable local amenities, 65–68;
constructing 100 percent affordable
housing, 97, 98–101; and impact of
land-use regulations in high-skill cities,
61, 63–64, 66, 69, 215n5; set-aside
programs, 97, 98; vouchers, 44, 54, 76,
85–86, 97–98, 185. *See also* fair housing;
residential mobility programs
Huang, Wei-Jang, 114
HUD. *See* U.S. Department of Housing and
Urban Development (HUD)
hypersegregation, 92–93, 94–95. *See
also* residential segregation by race
and class

immigrants: ethnic residential segregation
of the late nineteenth and early twentieth
centuries, 91–92; suburbanization
patterns, 42–43, 44
inclusive and equitable growth strategies
for American cities, 151–72, 173–91,
192–211; anchor institutions, 154–55,
162–66; applying a data-driven
approach to citywide community
investment, 187–91; Baltimore, 157,
164–66, 170–71; a broad commitment to
racial inclusion, 154; building from
strength, 189; Cleveland, 158–59,
162–63; and competitive cities/equitable
cities, 174; creating communities of
opportunity, 169; Detroit, 156–57,
159–62; enacting public investment
principles, 189–91; entrepreneurship
and small business, 154, 158–62;
epistemic communities, 192–211; four
broad categories of strategies, 154–56;
framework for policies, 152–58; general
goals, 152–54; identifying opportunities
for mixed-income communities, 190;
implications for regional leaders and
stakeholders, 209–11; maximizing jobs
and local employment through public
investment, 155, 166–68; measuring
role of social connection for growth,
198–201; measuring sustained growth in
CBSAs, 195–201, *197f, 199t, 200t,* 220n2,
221n3; New Orleans, 166–67; Oakland,
168; people-based strategies for the most
depopulated and poorest areas, 190;

Philadelphia case study, 163, 173–91;
Philadelphia's Neighborhood Transformation Initiative, 187–91, 220n10;
place-based managers and the center
city, 175, 185–86; Portland, Oregon, 167;
rebuilding from the inside out, 174,
178–91; rebuilding from the outside in,
174; re-norming of place to attract and
retain diverse populations, 184–87;
replacing older public housing
high-rises, 185; restoring public access
and shared spaces, 184–85; San
Francisco Bay Area, 157–58, 167–68;
school reorganization, 178–84;
stabilizing mid-value communities,
189–90; sustainable development, good
jobs, and equity, 155, 168–71. *See also*
epistemic communities; place-conscious
strategies to build shared prosperity
income inequality, 1, 15, 41; the educational
wage gap between college and non-college
graduates, 58–62, 118–19, 123–24; and
intergenerational socioeconomic
mobility, *10f,* 15; metropolitan Gini
coefficients, 15, 195, 196, 200, 221n3; San
Francisco Bay Area, 158. *See also*
socioeconomic mobility,
intergenerational
inside-out approaches to building shared
prosperity, 174, 178–91
intergenerational mobility. *See* socioeconomic mobility, intergenerational

Jargowsky, Paul A., 1–2, 3, 18, 43, 74, 76, 83
Jarmin, Ron, 142
Journal of Economic Perspectives, 209
JumpStart (Cleveland), 159
*Just Growth: Inclusion and Prosperity in
America's Metropolitan Regions* (Benner
and Pastor), 193

Kalamazoo, Michigan, 106, 113–14, 115
Kalamazoo Promise, 113–14, 115
Katz, Lawrence, 14, 123–24
Kimelberg, Shelley McDonough, 33
King, Martin Luther, Jr., 93
KIPP (charter schools), 181–82
Klein, Joel, 111
Kline, Patrick, 13–14
Kneebone, Elizabeth, 1–2

ACKNOWLEDGMENTS

The country has increasingly become divided into communities of wealth and communities of deprivation. To find ways to bridge the divide between these communities and to create a better future for all of us living in cities, the Community Development Studies and Education Department at the Federal Reserve Bank of Philadelphia has been investigating practical, research-based strategies to address disparity and build shared prosperity in American Communities. This volume is a seminal part of these efforts.

These investigations and conversations would not have been possible without the support of the Federal Reserve Bank of Philadelphia's President and CEO Charles Plosser, Senior Vice President Milissa Tadeo, and Department Manager Erin Mierzwa. We are also thankful for the generous support for this broader effort of the The Annie E. Casey Foundation, Penn Institute for Urban Research, Fund for Our Economic Future, Federal Home Loan Bank of Pittsburgh, and the Federal Reserve Banks of Atlanta, Boston, Chicago, Cleveland, New York, Richmond, and St. Louis.

This book is part of Penn Press's City in the Twenty-First Century series. We are grateful to the Press for thoughtful editorial direction in the development of this volume, with special thanks to Editor-in-Chief Peter Agree for his careful review of drafts of the manuscript and to managing editor Alison Anderson whose thoroughness and attention helped shape this volume. We appreciate the very thoughtful comments from two anonymous reviewers, which further improved the quality of the book. Thank you as well to Arthur Acoca, Cara Griffin, David Karp, and Anthony Orlando, who provided invaluable research and editorial assistance and kept the project on track. The intellectual contribution of Federal Reserve Bank of Philadelphia's Vice President and Community Affairs Officer Theresa Singleton has also greatly enriched this volume, and we thank her for her ongoing invaluable support and advice.

Without the dedication and research of the authors, there would be no book. Thank you to the individuals who contributed to this volume and whose work furthers understanding of, and progress to address, one of the most challenging issues of our time.